# Foxfire

## 25

# YEARS

# Foxfire

## 25 YEARS

Edited by Eliot Wigginton and
His Students

ANCHOR BOOKS
DOUBLEDAY
NEW YORK LONDON TORONTO SYDNEY AUCKLAND

AN ANCHOR BOOK

PUBLISHED BY DOUBLEDAY
a division of Bantam Doubleday Dell Publishing Group, Inc.
666 Fifth Avenue, New York, New York 10103

ANCHOR BOOKS, DOUBLEDAY, and the portrayal of an anchor
are trademarks of Doubleday, a division of Bantam Doubleday Dell
Publishing Group, Inc.

Library of Congress Cataloging-in-Publication Data

Foxfire: 25 years / edited by Eliot Wigginton and his students.
    p.  cm.
   1.  Appalachian Mountains, Southern—Social life and customs—Study
and teaching (Secondary)—Georgia—Rabun Gap.  2.  Folklore—Study
and teaching (Secondary)—Georgia—Rabun Gap.  3.  Progressive
education—Georgia—Rabun Gap.  4.  Journalism, School—Georgia—
Rabun Gap.  I.  Wigginton, Eliot.
F217.A65F696  1991b
370'.9758'123—dc20                           90-22834
                                                     CIP

ISBN 0-385-41346-7

Also available as a Doubleday hardcover
ISBN 0-385-41345-9

Printed in the United States of America

April 1991

10  9  8  7  6  5  4  3  2  1

FIRST EDITION

*This book is dedicated
to public school teachers everywhere*

—————————————————————

# Contents

# Introduction

In the life of a public school teacher, twenty-five years is just about a career. It is enough time, for example, if you stay in the same community, for your earlier students to present you with a new senior class largely made up of their children. It is enough time for those parents to become established, as former students of mine have, as teachers and veterinarians and landscape architects and principals and editors and fashion designers and builders and stockbrokers and cab drivers and civil engineers and—criminals. It is enough time for the thing to happen to you that just happened to me where Johnny, a former student now in a pilot's uniform, greeted me at the doorway of a United Airlines DC-9 bound for Chicago and said, "I've been meaning to tell you that the first time I ever flew in a plane was when you and I went to California to give a speech, and somewhere over the Rockies I decided I was going to be a pilot." It is enough time that you will have been best man at at least one wedding, and you will have delivered at least one eulogy at the funeral of a favorite kid; mine was at Gary's.

It is enough time that you will have been over the argument of whether or not teachers make enough money and receive enough recognition at least a thousand times, and you may well have decided, as I have, finally, to just leave it alone. Johnny and Gary and I know some things now, and the things we know together are so separated from that strife and controversy that sometimes it all just sounds like alien background noise. Yes, I know. Yes, it's important—but those experiences with Gary are deposits in a psychological bank account that count for something, too.

And it is enough time that you will have refined your craft to the point where you are either coasting comfortably on automatic pilot;

or you are drowning in repetition and are ready to retire and get on about something different; or, despite the fact that you have "topped out" in your state's salary scale, you are now hungry to take all you have learned to a whole new level of understanding and sophistication—to batter at a whole new set of obstacles and become, truly, a master teacher, reform a school, alter the course of a school district, contribute substantially to a state or national dialogue—make an indelible difference in the field.

Though I have never done anything but teach, I suspect the same is true in other fields. And though, really, there is nothing magical or particularly significant about a twenty-fifth year as opposed to a twenty-third or a twenty-seventh, it seems as good a time as any to reflect, to take stock, and to gather one's energies to make a decision or two.

This book, then, is in the spirit of reflection—of pausing along the way to catch one's breath and survey the landscape. Of asking, "What's next?" In part, it is an anecdotal record of an ongoing public high school adventure; in part, it is projection and hope.

It is not a history in the traditional sense of that word. One will not find here a chronological record of annual budgets, of each of the students and staff members involved and their years of involvement, of every scholarship and summer job awarded, of every project initiated and then carried forward or abandoned. Though pieces of that story can be found in other places, that's a different book.

Instead, this book is a natural extension of the kind of work for which we are best known. From the beginning, students have interviewed older community residents in an effort to document skills, traditions, experiences, and the resulting perspective. Through this, the students have presumably gained some appreciation for, and perspective on, the Appalachian experience they all share.

Now, for this book, current students again interview their elders, but this time the experience they all have in common is Foxfire. Just as former students have not presented a strict history of the Appalachian region in their *Foxfire* books, so too, this is not a history. Just as former students have not interviewed all of the thousands of older Appalachian residents in our region, so too, current students have not interviewed each of the some two thousand or more students who have taken at least one Foxfire course at the high school. How could they? Rather, like the students who came before them, they have selected those they interviewed on the basis of availability, willingness, and the relative richness of their participation during certain key periods of time or critical events (the creation of the very first magazine, for example) that seemed important to consider.

Thus this book, like the *Foxfire* books themselves, will be seen as flawed by some. It is not inclusive, but selective. It suggests immediately the outlines for another dozen books: a complete history; an oral history of those students who were not particularly affected by the program at all; or oral histories of staff members or administrators who were involved, or teachers and/or students who started similar projects elsewhere, or subscribers to the magazine, or readers of the Foxfire series.

This book is not any of those. Its rationale and its intent spring from an intriguing notion: that in the stories both current and former students tell of their most memorable and generally positive school experiences wherever they went, one can find the ingredients of a powerful approach to education—even the makings of a philosophy. More interesting than the specific products, then, that students produced out of single fifty-five-minute Foxfire classes—the magazines and books and records and videotapes—probably are the lessons teachers and parents alike can generalize from the process of that production: the wisdom of involving young people in small group work and peer teaching; of giving them real decisions to make and real responsibility; of producing something tangible, of substance, that the students value and that has an appreciative—even grateful—audience beyond the classroom; of wedding the community and the classroom and the curriculum together. And the wisdom of doing all this, and more, in a classroom atmosphere that is intensely collaborative, democratic, problem solving, analytical, and reflective.

Reading between the lines of the stories former students tell in this book, one will find those ingredients at work to varying degrees; reading the chapter where those same students reflect on their lives since leaving high school, one will find the results. Interviewing students who were not so positively affected by the program, one will routinely find that many of the principles above were not in place.

For the other students, though, and there are many, the results are significant. And through our work with other teachers in other schools, described in one of the chapters in this book, we are now finding that no matter what the age or class or subject—or project—is, when those core ingredients that create memorable experiences are in place, the results are, predictably, memorable experiences. In some cases, they change kids' lives. If I had children in a public school, they are the kinds of experiences I would demand for my kids—not just hope for. And as a teacher, the results of such work have led to my determination not to settle for less, and never to work for an administrator who dictates that I be on a certain page of a certain specified text on a certain date. When that happens, I move on.

This book has a second purpose. Many of you have followed the *Foxfire* books with keen interest. (The first book alone is now in its forty-fifth printing, having sold over 4 million copies.) Wherever I go, you ask me and the students who are with me the same questions:

"In every book, there are pictures of students with older people, but except for the introductions to the chapters, you can't really tell what the kids were thinking. What was going on behind the scenes? What were they thinking? What did they learn?"

"What has happened to those kids? Where are they now, and what are they doing?"

"What has happened to the people the kids interviewed—people like Aunt Arie?"

This book has been structured with those questions right in front of us, as you will see.

Its third purpose, of course, is to provide a group of current students, most of whom will be sixteen-year-olds about to enter their senior year when this book is published, the opportunity to have one of those experiences that is as closely based on those core ingredients as we can make it. I won't know all the results of that for years, but I do know that right now, as one direct result, I have a group of the most committed, skilled, and impressive students to work with that I've ever known. To a person, the visitors who flowed through our classroom this summer and watched this editorial team of seven at work on this manuscript, piles of paper scattered across the floor and Macintosh computers glowing in every corner, left shaking their heads in absolute disbelief. This book is one of our shining moments together. It may be the first time in the history of our public schools that such a book—an oral history of an oral history, a play within a play—has ever been produced. Personally, I know of no precedent.

Early on in this introduction, I mentioned "a decision or two." They've now been made. In part, through this book, I know we're on the right track. A capital campaign has been launched this birthday

year to double the size of our endowment; a vice president/adminis-
trator has been selected to enable me to take a leave of absence from
Rabun County to help create a new method of training teachers in
conjunction with several demonstration schools—impossible to do
here in Rabun County because of the absence of a college of teacher
education; a new, talented teacher will be hired to take over my
classes at the high school temporarily. Foxfire staff and students and
the network teachers and their students will add something of substance to the dialogue about public school education. The first
twenty-five years have been prologue. Now we take another step.

And I know that this whole effort will stand in the story of this
country's public education as one example of the good that can
happen when students, their families, administrators, teachers, and
members of a community come together, each willing to give up
something of self to a greater good.

In the process, everyone wins. I wish Gary were still here. He
would tell you so. But the letters he sent me remain behind, and some
have been woven into the fabric of this book. That's something, at
least. In one, he concluded, "My letters don't show it, but I think of
you often and the hours we spent working, talking, and just living.
I'll never forget that."

Neither will I, my good friend.
Neither will I.

—ELIOT WIGGINTON

# Preface

One afternoon in the spring of 1988, Wig walked into the classroom and said, "Hey, guys, I've got an offer from Doubleday to do a twenty-fifth anniversary book." Wig told us about some of the ideas for the book, and those of us who thought it would be fun to work on the project went with him to the library to discuss the idea some more.

A group of about twelve of us in the Foxfire I class went down to the library that day, and Wig started telling us about this idea to do a book about the past twenty-five years of Foxfire. One possibility was a compilation of the best chapters from *Foxfire;* another was to do the history of the Foxfire project as seen through the eyes of the students and adults who were involved in it. We got excited about the history idea and started meeting every Wednesday to figure out what the book might look like.

One of the first things we decided to do was a survey to find out what our readers would want to read. We did a rough draft and took it to our families, friends, neighbors, and to some of the classes Wig was teaching. We asked them to rank their interests in possible chapters like what happened to Aunt Arie and her house, interviews with former students about what they did in Foxfire and what they had done after high school, and interviews with other people who had been involved with Foxfire.

Based on the results we received, we revised the survey questions and decided to mail the survey out in *Foxfire* magazine. We divided the questions into four groups: the past, the present, the future, and the Teacher Outreach Program. We also left a space for suggestions. More than five hundred of the three thousand surveys we put in the magazine came back. That's about 17 percent, and the average response for this sort of thing is only 3 percent. Some of the more popular things that they wanted were things like: an interview with Wig, interviews with former students about what they had done since their involvement with Foxfire and how it influenced their lives, and updates of past interviewees who were favorites of our readers.

Based on the results from the magazine survey, we did a few interviews with people like Hilton Smith, a teacher at Foxfire. Then, we put those interviews into possible chapters. During the summer, Scott Cannon, Keri Gragg, Robbie Bailey, Jenny Lincoln, and I were hired to do what seemed like thousands of interviews. Most of the interviews we did we videotaped so that Mike Cook's video crew could do a documentary on the making of the twenty-fifth anniversary book. We were interviewing them about general impressions of the program, and stories of things they had done, but at that point we weren't sure what kind of information we wanted. We were working without any true knowledge about the people we interviewed or what was going on at Foxfire during the time that they were associated with the project. Also, Wig was gone most of the summer teaching university classes for teachers, and we didn't have his knowledge to draw on.

When the new school year started, there were many class discussions about what would happen to this book and what the sequence might look like.

As Scott Cannon says, "We picked the people who appeared most in the past magazines. Wig put the specific events up on the board, chapters like the 'First Magazine,' the 'Hopkins Year,' and the 'NEH Grant.' Then, the people who fit into the chapters were the ones we interviewed. Wig told us where everybody fitted."

One of the first things Shannon Edwards, Chris Nix, Scott Cannon, Jenny Lincoln, Lee Carpenter, Julie Dickens, and I did this summer was to finalize on the board the specific events we felt were important. These events formed the present chapters in the book. Then, we found that the interviews we had done the summer before were too vague, and didn't include many of the stories about the specific events needed to make the book interesting and informative.

To solve this problem, George Reynolds (Foxfire's Music/Folklore advisor) and I sat down, and rewrote and regrouped the questions we had used during each interview last summer. We divided them into four main groups: the specific events, the contacts they had interviewed, the effects that Foxfire had had on their lives, the things they had learned from their experiences and what they had done since graduating, and, last but not least, the "miscellaneous," with questions about special projects that they had been involved in (a newsletter, speech, or trip), and family and parent involvement. Next, we thought of generic questions to go under every group that we could ask the former students. Then, before each interview, we wrote in questions specific to the person we were going to interview, and sent them a copy to look over. This gave them some idea of what we wanted and gave them a chance to think.

We soon got into a regular routine of coming in in the morning, getting ready for the interviews that day, and editing when we weren't working on that. During the afternoon, usually after lunch, we had a meeting. This was our time to discuss things like who was editing what, what the interviews we had done the day before were like, how far along each interview was, and generally assess our progress.

Lee Carpenter says, "We just did the interviews from the questions. It was a tight schedule, so there were two or three interviews a day. We also edited and we transcribed some of the interviews."

After the interviews were transcribed, we edited them into sections like the "Hopkins Year," which is a specific event, contacts they interviewed, how their parents helped them, and what they had done after high school. Some of the people featured here had been interviewed twice. The interview from the summer before and the one from this summer had to be blended together. These sections were put in folders devoted to each chapter, and then we started trying to put the chapters in order. We interviewed Wig about each chapter and used that information to introduce them.

By the end of this summer we were still working after school tying off the loose ends: editing last-minute interviews like the one with Claude Rickman, taking pictures that hadn't been taken, like Felrese Bradshaw Carroll at work, developing pictures to go in the book, working on this preface, and keying the photos to the book.

There have been a lot of hard times with this book mainly because we have never tried anything like this before, but also because this work is all based on a deadline that slowly but surely worked a lot of frustration into our lives. We have worked for two years on this book now, and a lot of people have been involved with getting it finished. Thanks, guys! It's great to see it as a book.

Who would have thought that Foxfire would survive for twenty-five years? I can't wait to see them interview *me* for the fiftieth-anniversary book!

—LEIGH ANN SMITH

# Acknowledgments

In order for a project like Foxfire to have a chance, many people of good will and concern must either become actively involved—or at the very least agree to not stand in the way.

After the initial idea is uncovered, the first people to become involved are the school administrators and the school board. In our case, Morris Brown, the school's principal, was the single most positive influence on our work. As the best principals tend to do, his response to the initial idea was neither, "Yes," nor, "No," but rather, "Let's figure out together how we can make this happen." Other administrators like Karl Anderson and Donald Arbitter, as well as the members of Rabun County's school board and Raymond Smith, the Superintendent of Schools, endorsed and supported the project.

From the beginning, the majority of the students and their parents, the next potential obstacles, affirmed the worth of the project's goals. I cannot remember a single parent who opposed the idea, and though not every student participated fully, not one tried to destroy the enthusiasm the project generated. Not one piece of equipment was stolen or vandalized; no money was embezzled or misused. As far as students are concerned, my one regret with this book has been the fact that hundreds of students who could have been interviewed—should have been interviewed—have been left out. My vote would be to include them all, but this book would be thousands of pages long. The students have been, and continue today to be, the solid rock upon which Foxfire stands. They were, and are, magnificent.

Had the older residents of this county refused our requests for interviews, *Foxfire* would never have become the distinctive, special publication that it remains. In twenty-five years of publication, I literally cannot think of as many as ten people who asked not to be included. Because of their selfless generosity toward both the students and me, this has been the most instructive and fulfilling experience of my life. Many of those people are gone now, but I am thankful that, through countless hours of plain hard work, the students were willing to return their generosity and give them each some small measure of immortality. Now the words of the Aunt Aries remain behind to entertain, to inform, and to guide us all.

Yet another ingredient that must be in place before nearly any student project can be born is funding. For *Foxfire*, the funds needed to pay for the first issue were donated by the residents of Rabun County. Scores of them chipped in. The largest donations were for $25.00. Most were for $5.00 and less. No proposals were written; there were no grants. Interested parents, business people—even students—simply did the job themselves.

Soon after, individuals like John Dyson and Katherine Graham, and small foundations like the Coordinating Council of Literary Magazines expressed their faith in the importance of the effort with $500 donations. And thus, the creation of a nonprofit, tax-exempt corporation became essential. That meant a Board of Directors, which soon included John Dyson, Roy Sinclair, Howard Senzel, Mike Clark, and John Viener; as well as a national advisory board and a community advisory board whose many members have given, invariably, all we've asked.

By 1969, the scope of the work had already expanded to the point that the National Endowment for the Humanities was willing to invest substantially in our potential. There has followed help for special projects and initiatives from a staggering array of sources, all generous and all critical to the size and shape of our organization today: the Appalachian Regional Commission, Mr. Bingham's Trust for Charity, Georgia Arts Council, Georgia Commission for the National Bicentennial Celebration, National Archives and Records Service, New York Community Trust, Rockefeller Family Fund, Trust Company of Georgia; and foundations like W. N. Banks, Coca-Cola, Ford, Booth Ferris, William Randolph Hearst, John H. and Wilhelmina Harland, Charles Loridans, Lyndhurst, Andrew W. Mellon, Metropolitan Atlanta Community, Katherine John Murphy, Charles Stewart Mott, Rockefeller, Public Welfare, DeWitt Wallace-Reader's Digest, Asbury Warren, David, Helen and Marian Woodward, New York Times Co., and Rochester Area Foundation. Corporations like Apple and IBM have been extraordinarily generous with donations of essential equipment.

As the work takes hold, fueled by the generosity of corporations and foundations, and publicized by the media—which have been enthusiastic about our work from the publication of the first issue of *Foxfire*—a project grows beyond the capability of one adult and a group of students to manage. Inevitably, others are hired to help. In our case, some like Mike Cook, Paul Gillespie, Phyllis Ramey, Kaye Carver Collins, Linda Garland Page, and Dana Adams were former students who had helped create jobs for themselves at home. Others, however, were gradually hired who represented skills and areas of expertise former students had not acquired: Suzanne Angier, Bob and Margie Bennett, Millard Buchanan, Joyce Colborn, Delores Crane, Lyn Ellen Eubanks, Shelby Farmer, Joe Haban, William Henderson, Carol Elizabeth Jones, Connie Means, Ann Moore, Robert Murray, Kim Ramey, Larry Reinhardt, George Reynolds, Pat Rogers, Hilton Smith, Sherrod Sturrock, Jennifer Stutsman, Susan Walker, and Tanya Worley. All made, and/or are making, an invaluable contribution. This organization simply would not exist in the current size and scope of its mission were it not for them. Ann, Joyce, Mike, and George have stuck with me for nearly fifteen years.

The other central ingredient is you. People like you have provided the lion's share of our income and our determination to continue by purchasing our products and by thanking us for them. Your enthusiasm absolutely has been the fuel for our engines. Without it, this vehicle would be abandoned and rusting behind the house. You've been so loyal.

The students who edited this book have my awe and my eternal admiration. Carol D'Angelo, Jewell Murray, Lyn Eubanks, Ann Moore, Beth Lovell and Teresa Thurmond all pitched in to help type one final manuscript, and Al Edwards and Mark Edwards printed the photos. All have my gratitude—but especially Susan, who worked closely with me through several final edits.

And last, there's Dad, who brought me to visit Rabun County as a child, introduced me to Mary Hambidge, Claude and Edith Darnell, Margaret and Richard Norton, and Jack and Dean Beasley—and changed my life.

—ELIOT WIGGINTON

# Prologue

MORRIS BROWN, PRINCIPAL: I remember when Wig first came to Rabun Gap School in 1966. He was the only teacher that I've ever hired without a face-to-face interview. At that time, he was a student at Cornell University [and he applied for a job here], and we needed an extra teacher. It just so happened that I knew some people in the community that he knew, so I was able to make contact with him over the phone and [I asked him to come down so we could meet him]. He told me he couldn't come to be interviewed at that time because he had to finish getting his degree, and I told him I understood.

I talked with more people he knew, people he had grown up and associated with, to find out his background—what sort of person he was. I asked them questions such as if they were young and in school, would they like to have him as a teacher. Everyone I asked gave him a glowing report. Later, I called him again, saying, "Come on down. We need you to teach." He did, since he had finished his degree, and I was certainly never disappointed.

When some people around here first saw him, they thought he was strange. He was not the traditional "schoolteacher" type. Twenty-five years ago, men teachers wore ties and ladies dressed up; Wig was just Wig. He wore whatever he felt was comfortable. Many people had questions about him. During the first year or two, they'd look out of the corner of their eyes at him, and they'd ask me, "What sort of a fellow is that Wig?" This gave me the opportunity to brag on him. I think my knowing him and having hired him helped him get established in a shorter time than he would have otherwise, since I knew the community well, and people trusted me.

# The First Classes

---

FROM AN INTERVIEW WITH ELIOT WIGGINTON: I came to Rabun Gap to teach because I had spent time here as a child, and I knew this was where I wanted to live. When I first got here, they gave me all of the ninth- and tenth-graders, and I was supposed to teach English, five sections, geography, one section, six classes a day, about 146 kids. There were about 250 students in the school, so I had over half of them.

It was a situation I had never faced before, complicated by lots of things. One, of course, was it was my first year teaching. I had never done it before except for a semester of practice teaching.

Another one of the problems was that the population of the school was only half community students. The other half were dormitory students who had been sent to the school from places like Atlanta. The local students and the dormitory students were pretty different kinds of people. Typically, the dormitory students wouldn't know what the local students were talking about when they talked about milking a cow or baling hay or pulling fodder. The community students wouldn't know what the dorm kids were talking about with the kinds of things they used to do in the cities.

There was some friction there, also. The community students, for example, were free to go home at the end of the school day, and they were free to be out on the weekends on dates and things like that. They would come back in on Monday morning talking to the dormitory students, who were never allowed to leave campus, about what they'd done that weekend, and parties they had gone to, and the dorm students would get all agitated.

1

The other thing that complicated the whole picture was the fact that lots of the students had already decided that they didn't like English very much, and they were going to do what they could to make this new teacher's life miserable. Which they did. There were a lot of discipline problems. Things came up that I didn't really know how to handle. I had always assumed, for example, that if you took some students off to one side and really talked to them, and said, "Folks, we need to stop this kind of behavior; it's getting in the way," that that would be enough, and I couldn't figure out why it wasn't.

One of the things that I tried to do early on was find something that we could do together in those classes that might get them more interested in English. One of the possibilities that I suggested for something that might pull us together would be to start a magazine, and as we began to talk about some of the possibilities for things that could be in it, people began to get more intrigued.

I thought that probably what ought to be in the magazine was short stories and haiku poems because that was all I had ever seen in student literary magazines, so that's all that I could imagine. But we began to think about that together, and began to put lists of other possibilities on the board, and the list grew to the point where it included things like home remedies that people used in the area, and superstitions, and that all made sense, primarily because it was a logical, easy way to get students involved who didn't particularly like to write poetry. All of the community kids could go home and collect material. Even the dormitory kids could do interviews and collect material from local people because there were a lot of local people who worked on the campus. So as an experiment, we began to collect superstitions and remedies and post them on charts up on the walls, and add to them as students brought in new ones. That began to look interesting.

I began to turn more pieces of the project over to students as it became clear that we had other tasks that needed to be done. Money, for example. I couldn't pay for the magazine. The school couldn't pay for it. The principal, Morris Brown, did, however, give us permission to go to community residents and request donations. In fact, from the very first moment, he supported us in any way that he was able. So all of the students who wanted to pitched in to get donations from parents and neighbors and local businesses. The promise we made to them was, "If you give us money, we will put your name in the back of the magazine as one of the donors, and we will give you a free copy when it comes out, autographed by all of the students who put the magazine together." They raised over four hundred dollars.

We had to choose a name for the magazine, and all of the students contributed choices. We had long lists of possibilities. Finally when we thought that we had pretty much exhausted those, we got around to a vote. The name the students picked was *Foxfire*. It was their choice.

Someone suggested that we let people in the community put material in the magazine, too. One day I was talking to a woman named Sarah Rickman about the possibility of her putting some drawings in the first issue because she was pretty well known around the community as an artist. She agreed to do that, and did. She also suggested that one of the things that we might want to do would be to go and talk to her husband's father, Luther Rickman, who had been the sheriff when the Bank of Clayton was robbed in 1934. She said, "He's got a great story that would be fun to put in that first issue."

None of us knew what we were doing at that point because we had never done any kind of an interview before, but one day after school, I got four of the students together, and we went down to Luther's house to talk to him and to get him to tell us that story. It was a good one. When it came time to write it up to put into the magazine, though, the students had forgotten a lot of the details, and the story that they wrote out wasn't real interesting. It was pretty flat. It didn't sound like Luther talking at all.

We had a big discussion about what we ought to do, and somebody came up with the idea of getting a tape recorder from someone. We borrowed one from Bob Edwards at the Kodak shop and went out to Luther's house again one day after school and got him to tell that story again. We pretty much put that in the first magazine just the way he told it.

We also invited English teachers at the county high school in Clayton to allow their students to send some of their work in, and they did, so we had a section in the first magazine of work by students who were not at the Rabun Gap School. Slowly, but surely, the whole thing began to come together.

I didn't know anything about getting a magazine printed. I'd never done that before. But we did have a local printer, Mr. Cross, who put out the weekly newspaper, and could print a magazine like ours, so he explained how it would have to be typed up and how everything had to be pasted up neat and straight. When we had enough pages, some students and I took it down there and turned it over to him. We had the money we had collected, and we based the number of copies that we ordered on that. He promised us six hundred copies.

Then I began taking students down there after school to help out because I wanted them to see how the whole process worked. Actually, I also wanted to know how it worked myself. Mr. Cross had an offset press, but it was one of those smaller ones that could only print two pages at a time. They would print six hundred copies of those two pages, and then stack them on the floor. Then they would print two more pages, and then two more. So you would walk in and find these stacks of pages piled on the floor along one wall.

When they got those done, then they would print the backs. Then they would take all of those pages to a folding machine and feed them through and stack up those folded pages.

Next, they would put piles of those folded pages in sequence down the length of a long assembly table. At that point, Mr. Cross would bring in some people from the community, and pay them to stand there at those tables and assemble the magazines by hand. They would each get a folded sheet, and slide the next one in, and then the next, until they got down to the end of the table where there would be a pile of collated pages.

Then somebody would take those and put a cover on each, and then take them to a stapling machine, and then to a trimmer, and the finished magazines would get stacked in boxes and hauled back to a storage room and piled. The end result was that it was a *long* process. But whenever it was possible, I would take students down there to help out, and it would speed up the work a little bit.

Mr. Cross had to print *Foxfire* in between printing the weekly newspaper, so it was slow, but the students really did see how a magazine was printed, and they really got involved in the entire assembly process. That was good stuff.

When the first issue came out in March of 1967, the students were real excited about it. We took copies to stores and asked them if they could help us out by selling the magazines and giving us the whole purchase price instead of taking a percentage. Some wanted to take their percentage, but we were only selling them for fifty cents apiece so there wasn't much to go around. The magazine was costing us more than fifty cents per issue to print, so right from the beginning we were losing money. We hadn't taken the time to do the math to find out where the break-even point was. We just didn't know to do that. We didn't know anything. We just flew into it completely blind. There were so many people who wanted to see a copy of that first magazine that we wound up going back to Mr. Cross and asking him to print six hundred more of that issue, using a different color for the cover to distinguish it from the very first ones. By far and away, the kind of material that people liked the most was the interview with Luther Rickman and the superstitions and remedies. As far as most people were concerned, we could forget about the haiku poems. But the response to that first issue was overwhelmingly positive. People at the school loved it, the kids' parents loved it, and we had to restock stores almost every day.

Although the original plan had been to do only one issue, the students decided that we had to do another one. When we got down to a discussion of the contents, the decision was made to drastically reduce the amount of poetry and concentrate on local traditions. What we focused on for that second issue was all of the material we could find about how to plant by the signs of the Zodiac and the phases of the moon. That's what people wanted, so that's what we set out to provide.

And very quickly we began to get requests for the magazine from people who lived out of Rabun County. I couldn't figure out at first how that was happening. I finally realized that there were lots of people who were originally from Rabun County who had moved away. Lots of people from Rabun County had moved up to Michigan, for example, to work in the car factories, and those people wrote and said, "You've got to keep that magazine going, because we haven't been able to go back to Rabun County for years, and getting an issue of your magazine is like having a visit back home."

Thus it became clear early on that we had stumbled into something that made sense. Because so many students were involved in so many different phases of the operation, and because the response was so positive, and because it was the first time the school had ever had a magazine, and it was generating positive public opinion—for all those reasons and more, the students began to get intrigued and interested in a way that wouldn't have happened if we had just put out a literary magazine.

When I tell people the whole thing was virtually an accident, they don't believe me, but it was.

✄✄✄

BECKY COLDREN LEWIS: I was a community student in the ninth grade when Wig came to Rabun Gap to teach. I had him for English and geography. From the beginning, it was clear that he really had no faith in what he was doing. He really was struggling. If he was a woman, I believe he would have cried in class, and we knew that. We were terrible to him. Years later, I was in the Georgia State class he teaches on Wednesday nights, and even then he could name off the boys that made his life really rough those first few months of teaching. I'd forgotten them, but as soon as he named them, I remembered.

I wasn't in with Tommy Green on the day he tried to burn Wig's podium in class. I was in the back of the room writing notes to my friends. Wig would take up all the squirt guns and all the slingshots at the beginning of the period, but by the end of the period, they'd all be gone out of his drawer. We were awful. He was so nice to us, and he would try to be our friend, and we were terrible to the end.

But you knew that he really cared that we would become literate. One time, he took some kids out of my class who didn't read well, and read *The Yearling* to them. It was unusual and caring. He would take those kids out to the room next door and have us read silently while he was reading to them, but we just visited and talked. We didn't cooperate.

He also taught us geography. He was funny at times. He taught us things like how to fold a map. Nobody knew how, so he got a classroom set of Georgia road maps from Mr. Pennington at the Gulf station in Dillard and taught us all how to fold a map and read one, and that's geography. He tried everything with us. Sometimes it almost worked.

I still remember the exam we had in that class. It was, "If you were a businessman and you were going to set up a business in Rabun County, what are some of the components that you would have to think about?" The exam was a real-world thing. This was his first year, but even then, in the beginning, he was on the right track. Geography isn't just memorizing names of rivers. He knew then that to teach well it should be a real-world learning situation. At the time, we thought, "Well, what an easy exam. One question!" and we all knew that answer because of the teaching he had done. He didn't teach us the test, but the things we learned in that geography class had been things like how important the water supply is to a community, and how important elevation is.

Those first months were a real shock for him, though. I know there are people who wonder why he stayed. I remember the first few days Wig was teaching at Rabun Gap, he went to the school late at night and borrowed a typewriter to type up a ditto for the next day's class. He went up to the main building, and as he was coming out, this light flashes on him. A voice says, "Drop what you're doing!"

Wig doesn't know what to say, but he says, "I work here, and I just needed to type something tonight."

Now, this is my Uncle Henry Dillard, who's six feet, six inches tall, maybe four hundred pounds. He's with the Georgia Bureau of Investigation, and he's got a gun in his hands, and he says, "My name's Henry Dillard. Let me see your driver's license and Social Security card. You're under arrest."

Wig remembered the name and asks him, "Do you have a daughter named Henrietta? She's in the ninth grade. I'm her teacher."

Well, he didn't go to jail after all, but that shook him up.

Another time he was in a beer joint talking with a man there, and he found out he taught that guy's kid. The man calls up the school and says, "Did you know that you've got a teacher at the beer joint?" and he got in trouble. He didn't go back to the beer joint. I can't imagine all the culture shock he went through just coming out of college in the North in the mid-sixties.

The magazine really began with the tenth-graders. Wig tried to draw us into it, but we thought the magazine really belonged to the tenth-graders. I remember the contest to name the magazine. We all submitted choices. I also remember him saying, "When you go home, ask your parents if they have any superstitions or old home remedies." He tried to bring us in that way, but it was just our fault we didn't buy into it. The tenth-graders did, and the tenth-graders did the magazines the first year. We, as ninth-graders, had no ownership of the magazine. I think Wig was just trying to keep the room intact. There was no time for him to do or teach us anything much. It was our fault.

I really became a part of *Foxfire* the next year. I had always wanted to be in journalism. In the fifth grade, one of my poems was published in a school paper. In tenth grade, whenever Elizabeth Rickman, Emma Buchanan, Mary Garth, and I had study hall, we'd go over to Wig's room and answer letters and make deposits. I was a good secretary. I did a lot of transcribing of tapes and answering mail. That was truly my big involvement in *Foxfire.* It was a good way to get out of study hall, and we could get back there and talk while we were doing it, but there were skills that I acquired that I didn't realize I was acquiring. I didn't have a bank account at that time, so I guess that was my first association with banking.

I remember trying to interview my grandmother about making lye soap and quilts. She was hard to interview, though, because she didn't measure anything. Besides, I used to be embarrassed about using lye soap, and I was embarrassed that I had quilts instead of store-bought blankets. Wig was saying, "Go and interview your grandparents about how to do this," and I would think, "Why would I interview her, put it in a magazine, and send it to California for somebody to know that about me?" I didn't want people to know that I used lye soap and had never slept under a store-bought blanket. All this might seem neat to Wig or to somebody in California, but to me, I was trying to get away from it all.

But that's the kind of information people were demanding. I don't think anybody would have bought a regular literary magazine. People were writing letters and saying, "Lose the haiku! We want to hear more about how to make a log cabin." Wig was excited about the fact that his students were quiet for a minute. He was truly interested in everything, and that, along with the response from the readers, is what started the interviews.

I remember lots of the community kids doing interviews. They had contacts. I remember Wig also getting contacts from the community kids, but then including the boarding students on those interviews. I think the reason the boarding kids were into it was because they wanted to learn this stuff, and, also, they were stuck on the campus. When Wig took them off on interviews was usually the only time they got off except for church. There were also some of the community kids that were real involved, though, like George Burch and Jan Brown. They really enjoyed *Foxfire*. And there were a lot who didn't buy into it. My sister never bought into it. I guess no one thing ever works equally well with everybody.

ᴡᴡ

GEORGE BURCH: Wig was our tenth-grade English teacher. A new teacher for the tenth grade is like food for mosquitoes in South Georgia when a North Georgia person goes down there. "Oh boy, fresh meat! Let's see if we can tear him up a little bit." We were typical boys, and we'd push our luck every once in a while. But I always pictured

Eliot Wigginton as knowing what he was doing and having enough common sense to get it done, and that never changed.

Wig had never heard of terms like "run like a scalded dog." Everybody in Rabun County knows what you mean when you've got a hot rod that will run like a scalded dog; he didn't know. Some of these things intrigued him. He started talking about a magazine, presented it to the class as an idea, and we picked up on it and went from there.

When the project started, we got to interview people and work toward accomplishing the goal of producing the magazine. We had responsibilities, and we had to carry out those responsibilities. My responsibilities for the first issue were to help solicit funds and do some interviews. I'd also deliver the issues to the stores. I was involved with public speaking the second year the magazine came out. I went to the Rotary Club in Clayton, and to fund-raising events in Atlanta.

Donations were our biggest way to get funds. We went to Clayton, Highlands, Clarkesville, and Dillard. I believe everybody got tired of us. They almost walked out the door when they saw us coming. Sometimes we would even go to Franklin, North Carolina, to get donations, just to keep the magazine alive.

Everything had to be typed letter perfect because the text was photographed and printed photo-offset. If you made a mistake, you had to retype the section. I wasn't a very good typist, and I would have given one arm and maybe a leg to have word processors like *Foxfire* uses today. I would have probably given both arms and both legs to have a spell check like you have today. The modern technology has helped in every way except one: it still takes a person to write it. It doesn't matter whether it's handwritten or done on the word processor; it's still the author that has to do the work.

Everything about producing that first issue was pretty old-fashioned. I can remember going out to Cross Printing and having to run a stitcher when the pages were printed, and that would staple it. You would slip each magazine under the stitcher and stomp the pedal.

Then we would take the magazine to the stores to sell. I was amazed at the speed [with which] they sold. We were back into a second printing within a few weeks. At that point we decided it would be good to begin producing a magazine every so often. We started looking at doing it on a quarterly basis.

I knew we would publish that first magazine. At the start, I thought it would be a magazine, but I didn't picture Foxfire growing into what it is now. We were just trying to get that first magazine started, and it worked out.

I took out my old notebook from the tenth-grade English class the other night and I was reading it. Wig used to write comments in our notebooks such as, "Your notes are not organized enough or neat enough, B−." Looking back, I don't think he was any harder on us because we were the first Foxfire class. He walked in expecting certain things, and we should be able to do them. He did some nice things that changed the pace. We didn't work on the magazine all the time. For example, we read *Lord of the Flies* and *To Kill a Mockingbird*.

*Foxfire* was something that I knew I wasn't going to be involved in forever. Leaving after graduation wasn't a great sadness or a great joy, either one. You just had to move on.

ᴡ

JAN BROWN BONNER: I was in tenth grade when we started *Foxfire*. Wig was an interesting teacher. Even before the idea for a literary magazine was formed, we did things that we never did in other English classes. I remember we kept a journal, which I enjoyed doing, and we also listened to popular music and studied the lyrics as poetry. I remember trying to figure out meter. Not long ago, I found this silly poem I wrote in the tenth grade, and I read it to my children, and oh, they thought that was hilarious. I guess my classmates did too. But we were all good friends. We had all known each other for so long we weren't worried about what the other person was going to say if we had crazy ideas.

I enjoyed Wig as a teacher. I felt comfortable with him. I felt like I could talk to him. He wasn't quite the authority figure other teachers had been.

The first issue of *Foxfire* came about during our tenth-grade English class. Wig came up with the idea of a literary magazine which we, as a class, would produce. We wrote some poetry—haiku mostly— and other English classes in surrounding high schools were invited to participate. We decided which ones we wanted to use. I was very excited about putting together a magazine. English has always been one of my favorite subjects, and writing for a magazine seemed like fun to me.

We as a class were urged to make most of the decisions regarding content, name, how we should lay out the magazine, and the business decisions. I can recall Wig standing at the blackboard while we decided, "Yes, we are going to do this," or, "No, we aren't going to do that." He was at the blackboard a lot. Does he still do that?

There were a few cases when students didn't perform up to expectations, but mostly Wig kept us motivated and usually everybody did their fair share. Like all fifteen-year-olds, we had to have someone to motivate us. Sometimes Wig would get upset with us, but it was probably because we needed it. He was enthused about the project. It was something he really wanted.

When the first issue was published, we were proud of the magazine. But after it sold out completely, we were startled. We sold the first six hundred copies, and we thought, "Hey, this is *working!* Let's do it again." The success of the project kept us going then. We printed six hundred additional copies, and then we had class discussions about the direction *Foxfire* should take, if and when we should publish again, and what should be in the next issue. Most people liked the area folklore better than the poetry, so the focus began to shift. To tell you the truth, I rarely read the literary section. As I worked on the magazine I was interested in the stories, not the literary part.

When we decided to do a second magazine, we talked about how to finance it and how to organize the work. Fund-raising was always a problem in the early years. We talked about whether or not to use advertising, whether or not to offer subscriptions, and if so, how much to charge for subscriptions and individual issues of the magazine, and basically how to make ends meet. Letters asking for donations were sent to people.

Most of my responsibilities the first year or so had to do with the record keeping. I handled much of the mail that came in. The subscribers' names, addresses, and how many issues they had received, or were to receive, were written on index cards. Subscription records during those first few years were kept in little recipe boxes. When it came time to send renewal notices, we would find the ones who had received four issues and send notices to them.

The first year almost all correspondence was handwritten. As we got more money, we were able to print flyers to ask for renewals, gift subscriptions, and things like that. But that didn't happen for several years.

When we first started, we didn't know what we were doing. We did it because it was there to do. However, after we got into it and realized that not only were we learning something, but that we were, in fact, preserving some important parts of our local history, it gave us a motive and a purpose. But as time progressed, all kinds of exciting things were happening because of the interest that was generated by the concept.

We did a good bit of the work in small groups. Group work was not a difficult thing because we all knew each other, and the people who worked on *Foxfire* were committed to it. Therefore we were receptive to each others' ideas, and it seemed to work out okay. Actually, I think *Foxfire* brought my friends and me closer together. We spent a lot of time together after school and during the summer working on *Foxfire*. Mike Cook, Paul Gillespie, Tommy Wilson, Judy Brown, and I were all good friends, so going out on interviews was more fun than work.

My father was the principal at the school during the years *Foxfire* was based at Rabun Gap, and my mother was the librarian, and they were totally behind the project because they saw it was a good learning experience. Being in education, they saw the benefits, and how it could help me and others to become better students.

ᵂᴬᵂ

JUDY MARINDA BROWN PLANT: The funniest thing that comes to mind about Rabun Gap was the mix of students we had there. We had mountain folks like me who lived at home and were day students, and city kids who stayed in the dormitory. It was very interesting, therefore, to put that diverse group together. It also had an effect on *Foxfire*, giving it the benefit of a variety of minds and resources.

Since I had my grandmother and my mom watching over me, I had to work pretty hard to keep my grades up. I also had two older sisters, Becky and Rachel, who had done quite well as far as grades were concerned, so I had to try at least to meet their standards and to stay out of trouble. I was also in Beta Club and 4-H. I was in cheerleading, but I gave it up my senior year so I could spend my time with *Foxfire*.

I remember Wig's tenth-grade English class when we first came up with the name *Foxfire*. It was one of the times when he broke us down into groups, and we did some brainstorming. We went through quite a few possibilities, but no one wanted to hear any more after we read that one. I think it's an absolutely perfect name.

We had to work very hard to raise money for the early issues of the magazine. We had to ask people and businesses for contributions. There were articles that appeared in newspapers like the *Anderson*

*Independent* and *Atlanta Journal*, and when we started seeing the articles, which brought in a lot of subscriptions, it really showed us that people were expecting something from us, and we didn't want to let them down.

There were even a few times when we went to Atlanta and to Athens to speak at dinners in order to get people to contribute. We'd get a lot of subscriptions, and we got big checks in the mail, and we thought that was great. But then we found out that it wasn't quite enough to pay the printer, that we still needed more. It seemed like we were always a little behind. Sometimes, just to save a little money on stamps, we hand-delivered magazines to neighbors who had subscribed.

We had to be involved in all aspects of magazine production. We had a business editor and a subscription editor, and even though I was allowed to pass on most of that sort of work to someone else, since I was the literary editor and later the editor-in-chief, I still liked to get in there and address some envelopes.

I thought it was very exciting. There was always something new happening. It was also tremendous to see articles about something we'd done in the *Atlanta Journal*, for example. It was good to be published, but it didn't make us feel as if we were great writers. We had a lot of things we could improve on. Probably my favorite part was going out and getting the information. I liked doing the interviews better than I did the poetry and literary-type work.

**ヽ∧ノ**

R. E. Cross, PRINTER: Wig didn't know anything about making a magazine. He brought in a handful of material and said, "Here's what we have." It was a lot of work trying to get it organized, and seeing what needed to be done. He just had an idea, and he worked from that. We just had to work with him and get what he wanted.

We had a time getting everything [for the magazine] and publishing our weekly newspaper [the *Clayton Tribune*] at the same time. I'm afraid that we had to work after hours every once in a while, and it took weeks to get a magazine out. [When we were printing and assembling it] Wig would bring in two or three students at a time to help out. He was very cooperative and put forth the effort. He'd come in and help all the time. Sometimes, though, he'd come in on a Tuesday or Wednesday, and we'd have to tell him we couldn't do a thing because we had to get the newspaper out every Wednesday.

R. E. Cross, now retired,
printed the first issues of
*Foxfire*.

It seems like we started with about six hundred copies [of the first issue], and later it got up to about five thousand copies an issue. Each magazine had different colors of paper and ink. They each had to have a special kind of paper for the cover of the magazine, and we had a big time with that. There was some work, and some headaches with it, too.

Finally we had to stop printing them because we weren't actually able to handle the job. We didn't have the equipment to do it and the time to take to get it out once they got up to bigger quantities, so they found another printer. But I missed printing the magazine. I got used to jumping around to get it out, and all the rest. It kind of left a hole—not having something to do with it.

At the time, I didn't think *Foxfire* would go so far. It was just an experiment at that time. They have done real well. And I still have one copy of every issue we printed.

**WW**

MARY PITTS, POSTMISTRESS: I mailed out the first issue of *Foxfire* magazine in 1967. We had to get used to second-class mailings because we'd never had anything like that before. Wig would read the postal laws, and I'd read them, and then Mr. Dickerson would read them. We wanted to get it right.

**WW**

MORRIS BROWN, PRINCIPAL: Even before the establishment of the Foxfire program, the Rabun Gap School was fairly well known, especially for a school of its size. It already had a strong basis as a good, reputable school. However, *Foxfire* certainly enhanced this reputation. Instead of being only a northeast Georgia or Georgia school, it became known nationally.

Morris Brown, retired, was the principal at the high school when *Foxfire* began.

I really can't take any credit for the Foxfire enterprise itself, although I did try to create an atmosphere for teachers, whether it be Wig or somebody else, so they could use their talents for the benefit of the students or for the school itself. Knowing Wig, I had great confidence in him, and I certainly did not do anything to stand in the way of his program, which was something that would help the school accomplish its goal of giving students experiences they had never had before.

The only thing we simply could not help with was funding. When they were putting the first issue together, I told Wig, "We really don't have any money to help get it published." We figured that perhaps selling it would take care of most of it. Then when *Foxfire* did become financially stable, naturally the school received no money from that. *Foxfire* had a totally separate account, and all the money *Foxfire* earned went back into *Foxfire*'s operation.

*Foxfire* affected the school in many ways. When the program was just getting started, Wig would bring the local citizens about whom the students were writing to school, and many times we had programs built around these people. They had talents they would share with the students at assemblies—music, story-telling, etc.

Sometimes there were scheduling problems involved with *Foxfire* interviews and other trips. These were things the administration had to deal with. For example, if some students had to go on a long trip, we'd make provisions so that they could leave school a little early. In general, however, *Foxfire* was not something done in lieu of other classes; it was done to supplement those classes, and so it didn't create that many problems for me to deal with.

Also, in a school, when one teacher does outstanding work and gets a lot of publicity, other teachers may become jealous, but I never found this at all at Rabun Gap. We as teachers felt good when one of our own received recognition. We all shared in the success of Wig and the students.

When *Foxfire* was first started, I felt it would succeed. I had known Wig long enough to be sure that anything he undertook to do, he would see it through. I had no idea, however, that it would grow to what it has become today. I thought it would be a local project that would last for two or three years at the most and maybe get a little statewide publicity. I think Wig's quoted me a number of times saying that I didn't figure there'd be enough material to last over more than two or three years, not in a small community like Rabun County.

Even though I never dared to dream that what actually happened would ever happen, I was enthusiastic about *Foxfire* from the start, and after twenty-five years, I am still enthusiastic about it. I feel enormously privileged to have been in the school that gave birth to the Foxfire enterprise.

# 1968–69:
# The Johns Hopkins Year

WIG: During my second year at Rabun Gap, Geoff Hewitt, one of my friends from college, called and told me about a program at Johns Hopkins University, where he was at that point, and where you could get a master's degree in English through a special division called the Writing Seminars. Through that department, you would write constantly and have your work critiqued by a professional author and by other members of the class. When he sent me the information, I liked what I saw and applied for the program for several reasons. One was that I didn't have a master's in English. I had a master of Arts in Teaching, and I thought it would be valuable to have the other degree as part of my credentials. The bigger reason that I applied for it, though, was because I wasn't sure at that point that I wanted to stay in high school teaching or in Rabun County. I thought teaching at the college level might be interesting, and one of the things I liked about the Hopkins program was the fact that while you were getting a master's degree, you were also required to teach one section of English 101.

After I got accepted and decided that I would give it a try, the first question, of course, was, "So what are we going to do about the magazine?" I was working real closely with these student editors, and the magazine was going extraordinarily well, and they were unanimous in wanting to keep it going while I was gone. So I spent part of the spring and summer developing an editor's handbook, which laid out the various procedures we had designed together—something they could refer to if needed. I also added some messages that I hoped would pick up their spirits if they found themselves getting discouraged. After I got that squared away, I had a final meeting with the students, and we figured out some procedures for them staying in touch with me, and I left.

I was real curious to see how serious they would be about keeping *Foxfire* going. I felt sure they'd keep it going for the first several months, but I had some real concerns because I thought the enthusiasm might diminish as the pressures of their senior year began to take over. While I was at Hopkins, Judy Brown would call regularly and we'd have a conference on the phone. And there was a constant stream of letters from people like Judy, Jan, and George telling me what was happening, and the energy level never slacked. They just hit it at full speed from the beginning of the year, and they hit it all year long.

What really impressed me about what they were doing was that there was no adult at the school assigned to work with them, and so they were basically doing it all on their own. They didn't have a special class, and a lot was being done after school hours. They'd go to each others' homes and spread the stuff out on a living room floor and get it done there. The parents were also helping out by taking them to interviews.

Then, when a new magazine was pretty much ready to go, they would send me the material, photos, and all, and I'd go over it. At that point, I was typing up the final pages for the printer because I had access to equipment in Baltimore. When the magazine was ready, I would go to a business office and rent an electric typewriter, type up the final pages, send them to the printer, and the kids would take it from there.

I don't think I have ever seen a group of students work that hard for that long a period of time without an adult being right there with them to encourage them and push them along. I was really impressed. They had put so much into it over the first two years, and now it was clear that they cared about it in much more than a superficial way. They didn't want to let it die. That was the foundation of my conviction that even people that age can carry enormous responsibility, and it is largely because of that group of students that I returned to Rabun Gap and have been here ever since.

▞▚▞

GEORGE BURCH: We decided to have an editing board after the first year. Judy Brown was editor-in-chief, Jan Brown was in charge of subscriptions, Tommy Wilson and Charles Pennington were in on it, too. We all worked together to produce the magazine. I was voted business editor. By the time Wig left, we had worked on the magazine for two years, so we knew what we were doing. When he left, he handed us each an editor's notebook and said, "Here, gang, it's up to you." It had a lot of things: the articles we were working on, some of the previous covers, subscriptions, who to contact for help, and what we were trying to accomplish. Then we had the magazine alone for our senior year. We didn't have a class for the magazine, or a faculty member to work with us. We had study hall, though. We'd spend most of study hall reading articles and trying to organize them and finding which ones we wanted to print. We then typed them and sent them to Wig so he could read them. Time was a problem. It always seemed like we had a deadline facing us. We always had to get something finished.

Mr. Zero Webb was one of the people I helped interview. He was located up in Webbtown. You get up there by going up Betty's Creek and cutting back toward Otto, North Carolina. It's called Mulberry now. We interviewed him about splitting board shingles. I remember that we ate dinner there, and they didn't have screens, so we would shoo flies away and then take a bite of food. I wasn't all that sophisticated, being from Rabun Gap, but we had screens in our house. I just wasn't accustomed to not having screens.

There was another guy who lived at the top of Mulberry that we featured in one of our magazines. The day before Christmas holidays, Dale Justice and Jerry Lanich and I went up to his house in my truck to give him a complimentary copy. We got stuck and had to walk out. I had a load of cow feed on the truck, and boy, was my father mad!

But my best memory of a certain contact was that day at Webbtown splitting board shingles. I just thought that you took a bunch of logs and split them up any old way, but whenever we got into how to use the mallet and the froe I found out different.

I also remember one time we went on an interview with Mr. Noel Moore who lived up on Darnell's Creek. It was about syrup making. We had the tape recorder set up, but we didn't have a nice convenient thing like the ones you have. We had a regular reel-to-reel tape recorder. We taped the whole thing, and we got back and went to play it, and there was nothing there. We were in pure agony because we were coming up on a deadline and we thought we'd lost the interview.

As a high school student, George Burch spent an afternoon learning from Zero Webb how to split shingles out of white oak.

Fortunately, one of us had pushed the wrong button, or had flipped the tape over, and we were playing the wrong side. We finally flipped the tape around and found our interview.

Being business editor, I spent a lot of time getting money. My job was to get donations, get patron subscriptions, and take magazines out to certain locations. We'd give them so many magazines and then have to go back and collect the money.

That's something that students don't understand, and in thinking back a bit, I guess that's something we had to learn. What we were doing was important, but if we didn't get it done, it didn't get taken care of automatically. Working with *Foxfire*, you found out that was true. You wanted to have the printing costs covered for the magazine, so you went out and got them covered. You learned that if it's something you want you have to keep working at it. If you sit and wait, it won't happen, but if you want it and work on it, it has a good chance of happening.

We stayed together because it boils back basically to the same thing: we all had a job, and we all knew we had to do it. We ran into problems, but it was real nice in a way because there was no adult to say, "This is the way you're going to solve this problem." We sat there and solved the problems. We didn't have any other choice. After the magazine was established, none of us ever really thought of saying the heck with it, since we had the subscriptions and we were under an obligation, and we met the obligation. It was an effort by everybody.

▚▚▚

JUDY MARINDA BROWN PLANT: When we were in our senior year, we carried on with *Foxfire* on our own. It was quite challenging. We really had to think. We had more experiences than we'd ever had before in our lives. We were so busy, and when we got through, we still kept looking around for additional things to do. We made sure we didn't miss anything. We didn't want Wig to come back and say, "Oh no!"

I worked with Wig to get a lot of things done that he wanted us to do while he was away, and I did a lot of delegating to the other students. We had different people assigned tasks, and while he was gone, we were allowed to have a meeting during school time once a week. We met in the biology lab, and Mr. Brown would sit in on the meetings with us. We would review subscription money coming in and try to work on planning ahead on what interviews and what subjects we would be doing.

My grandparents were in a lot of the first issues of *Foxfire*. They also helped identify contacts for us. I interviewed them every single chance I got. This was an easy thing to do because they lived just up the road from where I grew up. I'd disappear from home for hours to go to talk to them. My grandmother showed me how to weave a rag rug, and then some linen towels. I interviewed my grandfather about making oak splits for chair making.

Margaret Norton was a valuable source of information for articles, recipes, and contacts on other subjects. She invited us to the quilting bee held by the Homemakers' Club of Betty's Creek. We talked to the ladies while they worked, taking notes and photographs. Each of the ladies had pieced together several squares of the poplar leaf pattern and then put them all together. Many quilts were made that way, and I think it was a fun social occasion, too. I can remember quilting upstairs at my grandmother's house with my mother and great-aunts. They enjoyed telling stories to the younger girls. A lot of times they would talk about romance. They inspired us by competition to get the stitches smaller. And they put someone beside us to look over our shoulders and make us take out every toe-hanging stitch we put in. Quilts were an absolute necessity during my childhood because we grew up without central heat. I liked the heavy ones, and I piled several on and pulled them over my head when the temperature dropped. I mean it dropped. You could see your breath frost up in the

Marinda Brown taught several students how to weave. She said, "I take my time in weavin'. It just don't pay t'weave a piece of material and throw it away, I found out. Weavin's just so satisfying. If you're interested in what you're doing, you can just sit down and forget everything. Last week I didn't feel too good. I was tired but I was doing something that I wanted t'get done. I kept right at it when I really didn't feel like it and my mind wouldn't stay on it. I'd have t'go back take some out. I noticed your feelings have something t'do with it. Like th'way y'work your beater. Sometimes you give it a harder jerk than y'do other times. And it makes your weaving a little closer together. It'll tell on you all th'way through." (*Foxfire 2*) Marinda passed away in 1985.

bedroom. About ten years after the *Foxfire* article on quilting, the Homemakers' Club of Betty's Creek quilted a king-sized quilt for me that I had pieced together. I feel like celebrities did my quilt, and I won't let it go for a thousand dollars. I was flabbergasted when I looked back at the article note indicating the quilts we pictured in *Foxfire* would be sold for $12.50. We actually sold that quilt to a *Foxfire* subscriber.

My family bought butter and buttermilk from Margaret Norton so I knew who to call on for our article on churning. It was cold the day we went to interview her, and she had a nice fire going in the fireplace.

Marinda's husband, Harry Brown, Sr., made stools and rocking chairs. At the request of then-governor Jimmy Carter, he made a rocking chair for each of the Southern governors. "We put in a pretty good bit of crops—corn, 'taters, beans. My woman had a good garden. We had our milk and butter, and most of the time a hog to kill. Nowadays we have to live out of paper pokes. I told someone the other day now it was bills and pills—that's all. [Laughter]" (*Foxfire*, Summer 1983) Harry died in 1978. Harry Brown, Jr., and his wife, Estelle, now live in their house and continue to produce crafts using their designs.

Margaret sat down beside the churn and went about her task while we talked. Wig had asked for an article from the standpoint that if people had to start churning again, what would they need to know? On churning, I knew you had to make the dash go up and down till you felt your arm would fall off, but he wanted more! I personally had churned butter more times than I wanted to, but it was a challenge to sit down and get the steps on paper.

Even though in one sense Wig wasn't there that year, in another sense he was always there. We heard from him regularly and we were able to talk to him on the phone and ask him questions. We got a tremendous amount of encouragement from him. He was always looking over our shoulders encouraging us, or giving us a kick when we were going in the wrong direction. He sent letters and packages to us about once a week. He made sure subscriptions were handled and that we had all the addresses we needed. He also helped us in contacting and working with or avoiding the press.

I remember one time when we had sent out an issue close to Christmas. Wig had gone to his parents' house. His father had asked us to enter a subscription for one of his friends. The issue arrived early, and Wig was really impressed that we had processed it before he got home.

Believe it or not, we didn't have any trouble at all getting people to work. It seemed like there were a lot of people who were willing to help with everything. As a matter of fact, some of the letters we sent to Wig were ones saying, "What else can we do? We're all finished."

By that time, we had set up a structure where people had to qualify in order to be able to work on the magazine. We didn't want anyone to be a member of the organization and not do any actual work. As new students like Mike Cook and Paul Gillespie came along, we put them on the junior board. George kept a special notebook, and anytime a member of the junior staff did anything to help, he'd write it down in that notebook.

Wig talked to us and gave us an opportunity to make decisions. We didn't set any limits as to what it could be made into. I really think he encouraged us to give it our best.

**WW**

HARRY BROWN, JR. [JUDY'S FATHER]: While Wig was gone, Jan and Judy worked together practically all the time. Where one of them was, the other one was. I took them on a lot of interviews, and I guess Morris did, too. All of them, I believe, enjoyed the interviews. Most of these old people around here were interesting to talk to anyway, and liked to talk.

ᵂᵂᵂ

JAN BROWN BONNER: Much of the record keeping, especially work involving circulation, was done at my house which was located just across the valley from the school. Judy would come over quite often and we would work at our dining room table or in my bedroom. We kept track of most of the correspondence and tried to answer any questions concerning subscriptions or, basically, anything else about which a person might inquire. Sometimes we would read a letter to one another aloud, look at each other with our mouths open (because we had no idea of the answer), and burst into laughter. Often we wondered how we ever got into the position of "experts" on mountain lore, but with the help of Wig or my parents, or through our own research, we could usually come up with an answer.

The notebook Wig left with each of us was invaluable. It gave us an organized set of procedures to follow. You should remember that our responsibilities were not limited to story ideas, interviews, and writing alone. We were actually running a small business. Unusual problems frequently arose. I remember once that we had a big order of magazines to ship and did not know exactly how to go about doing it. We had to go out and round up boxes, package them correctly, include all necessary materials, and then figure out how to mail the order properly—with the help of the postmistress.

Our daily routine varied. We were busy on weekdays with class, homework, and in addition, many of us were on the basketball team and had practice after school. *Foxfire* work was done during "in-between" times in the evening and on weekends. Many of us had been classmates for years, but our involvement in the magazine seemed to enhance our friendships. I don't remember too many arguments, but I do remember a lot of laughter and fun.

Of the people I interviewed, one person who really stands out in my mind is Kenny Runion. We were working on an article about herbs and wild plant foods, so he decided to take us up the mountain right behind his house and identify wild plants for us. The mountain seemed straight up. He must have been in his sixties or seventies then, and he had no problem at all. He just scooted right up the mountain, and we were grabbing onto tree limbs trying to pull ourselves up! I played basketball and tennis, and I was in good shape at the time. It made me feel bad that I couldn't keep up with a seventy-year-old man.

When we finally stopped to rest on top of the mountain, you could see all over. He told a lot of stories up there. He could ramble on for hours—he was not intimidated by the camera or by the tape recorder. He loved being asked questions and having his picture made. He would pose for the pictures. He was a performer! Sometimes I didn't

Kenny Runion was one of the most enthusiastic interviewees the students met. He entertained ten years' worth of students and hundreds of visitors from out of town: "Why, you *know* that there's a power if y'just look out. Now they talk about goin' t'th'moon, and they may of went. I don't know. But that moon. Is it standin' still, or movin', or what about it? Rises here [he points], and th'next mornin' it's here. Plumb across th'world. What d'y'think about that now? And when it goes, it's dark nights. And when it starts up, it's a bright light thing. It's little and gets bigger and bigger. What changes that? They's somebody—somethin'—behind it. It'll change. Then it'll get fuller and fuller till it's a full moon. There's a whole lot to study about in this world, boy, when y'get right on t'th'business. Shore is." (*Foxfire 2*) Kenny died in 1983, and his little house in Mountain City is abandoned.

know whether or not to believe him! He could come up with some of the wildest stories.

[Another contact that I remember is Jake Waldroop.] Once Mike and Paul and I were working on some material Jake gave us about how to make a turkey caller. He made all these noises demonstrating how the turkey call should go, and we were trying to transcribe the tape. It sounded like "chababbbbbba." I can remember just rolling on the floor laughing because we were trying to spell the sound so that if somebody read it they could understand it. It wasn't easy!

Beulah Perry, a black lady who lived outside of Clayton, was another person I enjoyed interviewing. One thing I visualize about that interview is how immaculate the inside of her house was, with all her little china teacups and things. She was such a lady, and she had an eloquent tone and poise that I loved.

Jan Brown interviewed Beulah Perry. Beulah Perry taught a generation of students that black Appalachians have stories and wisdom and sensitivity and humor: "Most of th'old womens [midwives] in those days smoked cobbed pipes. Our favorite old lady was called Aunt Haddy Corner. Well, if we saw that old lady comin' down th'road with that smoke from her cobbed pipe, we'd know that it was Aunt Had Corner, and we would watch and wait till she got near, and we could see that little black bag in her hand, and we'd say, 'Yonder comes Aunt Had. She's carryin' somebody a little baby.' " (*Foxfire 2*).

People in this area of the country have a certain sense of compassion that you don't normally see. Of course, growing up I had always seen that, but I didn't recognize it for what it was. Now that I have been around and seen how people are and how they react and how they think about things, I really believe, by comparison, that the older people here we interviewed have a determined yet compassionate nature that is all their own. I don't remember one interview that I wasn't treated nicely. I was scared to death as a teenager going up to strange places way back in the woods to do interviews. I didn't know how, especially when we first started. But they would welcome you so warmly, and always offer you something to eat or drink, make sure you were in the shade and comfortable.

I'm sure they probably recognized our inexperience, and they were very kind about helping us cover mistakes. Sometimes they were a little bit nervous until they got to know us and realize what the magazine was and what we were doing. It was important to them that we not portray them in a way that they did not want to be portrayed. Some were skeptical about what we were doing and a little standoffish—not in a rude sense, but in what they would say to us—until they realized that we were enjoying what they were saying. Then I could tell by the way they reacted that they felt maybe we were learning a lot from them; and I think once they realized that, then maybe they saw us the way we saw them—just special people to share with.

The reason we persevered during that year Wig was away—as I see it—was threefold. First—Wig had put his faith in us. We didn't want to fail. The project was very special to him and he was always forthcoming in his praise of us. We couldn't let him down. Secondly, we were committed. Imagine having what began as a simple English assignment blossom into a magazine read by hundreds and growing with each issue. In addition, the realization, as *Foxfire* began to find its niche, that we were indeed preserving a valuable piece of Americana gave us incentive and a sense of importance as high school students. Third, to me it was like having a job I enjoyed. We had fun, we learned, we were recognized. It proved we as teenagers could contribute, make decisions, organize our time, and learn from our mistakes. To have given a group of us the opportunity to go it alone during the year Wig was away and to see that we obviously succeeded, I believe, was one of the most important milestones of Foxfire's history.

◆◆◆

GENELLE BROWN [JAN'S MOTHER]: Of course, Wig was there—even though he was in Baltimore, he was with them all the way. And he had things well organized. He left them instructions on everything. And of course they could write or call him if something came up. He left them feeling they could do it because they had planned it all out.

But their stuff was all over the house. We had a mess here for a year! [Laughs.]

᭥᭥

EMMA BUCHANAN CHASTAIN: Mother was real excited when I came home talking to her about us doing a magazine, and when I'd bring the magazines home, everybody in the family would come and look at them.

My husband, Tommy, was also in *Foxfire*. He's a year older than I am. He was one of the reasons Wig started *Foxfire*, because Tommy was one of those boys who didn't give a rip about school. Wig was trying to find out what would occupy the minds of boys like him. Tommy liked *Foxfire*, and he's always kept up with it. He goes to the National Board Meetings with me, and he goes to the annual Foxfire picnic.

Pearl Martin was my first and only interview because I mainly worked on circulation. I liked that better. Those were the days when we kept our subscriber cards in little recipe boxes, and now you all have computers!

I got to know Pearl, of course, much better after the interview. When I went on the interview, all I knew was that she was Pearl Martin and that she was Andrea's grandmother. Since it was the first time I'd ever been on an interview, I thought, "Golly bum, what are we going to say, and what are we going to do?" But once we got started, it was easy because she was so sweet. You could ask her anything, and she'd grin at you and tell you all this stuff. She'd call us "younguns," and that would tickle us to death. She was just darling. The thing that impressed me most was her attitude toward us. She was so happy that we came to see her because that meant the young people were paying attention to the older people, and her attitude just made us feel so comfortable. Probably she thought we girls were crazy, but we could tell she really loved kids, and we couldn't really capture that in the article.

I'll never forget what she looked like. She had her hair up in a little old ball. She kept things nice and neat, and she was a very clean, pretty woman.

We had a real fun time the day of that interview. While we were up there, we got to talking about all sorts of little country things [like the weather and her garden]. Then we got to asking her about making lye soap. I'd never seen that done. She was definitely prepared to show us how to make it. She had the ashes sitting there, and she told us how they'd get the ashes out of their stoves and use them for the soap. She had a big black pot out in her yard, and she was constantly

Pearl Martin taught (l to r) Liz Rickman, Andrea Burrell (her granddaughter), and Emma Buchanan how to make lye soap . . . "I've got two feather beds and a straw bed. I'm goin't'keep that straw bed as long as I live. We used t', when we's a'comin'up children—you see, they'd cut and thresh their wheat and rye ever'year. Well, y'see we'd fill our beds up ever'year. Ever'year. And now, since they've quit that, why I had one full and I just kep' it. Just sun it and wash th'tick'n'things, and it's just as good as it ever was. I'm keepin' it for a keepsake. I don't have to use it at all, but I just want t'keep it. And I've got two feather beds. I've got one from my momma, and Oscar's got one from his momma. So we just swing along." (*The Foxfire Book*) Pearl died in 1978. The house she and her husband, Oscar, lived in is now owned by an Atlanta family.

standing there and stirring it. It looked just like pudding. She got all of us to help her stir it.

We asked her about washing her clothes in it, and she talked about how she'd washed clothes on the rub board and just scrubbed her little cold hands sore because they didn't have washing machines in her day. She sent us each home with a bar of lye soap. I kept mine for a long time, but I never used it.

From that interview, we could see how hard times really were back when she was growing up. We just go down to the store and buy a bar of soap now. Her generation, on the other hand, had to stand and stir for a day just to get a bar of soap. We have it a lot different than they ever did.

I can remember when we didn't have water in our house, but we had a little springhouse, and Mother kept the milk and stuff down there. I can remember all these changes, and I'm just thirty-eight. Pearl was probably seventy when we interviewed her, and the changes that she saw in her lifetime were just unreal.

▼▼▼

ANDREA BURRELL POTTS: When *Foxfire* was new, we didn't exactly know what to expect. We had Wig for English, and we liked him. He was in his early twenties at the time, and he made you feel energetic and want to do things. He was real enthusiastic. So even when he was gone, we kept going. We did a lot of interviews. I think the funniest thing that happened to me was when I went to interview Jake Waldroop. Frenda and I had pulled up and Mrs. Waldroop was standing out on the porch. She invited us into the house, and we got a glass of water and were watching some men in the field. Mrs. Waldroop shooed us out of the kitchen. The men were trying to birth a calf and she didn't think that we should watch it. She wouldn't even let us near the windows!

We also interviewed my grandmother, Pearl, about making soap. We set up the interview, and when we went over, she had everything set and ready for us when we got there. We asked Grandma if you could put perfume in the soap, and she just died laughing. She thought it was just hilarious that we would want to put perfume in the soap. Grandma said, "Sure, I guess you could if you wanted to!"

Maw used to work around the house in her old work clothes. Whenever we went to do an interview, Maw got dressed up. She would

Pearl Martin often went to the woods to gather sassafras branches. Here she chops them into pieces for making tea.

Jake and Bertha Waldroop taught us how to hunt turkey and bear, how to cook both, and how to tan hides. They also taught us about nature. Jake: "Chestnuts grow inside a burr, and it's a big thing, as big as your fist, and 'long about the fall of the year when it starts frosting they'll open. Then the chestnuts fall out, and later the burr itself will drop off. I've seen them a time or two in the fall, it's come a dry spell of weather and the [burrs] would open, but there wouldn't be enough moisture, and [the nut] wouldn't get loose of the burr, and it'd stay in there. I've seen hundreds of bushels hanging up, and you couldn't pick one to eat. Then it'd start to cloud up, rain some, and it was a sight on earth—just in an hour or two the whole earth would be covered with chestnuts." (*Foxfire 6*) Jake died in 1985, and Bertha in 1989.

fix her hair and have her rouge on. She didn't actually work that way. Soon as we got ready to leave, she would change back into her work clothes!

▚▚▚

MIKE COOK: Paul Gillespie and I just had gotten into doing things with the magazine when Wig left to go to Johns Hopkins. I was just doing photographs at the time. I had been in on some interviews and I was meeting with the staff.

During this space of time, I was basically a low man on the totem pole. I had been elected to the junior board, and I was involved with some of the work, but not the nitty gritty work that kept everything going. During the year, we kept everything very well organized. I remember working close to Tommy and Jan. We were all real good friends. We all lived close together. If you would look at some of the things I did with Foxfire, you would see Jan, Tommy, and me over and over. You know how things work when you're in school. Your buddy gets into something, and he says, "This is pretty neat. Why don't you get into this, too?" I remember clearly us sitting together for three days all day and all night putting an issue out. Everything went smoothly. It was a good year.

Wig kept touching base with people. I remember being dumbfounded one night when Wig called me long distance from Johns Hopkins. He was giving me notes and messages to give to other people who were on the staff. It was a big deal [to me] because I was in the tenth grade.

▚▚▚

PAUL GILLESPIE: I do not look back on the late sixties with corny nostalgia. I do listen to music of that period. Once in a while, I'll hear something from that era and it will trigger certain thoughts and images. Nineteen sixty-nine happened to be the year I started my association with *Foxfire* magazine. It was the third year of *Foxfire*'s existence. I worked on the magazine for a lot of different reasons, not the least of which was the pure enjoyment of feeling like I was doing something worthwhile. There wasn't a whole lot to do in Rabun Gap and Dillard.

My first big experience with the magazine was putting together the Summer 1969 issue, devoted to the construction of log cabins and related buildings like smokehouses and barns. Many of them were made the same way—the walls, the chinking, and the roof were about the same. On a living log cabin, they might have put in a puncheon floor and dressed it up a little bit more. In the log cabin issue, one of us was responsible for the foundation and the subfloor- ing; I was responsible for the walls and the notching; and somebody

When Paul Gillespie was gathering direc- tions for building a log cabin, he took a piece of poplar to Hillard Green, one of a couple of con- tacts who showed him how to cut a saddle notch. Hillard lived alone when we knew him, and was a great philosopher: "People nowadays don't live right. It's just how long they're goin' live, and how soon they're goin' die. Just what they can get in their hands *now*. Always wantin'. They just reach an'take ever'thing they can seems like. Ain't got no mercy on no one else. If I didn't depend on Him, I wouldn't have anybody t'depend on. You can't depend on a neighbor these days. Ever'body is for themselves. Ever'- body's looking out for money. They're not lookin' out for th'humans. We've got t'look out for ourselves. If we don't look out for ourselves, what are we goin't'do?" (*The Foxfire Book*) Hillard died in 1984, and his nephew, Dillard, owns his little cabin on Commissioner Creek.

For the issue on log cabins, Mike Cook diagrammed the saddle notch Roy
Thompson used for the cabin he was building.

else was responsible for the roof and the rafters and the shingles. It
was a very complicated process because it was a technical journal: we
were trying to tell people on paper, and with photographs and diagrams and narrative, how to construct one.

Wig was back by then, and we spent all summer putting that issue
together. We had just finished the tenth grade, and to me it was a big
responsibility. Our first interview was with Harley Thomas. It was a
muggy day in June in western North Carolina, and he had a little
work shed off Route 441. He made, among other things, fiddles in
that shed. That day he showed us how to hew dovetail notches and
saddle notches. I still remember the vision of his hands—what they
looked like, how he held his tools, and how they created. I also
remember how patient he was with us and all of our questions and
comments. Sometimes I wonder if Harley really knew what we were
up to, but he didn't mind. He allowed us to shoot several rolls of film,
draw diagrams, and said that we could come back anytime for further
help.

Work with the magazine always had national implications. I'll never forget, in Wig's class we had a map in the classroom of the United States, and we would put these pins in every city and town where somebody had a subscription to the magazine. You know, it was fun to see where all these subscriptions came from. And I remember we were very proud that somebody had subscribed from every state in the Union, even though many of the states only had one subscription. Somehow the word got out. I don't know how many subscribers we had in that year, but there were a lot. It was a big deal in high school.

I think your outlook on life, your attitude, and being able to live happily are important. That comes as a product of getting older. Sometimes, I think young people have a hard time seeing that. I know I did when I was in high school. I think back now about some of the individuals I was fortunate enough to meet and get to know through my Foxfire experience. They made a difference, and I still remember

Paul Gillespie, center, and his classmates hand-addressed envelopes for subscribers in the school library.

very vividly my encounters with them. I remember visiting at least twenty-five Foxfire contacts and what we did over the years I was involved.

I remember Lamar Alley and Alley's Grocery in Lakemont, Georgia. This summer, I was traveling through Rabun County, and I stopped to see if Lamar was still there. He was. There is something solid about going back and finding out that Lamar still has his store, still wears his watch up on his forearm, still has cold root beer in the cooler, and that he remembered who I was and would talk to me. In a world filled with convenience stores and people who really do not care, we need more Lamar Alleys.

# A Grant from NEH

Wig: About halfway through the year while I was at Hopkins, I decided that if the kids were going to care about *Foxfire* that much, I would go back to Rabun County. It was at that point that I realized that Washington, D.C., was only thirty-five or forty miles up the road, and I could probably get some help up there. We were always broke, and I felt somebody might give me some advice.

Simultaneously, one of my friends from college, John Dyson, had said it would be easier to attract support if we were a nonprofit tax-exempt 501(c)(3) organization, because then people could give donations and reduce their taxable income. There were also foundations that were not allowed by law to give grants to any organizations which were not tax exempt, so we were basically unable to seek money from a lot of potential sources.

John offered to have John Viener, an attorney he knew, draw up the papers and get them filed with the Internal Revenue Service. One of the things that you also have to have is a board of directors, and I had also thought it would be wise to have an Advisory Board that could give us some solid guidance in publishing and in collecting the material we were gathering in a more professional manner.

I began to spend time going up to Washington to find people who might be interested in what we were doing and might help. I remember clearly things like assuming that the people at *National Geographic* might be interested. I really didn't know what I was doing at all. I was just pulling ideas out of the air, but that one made a certain amount of sense.

I remember just walking into the *National Geographic* office building on Seventeenth and M one day and going to the guard at the desk, and telling him I was a school teacher from Georgia, and that we published a magazine that featured people and cultures. Then, reminding him that they did the same thing, I said there had to be somebody in that building who would be willing to talk to me. Well, he made a phone call upstairs and referred me to a person who turned out to be Ralph Gray, the editor of the *National Geographic School Bulletin*, which I didn't even know existed. It's a version of the *National Geographic* published for school kids, now called *National Geographic World*.

The guard sent me over there, and I sat and visited with Ralph for an hour or so, and the end result of that was he agreed to sign on as a member of our advisory group. He also wound up publishing several articles in that magazine about *Foxfire*, and they generated more subscription requests than any other articles that have ever been written about our work. I guess they resulted in five or six hundred subscriptions.

The same kind of thing happened at the Office of Education. I figured that in that office were the ones responsible for the federal effort to improve education in America, and surely there had to be somebody there who would be interested in what we were doing. I walked in there cold, and just like at the *National Geographic*, the person at the front desk picked up the phone and gave me Junius Eddy's office.

Junius was a consultant in the Office of Education on programs having to do with the arts and humanities. He sat and listened to what it was we were doing, looked at copies of the magazine, and got so interested in the story that he called Herb MacArthur at the National Endowment for the Humanities, which I had never heard of before.

Junius just made the connection for me right there in his office. As it turned out, Herb couldn't see me that day but agreed to talk to me later on. I couldn't make an appointment with him right then because it was getting close to the end of the school year, and the students who had been putting the magazine together were about to graduate. I had *promised* that I'd be there for the big event.

But I turned around and went back up to Washington later that summer, and Herb was the first foundation person that I had ever talked to. He got real interested in the work and said we should write a proposal. He showed me what one looked like, helped me understand the basic rules of formal requests for certain amounts of money, justifying the amount, and showing exactly how it would be spent. He took me through the form, question by question, made sure that I understood what was supposed to go in each of the blanks, and told me how much money to ask for.

I went back to Georgia with the form, filled it out, and sent it to him. When you send a proposal, you are supposed to send it along with about ten copies, which go to the various panel members who evaluate the requests. But there weren't any Xerox machines in our part of the world, so I called Herb up and told him my problem, and as evidence of what he thought of the work, he just laughed and Xeroxed the copies I needed. I've been a little embarrassed about that ever since, but I didn't know any better then. I just did it.

After they had their meeting in the fall, we received a grant for the full amount we requested: ten thousand dollars. We had never seen ten thousand dollars before. It was one of those situations where almost nobody could believe it—the students or the principal. It was a revelation that this organization called NEH nobody had heard of before cared enough about this silly little magazine to send us money to work with.

The money was used to purchase some equipment and supplies, and to hire students over the summer to do some serious work. They were so pleased with what we did that when we applied a second time, they gave us that one, too. Herb became a close friend also, and like Junius, joined the Advisory Board and helped work with our fund-raising efforts.

We were picking up one friend after another, and each performed the invaluable service of affirming that we were doing important work that should be continued. It still stands as one of the most pivotal, revealing periods of time in our history.

▼▼▼

JUNIUS EDDY: From the time he came into my office, I was impressed by Wig's eloquence, his sincerity, and the quality of his commitment to kids and to his democratic way of instruction. He is not a prepossessing man, obviously. He doesn't overwhelm you with his presence—but he's certainly not shy and retiring, either. He's a commanding figure, though, because of his educational thinking and his compelling, no-nonsense attitude toward life, students, and teaching.

I don't know the precise impact of that first grant, but I suspect it enabled them to continue and strengthen *Foxfire* magazine—maybe even to survive. Obviously, in the early days, the main worry was funding; they really had to scrounge for the funds to print those first few issues. But luckily, as a high school magazine, it was *so* different that Herb—and before long, other funders—realized this was support for much more than another high school magazine of poetry, short stories, and artwork. This was an endeavor in purposeful experiential education—to motivate learning by encouraging students to research and document people's lives in their own communities . . . and it made an increasingly strong impact on all of us.

ᵂᵂ

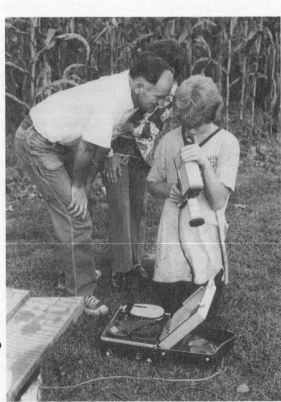

At the end of each interview we videotaped, students rewound the tape and played it back so the community people interviewed could watch themselves through the camera.

MIKE COOK: The NEH grant bought our first video equipment. Wig kept going around asking for money, and he would leave magazines everywhere. Wig might have found the money someplace else, because he has always been good about finding the resources he wants, but that was the first big grant that we had gotten. It made it possible to branch out into different departments, like the video one that I now run.

The grant also paid for some of the first summer salaries. I remember the first summer I was hired. There weren't as many Foxfire students then when I was in it as there are now. There was a small number of us during the summer.

Obviously, that grant made some nice things happen. You can chase your tail endlessly around trying to figure out what would have happened [without the NEH grant]. I think the magazine itself would have continued on without it. But tracing things back, lots of connections lead back to that grant. It really got things going.

▼▼▼

JAN BROWN BONNER: The first two summers I was in college, I worked for Foxfire. I think there were four of us whose salaries were paid by an NEH grant. That's when I first began interviewing our contacts on a regular basis.

We worked some fairly long hours, as I remember. We would be at school at nine o'clock in the morning and work the whole day. The interviews would sometimes run into the evening. I remember spending most of my time those summers working on *Foxfire*. We might have gone swimming some and played basketball some, but otherwise we spent pretty long hours working.

# Aunt Arie

WIG: After I came back from Johns Hopkins, I was given the juniors and the seniors to teach because the teacher who had had that position retired. There was a girl in my class named Andrea Burrell. She was a great kid, a good student, and she lived up toward the North Carolina line. She had friends in North Carolina just the way she had friends in Georgia. One of them was Patsy Cabe, and she went to the Franklin (North Carolina) High School because she lived over the state line. They cooked this thing up where Andrea would take a day off from Rabun Gap and go with Patsy to all of her classes, and then Patsy would come down to Rabun Gap and go to all of Andrea's classes with her. So Patsy was in my class with Andrea, and she heard the kinds of things we were talking about for magazine articles. After class, she came up and said, "I have a relative named Aunt Arie that you might want to meet because she knows a lot of this kind of stuff that you're collecting information about. It's basically the way she still lives."

I've always tried to have students follow up those leads, so I asked Andrea to get a couple of people together and go up there with Patsy and meet Patsy's aunt Arie. She rounded up Mike Cook and Paul Gillespie, and one day they just went up there with Patsy. They came back and said something like, "This one *really* looks good. She lives by herself in a log house way up on the side of a mountain, still cooks on a wood stove, wears the old-style dresses, and has a big garden and everything. She doesn't have any running water in the house at all. She draws her water from a well. When she wants to wash dishes, she draws a bucket of water, heats the water on the stove in a kettle, pours it in a dishpan, and washes the dishes outside on a little shelf. You won't believe it. It's just like going back in time."

Over Thanksgiving break, Paul Gillespie and I rode up there. Aunt Arie didn't have a phone, so we couldn't call her. We just went. We found the place—an old log house with siding on one end and a tin roof. We walked up on the front porch and banged on the door. There wasn't an answer, so we walked around to the back, thinking she might be in the garden. We found her in the kitchen, which had been added on to the back part of the house—a little one-story addition. She was standing there in front of this great big raw hog's head. I'd never seen anything like it before in my life. I didn't know what in the world was going on. It was an interesting jolt because we had just finished reading *Lord of the Flies* in class, and a hog's head really figures in that story!

Aunt Arie.

We introduced ourselves. Aunt Arie was real friendly—had this absolutely beautiful smile—and asked us to come in. She seemed relieved to have the company. I asked her what she was doing. She said the neighbors down the road had killed a hog for Thanksgiving, and they had brought her the head as a present because they knew that she liked to make souse meat. I was just amazed. It was hard for me to imagine that being a present to someone. You might bring somebody a ham, but. . . .

But in order to make souse meat, Aunt Arie had to get the eyeballs out of that hog's head. She'd already cleaned it and scraped it and gotten all of the hair off, but she couldn't cook it down and get the meat off until those eyes came out of there. She had been there for half an hour trying to get them out by herself, but she just didn't have the strength in her hands to do it. A hog's eye is set back in its head in a bony case, and it's hard to get to. Aunt Arie had never had to do it before because her husband had always done that kind of thing for her. Her husband was dead at this point, though.

Well, I had gone to Cornell with the intention of being a doctor, and I had taken zoology classes where we had dissected animals. I just said, "Sure. Give me a knife and we'll go at it!" Paul, meanwhile, had turned on the tape recorder and was holding the microphone in our general direction and spending most of his time looking the other way. He tape recorded the whole running conversation.

We finally got the job done. Aunt Arie was excited and happy, and then she wanted us to come into the living room and sit and visit. We kept the tape recorder going, and talked for an hour or so. Then she wanted us to stay for supper, so we stayed and helped cook it on the wood stove. What began to develop was this really powerful, sort of magical relationship with this woman who was so glad to see us and so grateful that we had come. That was a rather new experience because many of the people we had met up until that point were willing to be interviewed, and they endured it, and in some cases enjoyed the whole thing, but she was *grateful*. She wanted us to come back every day and couldn't understand why we couldn't.

When I said, "Can I send other students up?" she said, "Send anybody you want to, anytime."

That began a friendship that turned into something remarkably close and very special. It continued for six or seven years until finally she became bedridden. What was so remarkable about it, I guess, was not only the connection that Aunt Arie made with kids, but the fact that every time we went, she had new things to tell us. She was a walking encyclopedia of Appalachian expressions and stories and experiences. We did one project after another up there at her house that we just had never done before with people. For example, Beulah Perry had showed us how to make a white oak split hamper down at Clayton. Aunt Arie knew how to make baskets, and so we showed Jan Brown and several other students how to make her type. They documented the whole process. When Beulah saw that article in the magazine, she said that she had always wanted to know how to do that. So we loaded up Beulah in the car one day, rounded up some white oak splits, and took her to Aunt Arie's house. Beulah made a basket while Aunt Arie watched her and gave her some instruction. It was the first time Aunt Arie had ever had a face-to-face encounter

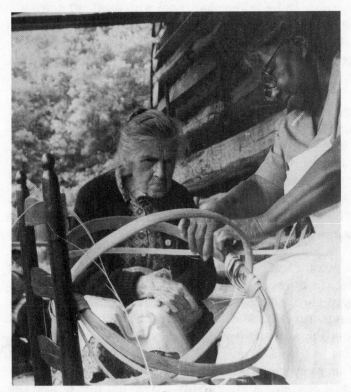

One afternoon when we took Beulah Perry to Aunt Arie's house, Aunt Arie taught her how to make a garden basket out of white oak splits—something Beulah had always wanted to learn.

with a black person, and it just astounded her. She wanted us all to stay for supper, which she always did. She kept exclaiming, with Beulah there, that she had never had a black person sit down at her table before. It was just like a revelation to her. It was all really good-natured—nothing prejudiced about it at all. It was just a new experience for her.

We began to realize how much she enjoyed having new experiences. I began to go up and get her, for example, and bring her down to school so that the students could meet her and interview her in class. She loved that. It turned out that she had been a Sunday School teacher for sixty-some-odd years. She loved teaching kids, but finally she had had to stop because her hearing began to go and she was afraid one of the kids would ask her a question and she would misunderstand the question, give the wrong answer, and mislead the kid. The opportunity to be in the classroom with all these new kids was one that she really enjoyed and would do anytime I invited her.

With us, she had her first meal in a restaurant. She ordered hamburger steak. Kate's Café only had about four tables in it, but she said, "Law, this is a big place, isn't it!" She couldn't get used to the idea of somebody being in the kitchen cooking a meal for her. She'd never had that happen before. When the waitress brought our meal, she looked at the waitress and said, "Ah, you didn't have to do that, honey. I could have done that myself."

When we were working later with a film crew to make a movie about Foxfire that other teachers could show their students, Aunt Arie was one of the people filmed. When the movie was finished, we had a little evening premiere showing at the school library with hors d'oeuvres and punch. Some of the faculty members came, and a lot of the kids came, and the community people who were in it came. I drove up with a couple of kids and brought Aunt Arie down to the school. She was the guest of honor. She sat and watched the movie. When it was over, she had this big grin on her face. Turned out it was the first motion picture that she'd ever seen. The first movie she had ever seen in her life and she was in it. It was just one thing after another like that.

She would get so excited that the kids couldn't help being excited, too, and they just got more and more involved in her life. I think the special quality that she had was an obvious, sincere, deep love for people. I would bring kids up there who had never been there before, and we would walk in the house, and she would grab every one of

At an evening premiere of a movie that featured Aunt Arie—the first motion picture she had ever seen—Beulah was one of many there to congratulate her.

those kids' hands and tell them how glad she was that they had come, and then she wanted them to sit down right away and start to visit. She'd pat them on the knee, and on the shoulder, and get all excited about the fact they were there. Some of the kids had been treated pretty rough by the world—had had a tough time—and they were the kinds of kids who, in some cases, weren't real sure if anyone cared about them or not. She just blew them away.

She would always ask, "Now will you'uns stay for supper?" And whenever we did, and we often did, we always went into the kitchen with her and helped her cook. None of these kids had ever cooked on a wood stove before, or peeled and sliced potatoes and put them over a stove eye.

There was never a half an hour courtesy visit to Aunt Arie's house. It always turned into a half a day, or a day. Sometimes, if she was sick, some of the kids would go up there and spend the night with her.

And whenever we got ready to leave, the kids, without being asked or prompted, would automatically line up at the front door, and she would be there, and she would grab each one of them in turn, one by one, and say, "Now you be sure to come back. I'm going to remember you and I'm going to think about you." She'd make them write their names down on a little scrap of paper, and she kept all those scraps of paper in a box so that she had a record of every kid who had been there. It was really a profound, human experience.

The other interesting thing to me was that for some reason or another, people who read the magazine and read *The Foxfire Book*, where we had that first Aunt Arie interview that Paul and I did, had almost the same kind of reaction to her. It was almost as though the people who read the magazine felt as though they also knew her. There was something about her face, and something about her situation, and something about the quality of the language she used when she told stories, and something about the compelling nature of the friendship that she had with the students that just absolutely captured everybody. Aunt Arie, unlike a lot of the other people who we'd interviewed for the magazine, began to get fan letters from all over the country. People sent her presents. She would mention in one of the articles that she had always wished that she had something, and she'd get it in the mail! She'd say, "I can't read this Bible anymore 'cause the print's too small," and within three weeks there'd be fifty large-print Bibles sent to her from all over the country stacked on her porch. She couldn't get used to the idea that people who'd never met her before could care anything about this woman who lived by herself up on the side of a mountain. I don't think she ever did understand that. I don't think she ever understood, either, what an impact she had on people's lives. It was as though she just jumped off the pages of the magazine right into their hearts.

We haven't met anybody since she died who comes close to having that kind of impact. And, to a person, if you talk to former students who met her, they'll say *she* was the one they'll never forget.

▚▚▚

HARRY BROWN, JR. [JUDY'S FATHER]: You know the time you showed Aunt Arie the first movie that she ever saw—the one about herself? I was at that. I never will forget the way she took on about that. That was worth going just to watch her.

**WW**

PATSY CABE KELLY, HER PARENTS, RUTH AND NELSON CABE, AND TONIA KELLY, PATSY'S DAUGHTER:

RUTH: Aunt Arie was really [Nelson's] aunt. We get a lot of people asking us questions about her. People don't realize that she really is our aunt because she was "Aunt" to everybody.

PATSY: Even at church that's what she went by. She was just an aunt to the whole community, I guess you could say. [Students] would go in [Aunt Arie's house]—ten or twelve of them—and she'd feed them. Just put them a spread out on the table and she'd feed them before they left.

RUTH: They'd take the ashes out of the stove for her, draw her water, and go get something out of the garden for her.

NELSON: [Foxfire students] carried her wood for her and dug taters for her.

RUTH: She was a sweet person. She loved all the people that came over; they were her children. And she loved Wig like he was her own child. Aunt Arie really did like him. She was kindly an idol to the younger people. She was an inspiration to them; they looked up to her.

PATSY: A few weeks ago we were in Milledgeville. Some of the kids down there found out that we were from Rabun County and they said, "Are y'all familiar with Foxfire?" Some of us spoke up and said, "Yeah, we know Foxfire." They would turn around and say, "Well, did you know Aunt Arie?" Then they'd corner me and start asking me all these questions about where she lived and what she was like. It's strange how people have come back and sort of focused on that one character out of all the people in the books.

RUTH: I was talking to Wig a few minutes ago and he said that he just couldn't get over, and couldn't grasp, how much of [an impact people like Aunt Arie who were in the first book had on people who never even met them]. The couple that bought her house after she died have not done anything to the house [except for] putting in a bathroom. They're living in the house now.

NELSON: It's like it was when Aunt Arie lived there. They've not changed nothing.

PATSY: [*Foxfire*] brings back a lot of memories to me. I can sit and read today, or I can still watch the Aunt Arie movie that was made. I will cry every time I watch it. It just brings back a lot of memories. Maybe [*Foxfire*] made me get a little closer to my granny Cabe and my papaw—all of them. It just made me more aware of the things I missed when I was growing up.

TONIA: Aunt Arie was my great-great aunt. I remember when I was little, I was maybe five or six years old, and I remember her being in a

Phyllis Carver, far left, and her classmates often dug Aunt Arie's potatoes for her. Some of them, like this one, were prizewinners—big enough to feed several people.

hospital bed in my grandmother's living room because they had to keep her. I remember sitting on the edge of the bed and talking to her a lot, but I don't remember her being at her house.

When my mom saw the Broadway play *Foxfire*, as a Hallmark television special, she just sat there and bawled because she really liked it. It reminded her so much of how Aunt Arie was and how she lived.

◥◤◥

ANDREA BURRELL POTTS: Aunt Arie was always thrilled to see us. I don't think any picture ever picked up the true warmth that she felt for us. She didn't have too many worldly possessions, but she valued friendship. You always left her smiling and feeling good.

Whenever we would leave, Aunt Arie would stand on the front steps of her porch and watch until our car was out of sight.

She had a small frame but she was very strong. She was partially paralyzed on one side, but she enjoyed life. Even through the hard times, Aunt Arie laughed. She wasn't down about what happened to her in any way. She had strength that came from hard times. She had been through the Depression and had grown stronger from it. She always saw the best side of whatever happened.

She had a black wash pot taken from her place. She laughed about it and said, "Now won't he look funny standing before the Lord with that black pot in his hands!" That came to my mind when my house was robbed about two years ago.

I went back to Aunt Arie's place a few weeks ago. It was the first time I've been back since I was young. Something affected me more than I realized because you could still feel the same feeling when you expected her to walk out on the porch smiling and saying, "Come in and sit down!" She would always stay on the porch when we started to leave and wave at us till we were out of sight.

MIKE COOK: The first time I went to see Aunt Arie, she was out on the porch tending to her flowers. As I was walking up, I got a big hug. As soon as she saw people coming, her face would light up. I will never forget that warmth. It was like she had known us forever.

The interviews that we did with Aunt Arie were about many different things. She was one of those magical folks that when you asked a question, you would just sit back. She could tell a story and make you see what was going on.

Paul Gillespie and I each wrote an introduction to that first article we did about Aunt Arie, and when I started teaching here, the students had a literature book in their English classes that had an Aunt Arie section in it. It had an excerpt from my introduction in the teacher's editions as an example of good literature. It kind of shocked me. It also shocked me that some of the pictures that we had taken for the Aunt Arie article got published in *Life* magazine. The Time-Life photographers have a reputation of being the best in the world, and to be published alongside these people gives you that kind of feeling. When something you did gets bigger than you have ever dreamed it would, it flips you out. It's a big dream, and you keep on dreaming.

For many of the interviews with Aunt Arie, we would gather on the porch outside her kitchen—in this case, to learn how to make a foot mat out of corn shucks.

Aunt Arie's house is now owned by the Hollands, a couple from Florida, who have preserved it largely as it was when Aunt Arie lived there.

PAUL GILLESPIE: I was in the eleventh grade. It was November 1969. My parents always traveled to see their friends at Mississippi State University at Thanksgiving. I was old enough to stay home alone, and I had a basketball game Tuesday night before break, so I stayed in Rabun Gap. Since I was home, Wig and I planned to go see Aunt Arie.

Andrea Burrell, Mike Cook, and myself had gone up about a week before Wig and I went. I will never forget it. I was driving, and I had learned to drive on my father's jeep. The gears on the jeep were in the floor. Well, I was driving Wig's Bronco, and the gears were on the column, and I hadn't quite got the hang of it. The last part of the road to Aunt Arie's was treacherous, and we were on a hill and I was struggling with the gears, clutch, and gas pedal. Somehow I let out the clutch, Mike gave it gas, and Andrea shouted encouragement. The Bronco lurched up the hill, and we made it.

I met Aunt Arie for the first time, and it was very special. Here was this ninety-year-old lady who lived by herself in this old log house out in the middle of nowhere. I sensed her love and concern immediately, even though she had never met Mike and me before. She treated us like long-lost grandchildren.

Then I took Wig up to Aunt Arie's and we ended up eating Thanksgiving dinner with her. She would have eaten alone, and so would we. Anyway, we walked in on her on Thanksgiving morning. She had her back to the door, and we startled her. There she was trying to carve the eyeballs out of a hog's head. I was almost sick to my stomach, so Wig helped operate on this hog's head while I turned my head and "held the microphone of the tape recorder in the general vicinity of the action."

They struggled for at least fifteen minutes, maybe more. And then I witnessed one of the most amazing events of my life. Aunt Arie took an eyeball, went to the back door, and flung it out. When she threw it, the eyeball went up on the tin roof of an adjoining outbuilding, rolled off, snagged on the clothesline, and hung there bobbing like a yo-yo. I had Wig's Pentax so I took a picture of it, and it appeared in a subsequent issue of the magazine. It was very funny, remarkable.

After dinner, I will never forget sitting there in that straight-back chair in front of the fireplace listening to Aunt Arie. Wig went outside to take some pictures and left me in there alone with her. I was scared and I was supposed to ask her all of the right questions, or so I thought at the time. I asked her questions like: "What is your most valuable possession?" or, "Would you rather live now or back in the old days?" Some of them were probably pretty stupid, but I was doing the best I could. I was just a sixteen-year-old kid. Wig was out taking pictures, and he did it on purpose, I think, so I would be in there on my own.

I cannot begin to describe all the images. In *The Foxfire Book* I described her house, the pictures on the wall, her lifestyle, and what she perceived as being important. I will remember her patience, wisdom, understanding—and her spirituality. I will never, ever, as long as I have any semblance of a decent mind, forget my visits with Aunt Arie. A lot of people say that, but I was really fortunate. Armstrong and Aldrin will always be able to say they were the first to walk on the moon. I will always be able to say I was among the first of many Foxfire students to know Aunt Arie.

For one interview, a barefoot Jan Brown walked with Aunt Arie up the driveway to her home. With Jan were classmates Mary Garth and Stan Darnell, carrying a bundle of white oak splits for basket making.

With Jan's fingers holding, Aunt Arie began to weave a basket.

The finished basket was rough, but Aunt Arie said she was as proud of it as of any she had ever made. It is now in the Foxfire collection.

JAN BROWN BONNER: My favorite article about Aunt Arie was the one we did on basket making with white oak splits. The oak splits we had were awful. But I was amazed at the baskets Aunt Arie was able to make out of them, even with the splits we had. Aunt Arie's hands were so gnarled she had to have our help in weaving the splits, but we actually learned more that way.

We had big dinners at Aunt Arie's. I remember when we would eat with her, she would always have souse meat. She would insist that you try it. She spooned it onto my plate and I couldn't bring myself to eat that. I can remember putting some in my plate and flattening it all up, so it would look like I had eaten it. I hid it under bread and everything! I never did eat a bite of souse meat, but I'm sure it wouldn't have been as bad as I imagined it. Once you imagine her

Besides cooking on her wood cookstove, Aunt Arie also sometimes cooked potatoes for us in a Dutch oven on the fireplace hearth in her living room.

Whenever she fed us, her kitchen table would be loaded with food. Here, left to right, are Craig Williams, Laurie Brunson, Greg Strickland, George Freemon, and Mike Cook.

with a pig's head laid out in front of her making souse, it's not real appetizing. And that black, black coffee she used to make. And the bread she used to make in this hot oven. She would really slave over that old wood stove, and it didn't bother her at all. No matter how many people were up there, she always seemed to have enough food.

Aunt Arie's generous nature is what I remember most. All the people we interviewed had the same trait—it ran true for all of them—but Aunt Arie was such a special person to us, and she was always so cooperative. She always had such a wealth of information to give us. I still see her standing on the end of the porch every time we would leave, waving good-bye, and there was a sadness on her face every time we left.

◆◆◆

Often, we'd then take our plates outdoors and eat. Left to right: Mike Cook, Craig Williams, Paul Gillespie, Laurie Brunson, Frenda Wilborn, Andrea Burrell, and George Freemon.

BOB KUGEL: My mother was a nurse in Detroit. She found out about this school from one of her friends. I was getting into a lot of trouble and she wanted me to get out of the city, so she sent me to Rabun Gap because I could go to school and work on campus to help pay my tuition.

When I got down there, it was a whole different world. When I signed up for Foxfire, I had no idea what I was getting into. We had about twenty-five to thirty people in our class. When I went on my first interview it was fun and exciting, because you are dealing with people that are so different. That's part of your learning process. You take all these little pieces of information into your head and it all begins to come together. It will come out sometime—may take twenty years but it will finally come out.

My favorite was Aunt Arie. She was like something out of the past. I remember going over to her house to make some homemade jam.

Everything was cooked on that wood-burning stove. I still think about her sometimes.

ᵂᵂᵂ

BIT CARVER KIMBALL: Sometimes I went to Christmases at Aunt Arie's house. We'd all string popcorn and make little rings out of construction paper. The guys would get her a tree and bring it in for her.

She was a good, good, good person. I felt like she was special, partly in her own right, don't get me wrong, but mainly she was also a symbol of what the mountain people her age were. They all went through the same trials and hardships that she went through. They all were good, religious people, and they lived their religion. They didn't just speak it.

Some kids visiting from Alaska were interviewing her for the *Foxfire* film, and they asked her, "What's the one piece of advice that you'd most like to give a kid?"

She said, "The one thing I'd tell them is not to ever do anything you don't want your mama to find out about. If you don't want your mama to know it, then you must be ashamed of it, and nine times out of ten, she's going to find it out, anyway." It's what I tell my son now.

ᵂᵂᵂ

CLAUDE RICKMAN: Warfield and I would go up there a lot to see Aunt Arie. Just take off and enjoy it. From the first time I met her, she hugged me and said, "I love you kids." We'd go up and sit with her, eat with her, plow her garden, help her plant stuff, chop wood—you know, whatever she needed.

One time we went up there and the handle of her refrigerator had broken off, and she couldn't get it open. She'd been living off what she had in the cellar, and she hadn't had any meat in five or six days. Three of us fixed the handle, and that's when we took her out to Kate's Café. We sat down, and she'd never gone to a restaurant. They came around and asked us what we wanted to eat, and she ordered something and they brought it. She said, "I've never been so embarrassed. I've never gone somewhere and sat down and not helped 'em serve." She said, "Honey, I'll help you wash the dishes." She didn't know what to do. That girl just looked at her. Aunt Arie never did catch on that we were paying and you didn't have to wash the dishes or set the table or anything else. I never have forgotten that. But she thought that was the greatest thing. When we left, all the way home, she just said she hoped they didn't hold it against her and think she was sorry and no-count because she didn't help.

It was a good experience for all of us. I'd been raised around my grandfather, but Warfield came from Florida where he wasn't around that kind of stuff, and to see somebody that was as nice and as genuine as her. . . . That helped build a real strong friendship between us, up until he died. Not only were you learning a lot about where you lived and what your family probably put up with in the past and how they made it through life, but you also built something that you'll have till you die.

▞▞▞

GARY WARFIELD: I am sure she knew she fed me, shared her life experiences with me, and once gave me a place to sleep in a bed that was stacked one foot high with quilts. But I doubt that she knew that she renewed my faith in mankind and taught me what unselfish generosity was. No one could outgive Aunt Arie. I never left her place without something . . . a full stomach, vegetables from her garden, a strangely good feeling.

Aunt Arie also taught me that things like honesty, caring, loving, selflessness, trust, and faith in God were legitimate, honorable virtues—virtues that you didn't have to be ashamed of possessing. In fact, Aunt Arie proved to me that "good guys" don't always finish last.

Aunt Arie knew right from wrong like night from day. She didn't beat around the bush, pull punches, or straddle any fences. She told it like it was and meant every word she said. She had a great sense of self-worth and inner peace. She didn't care what others thought of her. She knew that she was a fine person and had lived a good life.

Aunt Arie also reinforced the fact that we need to take the good with the bad and meet difficulties head on. She impressed me with her ability not to gripe or complain and not to wallow in self-pity. Aunt Arie took pride in everything she did. Even though she drew her water from a well, cooked with wood, and lived in a house that only slowed the wind, Aunt Arie was optimistic, happy, and "up" on life. She always had a kind word to say and a positive outlook. I rarely saw her angry; when she was, it was when she would relate some injustice or inherently wrong circumstance.

Aunt Arie also impressed my hard head with the fact that I wasn't the brightest, wisest soul in the world. I learned shortly after our first visit that the longer one lived, the more one learned. It was evident that Aunt Arie knew more about life and people than most individuals ever will. And what is amazing is the fact that she probably never traveled more than fifty miles from where she was born and wasn't well read or college-educated.

I hope that in the twilight of my life I will have Aunt Arie's vitality, enthusiasm, dignity, and inner peace. I hope that, like her, I can "set my feet under the table" with friends and dine on the cornbread, leather breeches, and lye hominy of my time.

[From *Aunt Arie: A Foxfire Portrait* (New York: E. P. Dutton, Inc., 1983) 204–6.]

### Aunt Arie: "Livin' by yourself ain't all roses—and it ain't all thorns"

The nineteenth day a'November, I'll be here seven years by myself. When Ulyss' died, they didn't want me t'come here and live by myself.

I don't know at th'people that wants me t'leave here. They don't want me t'stay here atall, but I never have been afraid *a'nothin'* s'bad that it would make me move away from here. They said, "You never have been afraid?" I said, "No!" They thought since people has got so mean, somebody might come and scare me, but it's just as peaceful here as it can be. A night 'r two ago, I thought I heared somethin'. I'm as easy waked as a cat. I never have got bad scared, though. Not since I been here.

Besides, I've got enough of a temper t'take care a'number one. I don't let nobody run over me. Th'Bible tells you if anyone slaps you on th'one cheek t'turn th'other cheek. I don't do that. I don't. I don't want nobody slappin' *me* about! I told Ulyss' [my husband] once, "You go t'strike me a lick, you make *sure* and make it count cause you'll never strike me another!" I'm half white and free born and I never have took a lick off a'nobody, and I aint' a'gonna commence takin' nothin' off a'nobody now! If y'let people commence runnin' over you, they'll tramp you under their feet. I don't do it. I'll say somethin' back. I'll say it even if I have t'say somethin' and run! [Laughing.]

And I've got a good number twelve shotgun in there if I need it. I've shot it many a time. I use t'shoot with th'boys, and I was pretty good with a gun. Use t'be. I ain't shot none in a long time. Last gun I shot I killed that possum I told you'uns about. That's th'only thing I ever shot at t'kill it. But I know how t'use it. I was raised with boys, and I mean I was *raised* with'em, and I done just what they done. Yes sir. They was always lotsa boys at our house that come there t'be with my brothers, and I've shot with'em lots just t'be out in a gang a'boys shootin' at spots.

Some of'em wants t'buy that gun I've got, and they're not gonna get it. I've got it hid. I hope t'God I never have t'use it, but I might sometime. I don't know. Y'don't know what you'll do. Some people make you do things you won't do.

I know one woman who got her a pistol. I'm scared t'death of a pistol. That's th'truth. I never shot a pistol in my life. She said I oughta have a pistol up here t'protect myself. I said, "Lord, I ain't gonna have no pistol." I might get shot with it. I might.

But she got her one because they was some mean boys down where she lived that done her wrong. She had a grapevine right below th'house and them mean boys'd slip under her grapevine and steal her grapes till they'd hear her open th'door. Then they'd run down th'hill and they'd laugh like they'd die. Didn't care for her feelin's a bit more'n a big groundhog up there on th'mountain. She got tired of it and got her a pistol. They calmed out and she never did have t'shoot none. I said I wouldn't a'cared much if she *had* shot *at*'em. I don't mean *shoot*'em, but shoot *at*'em and just scare th'hell out of 'em. That was meanness. They never did do me that way. I wouldn't'a shot'em, but th'first time they'd done me devilment they'd a'got run off, day'r night either one.

And I'm not a'gonna be like Grandma Henson. She was afraid a'anything. Th'mules got loose one day and come towards th'house, and she seen'em a'comin' and she run up on top a'th'springhouse! Yes sir, she sure did. That's just how afraid she was a'anything. I'll not be like that.

Livin' by yourself ain't all roses—and it ain't all thorns. On real dark lonesome nights when a thunder comes, 'r lightnin' comes right down here, and I'm settin' here and it comes all around me, and it seems like it comes right down on th'house, I get in th'bed pretty soon! I do. I ain't afraid of it. I just ain't what you'd call *afraid* of it. But it uneasies me. Now I don't know whether you'uns will agree with me 'r not. If you don't, you don't, and if you do, you do. It's all right. You ever heared tell that if it comes a storm t'lay down on a feather bed and you never would get struck? That's what I do. I got a feather bed. [Laughter.] You don't know how little you feel layin' there by yourself, though.

But I ain't like ol' Maggie down here. Now with all due respect t'her and all th'women in th'world—I don't mean t'make fiddle and fun a'nobody—and if she's afraid of a storm, she's afraid of a storm. She can't help it. Well, when a storm comes she just cries her eyes out, nearly. She cries like a whipped child. She just can't stand it. Now I don't cry and I don't get scared, but you feel bad. You set down here by yourself and know y'can't make nobody hear—I couldn't holler and make nobody hear—well, y'don't feel good. Then's when y'know God is takin' care a'you. You feel it. You understand it. Yes sir.

Still, it gets a little bit lonesome—'specially if y'get t'hurtin' right bad. When there's nobody here but me, and I feel bad, I lay down pretty soon. Now my heart took a bad spell a'hurtin' th'other night—aw-w-w-ful. I don't know what done it. I went on t'bed. I lay there and tumbled and tumbled and tumbled and I couldn't go t'sleep and I got up 'bout two o'clock and took another aspirin tablet and finally went t'sleep. Sometimes this hand hurts and keeps me awake. It took a spell th'other day and it like t'drawed me t'death. I put alcohol on it t'keep it from drawin', and if I go t'bed and take a bad case a'th' "slick foot," I call it, and can't go t'sleep, I get up and take me a aspirin tablet and sometimes I get t'sleep. I have m'bottle filled at th'drugstore. I get Ruth t'take it and have it filled for me. I don't do without it. If I do without, I can tell it just in a few minutes. I *want* t'do without it, though. It costs like everything. Just a little ol' thing like that cost three dollars. One time I said I'd just do without it. Ruth, she begged me not t'do it. I said, "Next time I get out a'that little ol'medicine, I'm gonna do without it awhile." Shew, I done without for two'r three days and my hand commenced t'drawin'. That's what it commenced t'doin'. I just can't do without it. If I have t'sell this place t'buy my medicine, I guess I'll just do that. I'm just gonna live so long, anyhow.

That and high blood medicine is th'only kind a'medicine I use. Dr. Kahn makes me take that ever'day a'my life. He's a good doctor. He's been here t'see me two'r three times. I got s'tickled at him. He come one time and I was layin' on th'lounge, and he hadn't been here before. He come in through th'kitchen door and set down there and wanted t'take m'blood pressure. I had on m'dress, and he got out his knife and I wished you'd see'd that man rip my dress sleeve. He never cut no hole in it. Just cut along th'seam. Just as particular with it as he could be. Way on after that I went t'his office. I asked him if he remembered rippin' m'dress. He said, "Yes, I do." I said, "You was so particular; you that afraid you'd cut m'dress? What made you so afraid?" He said, "I was afraid you'd cuss me out." [Laughter.] That's all he said. That just tickled me t'death.

Dr. Kahn's a good doctor. He's good t'me. And I've got good neighbors. They's hardly a day passes here without somebody comes t'see me. When nobody comes is when I get worried. Then's when I wonder if I'm doin' th'right thing, stayin' here. It's not all sunshine, I can tell you, stayin' by yourself. I hope you'uns'll never have t'do it. I do. I hope you'uns never have t'do it. But if y'do, and if y'live t'be as old as I am, you remember what I tell you'uns. [Slowly and deliberately.]: You *learn* t'make yourself do lots a'things that you *never* did think you *could* do. I have t'*learn* t'make myself not be lonesome. I have t'do that a lot here lately since Ulyss' is gone and nobody here but me, cause if y'give out a'heart, ever'thing goes t'th'bad right *now*.

I nearly go into fits when I have t'set here all day when it's rainin'. I just get s'lonesome I just can't hardly live. It's them days when I think bedtime'll never come. Y'listen t'th'radio, but y'listen to it, and you can't say nary a word *to* it. When y'listen t'*somebody*, they can answer you back 'r you can answer them back. But y'learn t'pay no 'tention t'things like that.

Somebody asked me th'other day didn't I want a telephone. I don't believe I could hear good enough t'answer it. I don't believe I could. And I don't want no television. Ain't got a bit a'use for television in th'world. Th'way it flitters it hurt m'eyes. You look at that wiggly thing too much and it'll ruin your eyes, and m'eyes are th'best thing I've got. That eye specialist I went to examined m'eyes and he said he couldn't find a thing wrong with'em and me as old as I am. Yes sir. If God was t'take my vision away from me, what would I do? Course I don't see as good as I *did* any more. You'uns get my age and I guess you'uns'll not see good either. [Laughs.] I *hope* y'do. Hope you can see as good as *I* do.

Yes sir. That goes with th'Cabe generation. My grandma Cabe, now she died and didn't have t'use specks. I don't have t'use specks now. But they's some a'that little tiny print on th'medicine bottles that I can't read. Another thing I can't do is run a reference in th'Bible. That's somethin' I hate s'bad that I don't know what t'do. I still read th'Bible. It's a good pastime t'me. I've read it plumb through more'n once. You teach Sunday School class sixty-odd year and see if you don't, too. Commence from one side and go right out th'other. Not all at one time, but you know what I mean. And I still read in it, but now them little bitty letters when they run a reference—I've got so I can't see that good, and that worries me.

Readin's good, though. I read more, I guess, than I ought to. They bring me th'Asheville *Citizen* and th'Franklin *Press* and all kinds a'papers up here and let me read'em. I'm awful t'read. I'm a paper bug. I sure am. But it's not like havin' somebody here, either. I'll tell y', there are some times you get pretty lonely. Sometimes you get mighty blue. Sometimes you feel like gettin' up and goin' *somewheres*—no tellin' where. Th' "allovers," I call it. Th'worst time is winter when they's snow on th'ground. Now when it's warm weather, in th'daytime, if nobody comes t'visit, I can walk t'th'mailbox and see somebody. I can even do that in th'rain. But when it snows I just about have t'stay in day and night. I just about freeze myself t'death and can't walk in it. I keep a good fire in th'livin' room here, but I just have t'stay and I never get out th'door. I use a chamber [pot], y'know, cause I can't walk in th'snow t'save my life. I just squenge. It squenges me all over. I've learned when it snows t'stay at home. Yes sir.

Winters are th'hardest time. One winter not too long ago, that food cellar door out by th'well got froze shut and I like to a'starved t'death. I got sorta uneasy then. Now that's th'truth! [Laughter.] When they fixed my cellar that fell they left a seam right in front a'th'cellar door, and when it come that hard freeze, it froze that seam till it pushed up and locked my cellar door. I couldn't open it and I didn't have a bite of a thing in th'world in th'house, only bread t'cook. Not a thing. I had a-l-l my taters and everthing in th'cellar. I couldn't get it open. I got me a rock and beat on it and beat on it and beat on it t'see if I could rock off th'hinges. Boys, I sorta got scared. Y'can't get your hand on nary thing t'eat, cook . . . I can cook but couldn't get m'hands on it *to* cook. So I said, "Well, I reckon th'next thing best t'do is t'boil a big kettle a'water . . ."

First thing I done when I went in th'kitchen th'next mornin' was t'go see if my door'd open so I'd have somethin' t'cook for dinner, and it opened just as pretty as it could be. Lord, I rejoiced! I did. I rejoiced and run in there and got me a can a'beans and put on t'cook. You set down t'nothin' t'eat but only bread, and y'can't hardly eat that by itself. No sir. [Laughter.] Y'*could* eat enough t'keep from gettin' hungry, though. I'd betcha that. [Laughter.] Yes sir, y'sure could.

I wadn't as bad off just by myself, though, as I would be if somebody was t'come in and I was thinkin' I oughta give'em maybe a little somethin' t'eat. "A little nothin'," I call that! A little nothin' t'eat! [Laughter.]

But I'm makin' it all right. Stayin' right here. I don't know what I'll have t'do before I die. May have t'lay out in th'rain somewhere. I hope I don't. I think God will take care a'me. And they's lotsa pleasure in bein' alone. They's nobody t'quarrel at y'. And when I need 'em, I've got awful good neighbors, I'll tell you. Y'know how t'live and make neighbors? Be a neighbor. Be a neighbor and you'll have neighbors. I've tried that. Now I've tried that by experience. I do try t'be good t'everybody, and there's one thing I'll never do is insult anybody in my house. Mommy taught me that when I was young.

I try t'treat everybody just as I'd have them treat me. Do unto others as you'd have them do unto you and you'll have a good time. Well, anyhow, that's what I do. And look what I've got in return. There's Marie. She helps me do anything and everthing. Comes nearly ever' day. I can't do without her hardly, and that's th'truth. And Ruth comes up all th'time. I don't never have t'tell her t'come and bring m'rations. She brings m'coffee and medicine and sees about me. I just can't eat without coffee, I don't reckon! I'll tell you what I use t'do, now. I use t'drink nine cups a'coffee a day. You'll think that's awful, and I do, too. Three for breakfast, three for dinner, and three for supper. I quit th'coffee and never drunk a drop for three years. Now, like I did today, I pour me a little out in a saucer. I never do pour me out no coffee in a coffee cup. Hardly ever. Pour it out in a saucer and drink it while it's hot.

And then these neighbors that live up there in that trailer are as good t'me as they can be. They bring me stuff t'eat, already cooked, and ever'time I go up there they want me t'eat somethin.' Last time I was over there I said, "I'm gonna quit comin' up here. Ever'time I come you want me t'eat!" He said, "We don't care if y'eat everything we got!" Tickled me, and I said, "Oh my, I can't do that." Th'other afternoon when she come up here, she brought a piece a'ham already cooked. It was ever' bit that big. I guess my hand wouldn't cover it. All I'd have t'do was warm that. I built up a fire. I just don't eat cold rations. I took me a knife and stripped that into three pieces and laid that in a fryin' pan and poured cornbread gravy on it. And it was *so* good.

Then I get lotsa visitors I don't know. Course I never see no strangers. They're all just as welcome as they can be. Four'r five boys come th'other night. I didn't know nary one of'em. As it happened I was eatin' when they come. Somebody come t'th'door and knocked, and course I hollered, "Come in!" Sometimes they'll come in and sometimes they won't. Now you'd come in if you was t'come here cause you're use t'me. But a lot a'people ain't use t'me and they won't come in. I got up and went and started t'th'door, and they all come on in, and of course they all told who they was. I'll never remember even one name. Use to I never forgot nothin', but m'mind ain't as long now as it use t'be! It just can't be. It's been wore out too much!

Then there was a man and a woman come here a'Sunday. Said they had drove four hundred miles a'purpose t'see me. They stayed here and took pictures all out there and developed'em while they was out there. I wanted one of'em s'bad I didn't know what t'do, but I never said a word. They didn't give me one and I didn't tell'em to. I just hated to. She said she'd a'brought me somethin' if she'd knowed for certain she'd a'got t'see me, and when she got ready t'start she give me fifty dollars in money. Said she had read all about me in th'*Foxfire*. I said, "Yes, who ain't?" [Laughter.] Poor Eliot done me a good favor.

Use to I didn't know what t'do when people give me money like that. First time it happened this man was here, and when he left, he left a letter in th'mailbox. I opened th'mailbox and there was this letter about so high stickin' up in th'back, and there was a twenty-dollar bill in there. He never said what t'do with it. Never said what t'do with it. Y'know what I done with that? I kept it two year before I ever spent it. I put it on this road. I finally said, "Put that on th'road." Spent four hundred and forty dollars and so much on that road. That's how much they charged me, gettin' that road fixed. That took all I had and more, too. But that twenty dollars helped out, and I never asked for that.

You don't know how bad I hate t'ask people t'do things. Like that clock there on th'fireboard. Now I can't wind that clock t'save my life. I just can't. Well, just as quick as anybody comes, I ask'em t'wind m'clock for me. I hate t'do that. Use to I wouldn't do it. But when it comes t'*have* to, children, you don't mind it a bit in th'world. You just go ahead, and I don't believe anybody in this world cares a bit t'help me do things like that, and I appreciate it from th'bottom a'my heart. I can't express th'appreciation that I have for what people does for me. I just can't do it.

They come in here and help me do anything and everthing in this world: plow, fix th'garden, fix th'bean patch. Th'poor ol'feller that plowed my bean patch last time done it all wrong and it had t'be done over. I'll say it this way, with all due respect t'him and everbody else—I was tickled t'death, honest, I was—but I was s'sorry for him I didn't know what t'do. He laid them bean rows off straight as a gun barrel. He sure did. That was t'do all over. But he's a big help t'me. They all are. Th'other day he said he was goin' t'bring his son and his son's wife and children if I didn't think they'd run me crazy. I said: "You think I'd run crazy? Ever' youngun on th'hill comes up here, and I'm not run crazy!' No sir. I'm use t'younguns. Love'em t'death. I'd rather see younguns come as t'eat sugar. Course I enjoy it when *anybody* comes t'see me. And I'm just tickled t'death whenever anybody comes t'*stay* a few minutes. I'll tell y'what I don't like. I don't like it when anybody comes in this door and goes out that door and never sets down t'stay there a single minute.

I always have time—*take* time—t'set down and talk a few minutes. Mr. Stiles come yesterday evenin' and I was in th'garden. I went on in th'house, and he come in and he said, "Can't stay but a few minutes." I said, "You can stay a *few* minutes!" And he did; he stayed a few minutes. And these boys come this mornin', while I was fixin' pickle' beans, and they helped me. They helped me fix ever' one of'em. I was tickled t'death with it.

So God does all things well. Just look how he's blessed us. Boys, you need t'never fear t'trust in th'Lord. Cause I don't care what you do, if you do it in th'right way and in th'right spirit and do it for th'glory a'God, He'll return you fullfold. He'll sure do that. Now I've tried that. Me and Ulyss' both tried that. Yes sir.

And I've had lotsa happiness in my life. I guess th'happiest was when they was all here—Poppy and Uncle Bud and Aunt Avie and Berthie and Ulyss'—all havin' a good time t'gether just like we are today. All happy as we can be, I call it. That's th'happiest time in your life. Lord, I tell you time passes by, don't it? Now I never quit talkin'. Ulyss' said I could outtalk a flyin' jenny! Oh goodness alive! [Laughing.] When I had that stroke a'paralysis, y'know it got half of me. Yes, it got half of me. Even half a'my nose. But I said I was s'glad it didn't stop my tongue I didn't know what t'do! If I'd get t'where I couldn't talk, I don't know what I'd do. [Laughing.]

Yeah, I talk a lot. Wouldn't be a woman if she didn't talk. That's th'reason they out talk s'many men! Oh Lord have mercy! [Laughter.] I just keep clattering away. That's all they is to it. I know I've talked more'n Ulyss' has in his life. He was a pretty good talker, but he wadn't like me. No sir. Y'have t'get up before daylight t'beat me!

And I'll tell you another thing that was th'happiest time in my life was when we use t'have a revival meetin' in Coweeta and everbody in the church would get t'shoutin'. That's th'happiest time I ever see'd in my life. Everbody was as happy as they could be. You don't see many a'them days now, though. Scare a body t'death if they's t'see anybody shout nowadays, wouldn't it? [Laughter.] Sure'nough, I ain't seen nobody shout lately. That was th'happiest time in my life, when I got back t'that church. Now that's th'truth. Words can't express th'feelin' you had. No sir. I was just th'happiest that I could be.

Course there were th'sad times, too—seein' your mother and father go out and knowin' they'd never be able t'speak t'you again. Knowin' that's forever. I don't believe anyone in this world can express that feelin'. I can't. Words don't come t'express it.

Ah, you get t'studyin' back over where you've been and what you've done, I get amazed t'death. I certainly do. I don't see how I ever done it. Eighty-eight year t'tag up and down this road is a long time.

I used t'be awful stout. Worked pretty hard. I enjoyed it, though. I'd rather work as t'play. Heap rather work as t'play. Still that way. Th'other day, I tried t'do a little bit in th'garden and found out I couldn't do that. Come in here and set down and rested a little while. Then went t'th'mailbox, come back, and went in th'garden again. I thought I *could* do *somethin'*. So I took that chair out there and set it in between th'rows and set down in it and got t'pullin' weeds out a'th'peppers. I love t'work, but now I'm as slow as cream a'risin.'

Th'saddest thing that's come my road, though, is not bein' able t'do near what I use to. I can't get about and get stuff t'give people like I use to. I use t'have a lot a'stuff t'give t'people, but I just can't do it now. Can't give away quilts now like I use to cause I can't quilt. Can't cook'em somethin' good t'eat and give'em a good drink a'water like I use to cause I can't hardly cook.

And there's s'many things I'd love t'be able t'show you younguns how t'do, but I can't now. Can't crochet any more. Can't card and spin any more. Can't make willer baskets and bottom chairs any more. Can't do hardly anything I use t'do.

But I can still love.

Tenth-grader Randy Starnes took this photo of Wig and Aunt Arie saying good-bye one evening. She died in 1978.

# *The Foxfire Book*

---

WIG: It's surprising looking back to see how many things have happened to this organization almost by accident. *The Foxfire Book* is a good example. One of my fraternity brothers, Mike Kinney, became an assistant editor at Anchor Books, which is a division of Doubleday. Mike had stayed in touch with the magazine and its evolution. I had also sent letters to Mike from time to time talking about what we were doing, and in one of the letters that I sent him, I mentioned that more and more people were finding out about the magazine and they were requesting back issues. We didn't have enough money to reprint those, so I was beginning to explore some ways to get that information into the hands of the people who were requesting it. One of the ideas I was playing with, for example, was to take single special articles from the magazines and just reprint them and sell them for twenty-five cents apiece.

Mike said, "What you might want to consider doing is taking the best articles out of the magazines and putting them together into a book." I hadn't really thought about that; it was a new notion to me. The thought of having the best material all collected between two covers, though, and the thought that some other entity might actually pay for that, and the thought that it could generate some income which we really needed made the whole thing pretty intriguing.

Mike wrote, "If this idea interests you at all, then why don't you come up and let's just sit and talk about it." So on a trip to New York, I went over to Mike's office and we talked for a couple of hours about the possibilities. I didn't know anything about putting a book together. I didn't know whether you could just cut the articles out of the magazine and stick them on a piece of paper and hand them in, or whether you had to retype everything, and if so, what format it had to be in. I didn't know about contracts, royalties, percentages, distribution, publicity, any of that. Mike explained how all of that worked and said, "If this is something that you folks decide you want to do, send me a letter that describes what might be in this first book, and I'll take it to the people up here and see if I can get some enthusiasm going for it and get permission to offer you guys a contract."

I took the idea back to the students, and they wanted to go ahead, so we sent the letter, Mike got us a contract, and we signed it. Doubleday sent us an advance against the royalties. It wasn't very much—about fifteen hundred dollars—but it was enough to hire a couple of students during the summer to give me a hand pulling that material together into some form, and, in a couple of cases, doing some follow-up interviews to make a chapter a little bit richer. We pulled the manuscript together in a matter of a few months and sent it off.

I remember sitting with our editors and then with the kids wrestling with the title for this thing. We had all of these suggestions from editors who thought it should be called something like: *The Foxfire Book of Country Crafts and Wisdom including information about.* . . . Crazy long titles that nobody liked. Finally all of us—students, myself, everybody—just threw up our hands and said, "Let's just keep it simple and call it *The Foxfire Book* and leave it alone." I think that turned out to be the best decision we could have made.

By that time, Mike had left Doubleday to take another job. Getting Foxfire under contract with Doubleday was one of the last things he did before he left. He turned the project over to Ronnie Shushan, an editor at Anchor, whose assistant was Bill Strachan. Several years later, when Ronnie left, Bill became our editor and one of the members of our Advisory Board. Both are still really close friends of ours, as is Loretta Barrett, who was their immediate supervisor at Anchor.

The book came out in March of 1972, and what happened then was one of those crazy moments in publishing where one thing leads to another and it just runs away from you. Doubleday/Anchor Books sent out advance copies of the book to publications that might want to do articles about it. The editors at those publications were just as captivated by this whole notion that high school students were talking to older people and documenting their customs and traditions as people at places like *National Geographic* and the Smithsonian had been. All of them reviewed the book: *Time, Newsweek, Life. Life* sent a couple of photographers down here who stayed a few days and followed the students on interviews. Doubleday approached the "Today" show about having us on there. We got an invitation immediately to come up with a couple of students—in fact, it was Paul Gillespie and Claude Rickman who were with me up there. The publicity was overwhelmingly positive. Bookstores kept placing more and more advance orders, and Doubleday was printing them as fast as they could, and the scarcity of the books just added to the demand, and the whole thing just took off. It was just one series of lucky coincidences after another, one being, of course, the fact that the book came out at precisely that time when the public interest in this country was focused on looking at simpler lifestyles and at a time when things weren't quite so complicated, rushed, and crazy. A huge population out there was hungry for information about how to build a log cabin. All of those factors just converged, and the notion that high school students were doing this work absolutely entranced people.

The end result was that orders from bookstores were coming in so fast that a third printing of the book was ordered by Doubleday really before the first books hit the bookstores. They realized in the midst of getting ready to ship the books to bookstores that this thing was out of control. By then they basically stopped the plant and said, "Just run *Foxfire* books. Take everything else off the line and just start putting them out there." There were thousands, and thousands, and thousands of copies of *The Foxfire Book* being shipped out of that plant. The end result of all *that* was that the book went straight to the top of the *New York Times* best-seller list, and that just simply became one more factor that added to the demand. Every one of these elements jumped the whole thing up another notch until it was just out of control. It stayed on the best-seller list for about thirty-five weeks.

We were besieged, and I mean suddenly besieged, by requests from television stations and newspapers and radio shows that wanted to be allowed to come down to Rabun County and see the students at work and interview them and follow them around. Requests for speeches came in from everywhere.

The book was so successful that Ronnie Shushan, the editor, was on the phone only a few weeks after the book had come out saying,

"We've got to have a second book right away. You guys might as well put the manuscript together. We've got to have it." I had to tell Ronnie that we weren't even close to having a second book ready, and that I wasn't going to slap something together and have it be less than really solid work. She understood that and said, "Just see what you can do about putting one together as soon as possible." She said, "Bear in mind the longer you wait, the more the sales may be affected." It turned out that by the time *Foxfire 2* came out, it was virtually the same story all over again because there were all of these people sitting out there saying, "They did it once, but they'll never do it again." When the second book was better than the first, the whole thing just repeated itself.

One result, of course, was that, for the first time in our lives, we found ourselves with some serious income. All of a sudden we were getting checks for tens of thousands of dollars as our share of the proceeds. Suddenly we had the ability to really expand the summer jobs program, to initiate and expand a scholarship program, and to buy new equipment. We had the possibility in front of us of actually hiring some other adults to work with us. So the publication of that book wound up changing everything.

And it had the result of simply confirming once again to the students, the school, and the community that the work that was going on here was pretty special stuff, and it invested the program with a sense of importance that it hadn't had before. Whereas before, individuals had become interested in the work and had confirmed that it was important, what actually happened when *The Foxfire Book* came out was that the nation affirmed that the work needed to be continued, and the kids heard that loud and clear.

I wasn't expecting the book to be a best-seller. I just hoped that we could buy copies from Doubleday at half-price and sell them ourselves down here to subscribers and to people who were writing letters asking for back issues, and make some money that we could use to buy new cameras and print new magazines. I figured we might be able to make several thousand dollars a year in extra income on top of what we were making from subscriptions. None of us were prepared for this. Doubleday wasn't prepared for it. It swept over us all like a big wave.

LORETTA BARRETT, EDITOR: This started out as a sleepy little project. Wig thought he could sell some copies down in Georgia. The people of Doubleday didn't think there was a big market for oral history, either. They were saying, "You're going to print a book with an old lady getting the eyes out of a hog's head? What? Are you crazy?" Some of us, on the other hand, thought we had a big thing—but never this big. We just didn't know.

What happens is our sales reps go into the bookstores about three months before a book comes out, show the jacket, describe the book, and take orders. Well, the bookstores went insane over *The Foxfire Book*. The orders were five, six, seven times the usual advance orders. We expected a small advance order, certainly under ten thousand copies, but this was advancing forty and fifty thousand. The phone calls were coming in, and people at Doubleday were saying, "This is huge. What do you have? What is this?"

The problem is that when publishers fill the orders and send the finished books to the bookstores, every one of them can be returned if they're not sold. So you can get *very* nervous if you advance fifty thousand copies, print them, and send them out. The bookstores are buying the book, but the customer hasn't come in yet to the store to buy it. So bookstores kept ordering *Foxfire*, and there was a real fear here that there were going to be piles of these books stacked up that high [gesturing toward the ceiling] and they were not going to move out of the stores. The bookstores just ran away from us, and some people were scared that because the books cost us a couple of dollars apiece to print, and we'd printed sixty thousand, that if we got forty thousand back we'd lose our shirts. There was this lapse of time between printing and delivery to the stores, and more orders coming in every day, and we were sitting here thinking, "Oh, my God. Should we print twenty thousand more? We're crazy, folks."

But the bookstore people knew. They knew it was a winner. We didn't get the books back, and we were out of stock in the best sense of the word. All of a sudden it took off and hit America. We went into a second printing, and a third. It got so big for Anchor, the department I was running, that we literally took the *Foxfire* figures out of the Anchor budget and accounted for them separately.

And everybody forgot it was sixteen- and seventeen-year-olds doing it. They didn't believe it. They thought Wig had written it and Doubleday was covering that up. They were saying, "Kids couldn't do this. What's the real story? Where's all the money going?" which is a legitimate question when it got into the millions of dollars. I remember bringing down a huge check one time personally and delivering it to the kids in their class.

It was just wild.

▚▚▚

EMMA BUCHANAN CHASTAIN: At first *Foxfire* was just a magazine, and I was shocked to death when I found out they had decided to make a book out of it. I was really shocked. I thought, "Golly bum, you mean it's gonna be a book? It's going to grow *that much?*" I was amazed.

I was already out of school once they decided to do *The Foxfire Book,* but they used our article on soap making in it. I was proud of that.

▚▚▚

ANDREA BURRELL POTTS: [I can remember] going to see the editor at Doubleday in New York about *The Foxfire Book.* It was getting ready to come out, and the guy laughed at me about the way I talked. He said, "We need people like you to go around and advertise the books!"

▚▚▚

MIKE COOK: I remember the final editing of *The Foxfire Book* was done by Wig. Students were involved in strengthening certain sections. Our main contribution to the book, though, was basically what we had already done for the past magazines: going on interviews, taking pictures, and writing the articles that went into the book. That was our responsibility.

Before the book came out, we would print one issue of the magazine, sell it, and get enough money to pay the debt for the one that had come before. We were always behind. My senior year we were trying to raise $1,800 to pay for the magazine to try to get ahead. We had one of those thermometers that keeps track of how much money we had raised. I can remember being close to that goal. Later, I remember Wig saying, "Do you want to see something?" He handed me a check for $160,000. I stood there just looking at it. We had been struggling to raise $1,800, and here Wig handed me our first royalty check from Doubleday.

PAUL GILLESPIE: [After the book was published] if you had journalists coming into town, and they wanted to see some Foxfire contacts, which they always did, Kenny Runion was one we'd often take them to meet. You never had to call Kenny. He was always glad to see you. Except one time. We took Geraldo Rivera to his house. We took him and his crew down there and I said, "Look, don't mistreat this guy. Be good to him." When we got there Geraldo commenced to run a cord up Kenny's pants leg for a microphone. Kenny completely freaked out, and it was a bad scene.

We also had some journalists that came that were outright rude and thought that we were all hicks, and thought with their New York business that they could run roughshod over us and get what they wanted. I used to have some real falling outs with them. We disagreed on stuff all the time. They would promise things and wouldn't come through. They would say that they would take a day on shoots and they would end up taking three days. Their footage was excellent, but it took a lot of pain and time to do it. Sometimes the contacts would get money, and sometimes they would get pictures. On balance, I guess it was beneficial for everyone, but sometimes it strained everyone's patience to the limits.

₩₩₩

JAN BROWN BONNER: When *The Foxfire Book* came out, I was already out of high school. It was scary to see my work in a book. I remember not wanting to read it. I thought, "Gosh, what kind of grammatical errors did I make, or how could I have phrased that better?" It's hard to read your work in a book. You're almost afraid to pick it up.

₩₩₩

MORRIS BROWN: When *The Foxfire Book* started selling and the first royalty check arrived, we were dumbfounded. I think Wig was, too. I think he was just as much surprised as we were when it became a Doubleday best-seller.

We all got to see the royalty checks, and they were very sizable! Of course, Wig was getting a teacher's salary, so there was no question as to where the money would go: only to the Foxfire organization itself. There were so many things it was needed for: equipment and a darkroom, for example. I never heard anyone in the community say that they thought Wig was getting rich, because they knew none of it went to him.

# Music, Radio, Video, and Outdoor Education

WIG: After *The Foxfire Book* was published, we had enough income to be able to consider the possibility of hiring some other adults to work with the program. One of the areas that I really wanted to pursue was video. We had asked in one of the NEH proposals for enough money to buy a video recorder and camera so that when people were demonstrating how to do certain kinds of things like shear sheep, or spin wool, or make baskets, we could document what they were doing not only with still photographs but also with videotape.

At that point, all that was widely available was little black-and-white, half-inch Sony equipment, but the National Endowment for the Humanities thought that was an interesting enough idea that they allowed us to purchase one of those units. Because I was also allowed to hire students during the summers, we began to have students videotaping all of the interviews.

One of the students who was involved with that work was Mike Cook. Mike went on to the University of Georgia and majored in journalism. One of the happy coincidences of many that have characterized this whole venture was that he graduated from school at just about the time when the royalties checks began to come in. By the time Mike graduated from college, he was pretty sophisticated about this whole venture and what it stood for, and he had been involved in enough teaching situations that I didn't have any reservations about whether or not he could teach.

The idea of hiring a former student who wanted to come back to Rabun County after college, and the idea that our organization might be able to grow to the point where we really could offer a number of people jobs, was so intriguing, that as soon as Mike graduated, we just hired him. I don't think any of us thought very much about what we were getting into. We weren't thinking, "One of these days the *Foxfire* books will stop selling and we'll run out of money, and here these people will be that we've hired, stranded." We were just jumping at opportunities and saying, "We've got the chance to do this; let's not think it to death. Let's just do it."

With the permission of the principal at Rabun Gap, and the permission of Karl Anderson, the president of the school, we added Mike to the staff. Luckily, Mike had been a really good student there. His father was a teacher and a coach there. The whole family was well respected, and nobody in a position of authority at the school had any qualms at all about somebody like Mike being part of the work, because they trusted him completely. They knew that he was one of the best students they had turned out of that place. I think if I had had to try and hire a stranger, it would have been a completely different situation, but people were unanimously excited about the thought of Mike coming back and working with students. So they gave me permission right away to add him to the faculty as long as Foxfire paid his salary. One of the first responsibilities that he had was to expand the work that he had already helped start in video and to just take that and see where it could go.

Then we began to look at what some of the other possibilities might be. At that time, I was on the board of the Highlander Center in Knoxville, Tennessee. One of their staff members, Guy Carawan (who had been partly responsible for reintroducing an old Negro spiritual into the Civil Rights movement and turning it into the anthem of the movement—"We Shall Overcome"), had agreed to serve on our Advisory Board. I had invited him because of his expertise in working with other cultures and documenting music. I didn't know anything about music, but Guy reminded me that preserving or documenting some of the traditional music around here might be just as important as documenting skills and crafts. It might also, like video, stretch the students in some interesting ways.

I said, "If you hear of anybody, let me know. I'm willing to consider it as a possibility."

He said, "Let me bring one possibility down so that you and the kids can meet him." So Guy brought George Reynolds down one day. George had just gotten out of college, had his degree in folklore, and was a musician himself—banjo picker, guitar player. Guy said, "In order to let the students get to know George a little bit, why don't you let us do a concert for the school?"

The school gathered in the auditorium, and Guy and George did a forty-five-minute concert. Afterward the students who were in the program got together to interview George. It turned out that the students really liked him, and they wanted to have him work with us. I liked him. The administration liked him. Everybody liked him.

So we offered George a job. He and his wife, Sherrod, moved down to see what we could do not only to document traditional music, but also to produce a series of record albums.

Yet another addition was Bob Bennett, Margie's husband, an avid outdoorsman who was constantly taking kids on camping trips up into the mountains. The job I gave him was to design and initiate an outdoor education division inside the science department at the high school. With Project Adventure's staff and our students, he built a ropes course in the woods behind the school. Then with Peter Gott, he and the kids built a log cabin there to be used as their classroom. A whole series of programs flowed from there, including water quality

At an early board meeting on the Foxfire land, George Reynolds is visible sitting on the floor in front of Guy Carawan. Wig is on the stool to Guy's left, and barely visible on the floor in front of Wig is Ralph Rinzler of the Smithsonian's Festival of American Folklife. Behind George are Margie Bennett and Ann Moore.

Gary Warfield (holding camera), Karen Cox, and David Wilson documented a quilting using our early video equipment.

testing of area rivers and streams, the design and building of proto-type passive solar water heaters and fuel-efficient wood stoves and the study of native plant materials.

Experiments like these are what led to our conviction that Foxfire could be much more than a magazine.

## A. Video

MIKE COOK: When I first came back to Foxfire after college, my respon-sibility was to create a community resource with high school students using videotape equipment. We started out doing nothing but cable programming. We did basketball games and interviews with people in government here in the county; we had people talking about service organizations; we had interviews with musicians, interviews with people who visited the school, and interviews with students who were doing special projects.

We didn't have a video editor. We would point the camera at you and say, "Okay." There was more to it than that, but not much. We'd add graphics by pointing the camera at a sign that said, "This is so and so." You wouldn't believe how primitive the equipment was. Right now, if you've got a camcorder, you have much more sophisticated equipment than anything we possessed back then.

We finally bought a decent little editor. It didn't have a computerized console like you've got now, where you go find the edit points and lock the numbers in, and the computer goes and finds them and performs the edit. You had to do it manually. You could work for hours to get one little piece done.

We put on a new cable program every week. We had worked out a deal with Rabun Cablevision. They let us put shows on, basically, anytime we wanted. One channel on the cable was reserved for local people to use. To put the shows on, I had to get in the car with whatever student it was who wanted to go that day and head for the top of Black Rock Mountain, go through the gates up to the cable head, connect the machines to the cable, put the shows on, sit there with them, put the machines back in my car, go back down the mountain, take the student home, and then go back home myself. Now it seems just ridiculous to have had to do all of that, but we did it that way for a long time.

Later, we decided we wanted to do color, so we bought a color camera. I think it cost fifteen hundred dollars. When we would go to tape with that color camera, I would have to load my car full of equipment. There would be a camera, a tripod, a recorder, a light kit, a bunch of separate lights, and big cables for the lights. Because of the old technology, you would have to light everything so bright that it would almost hurt your eyes. The kit itself was three 650-watt lights. We usually took other lights that were 1,000 watts each. You start adding that up: 6.5 amps for each kit light, 10 amps for the 1,000-watt lamps, and pretty soon you're kicking people's breakers.

We used one old JVC 6300 industrial model tape recorder for everything we taped. That machine and the camera and whatever else we could build was all there was for a while.

One summer I hired some students to build a studio in Clayton in a space provided by the local cable company. We got the studio built, and I hired Andrew Lampros and some others to produce cable shows.

Andrew and that bunch were an experiment because I had to go to school that summer. They worked without supervision. I would come back in the afternoons and see how things were going. They thought it was stupid to try to do all of those shows with no good way to edit them, and on their own they put together a proposal for a good editing machine. Of course, we had talked it over beforehand. They presented the proposal to the staff and got the okay to spend ten thousand dollars, which is what an editing system cost at that time. After we got the new editing system into the studio, we began to do classes in two-hour blocks there. We'd take the students in the van and then drive them back to school.

Frank Dyer and Danny Flory came into the program after the studio and the editing system were up and running. They were in the first class I remember to take full advantage of the foundation built by earlier students. Both of them are in law enforcement now, Frank with the local sheriff's department and Danny with the police department of the city of Clayton.

DANNY FLORY: We did a lot of the editing from the basketball games when they videotaped those. We taped them there at the school, then went from school on up there during the class and edited them and put in the commercials. [The games were cable cast, and the ads were sold to defray part of the cost as well as offer an opportunity for the students to do serious video work.] We went around to the businesses in town, and some of them bought an ad for ten or fifteen dollars.

FRANK DYER: [Students] went out to do the ad sales, and we had another crew go out to whoever bought the ad, like to Foodland, and take the shots outside and inside and then bring the footage back and piece it all together. We would show the script to the business folks before we started to shoot.

DANNY: It was hard to figure out a script to fit into a thirty-second time slot, but it was all a learning experience.

We did one show that was out at Tate City. Curtis Blackwell's band came out for a get-together out there. I suggested to Mike that we go there to get some videotape of the band. We all made a day of it. It was bluegrass music out at the Tate City church. It rained that day, but everything still went pretty good.

Frank got to go to the World's Fair in Knoxville.

FRANK: Sho' did. And you ain't liked me since. Going to the World's Fair first of all, was an experience. [You'd] hear all kinds of stories about what all they had there. Mike thought it would be a good idea to get a tape of the Foxfire String Band playing up there—that was George Reynolds [Foxfire's music advisor], Richard Hembree, Mike Hamilton, Tom Nixon, Wayne Gipson, Dean English, and Steve Mc-Call.

We taped both their shows that one particular day. We had an afternoon show and an evening show. The afternoon show was in direct sunlight. It was, I would say, in the neighborhood of a hundred degrees. Had two cameras set up. Took the special effects generators and everything.

The funniest part of that trip was on the evening show, the second tape we did. They were singing a song called "Daniel Prayed." It's sung without instruments. Dean was the vocalist on there, and he'd sung it earlier with no problems. During the evening show, they got through the first verse, and they had just started on the second verse and he just stopped and just cracked a big ol' grin. Everybody else turned and looked at him and he just grinned real big and said, "That's twice I've done that." He'd forgotten the words. Got that all on tape. Audience got a big kick out of it. Even applauded. He was honest enough to say he forgot the words, and he got up there and apologized and then tried it again. He went back through and got that song all right.

Then there were the basketball and football games that we taped. Those were an experience in themselves, especially basketball games. One time we were sitting on the front bleachers, and Rabun County, I believe, had just scored and got a foul called or something against whoever they were playing. The one that had the foul called on him had the basketball in his hand. He got mad and he threw it right into the camera. I think Jeff Giles was the one running the camera and was in the process of fading over to another shot. Jeff [was] pointing it right at the fellow and that basketball was coming toward the camera just as it faded off. I had a summer job with Foxfire the summer of '84. I mainly just edited shows that were shot during the school year. Felrese's show that I remember that summer was one about Keith Yates. He is a singer over in White County who wrote songs, basically bluegrass and country.

FELRESE BRADSHAW CARROLL: [Keith Yates] was in Helen [Georgia], and the way I found out about him was through my uncle. Keith played all kinds of unique songs, so I thought it would be kind of interesting to interview him and to listen to some of his music. So we got what turned out to be this major production together.

After I met Keith, we set up the time, and he came into the studio above Rabun Cablevision. We had two cameras set up and the special effects generator. That was so much fun because I got to run the special effects generator and talk to the camera people and tell them what to do.

[For one of his songs] he had a knife and he had a guitar. This is the thing I remember most about the show. I think it was "Amazing Grace." He used that knife [sliding it on the strings] and it was beautiful. He played the guitar in his lap for that song. Keith Yates was the best one I ever did [laughing].

It sounds kinda strange, but what I remember the most about the time, I guess was using the special effects generator. I could do these really cool fades in and out, using the two different cameras, and I think I got lucky and did some really good fades and switches. Luck is involved.

I guess the show that was most fun and interesting subject-wise was the water dowser, Bob Slack. He actually did dowsing for people who were building houses and helped them find water. I think his accuracy was very good. We got pretty good at it ourselves and it got to the point where I was kinda scared. I buried my rods somewhere, I think, because it got too eerie.

Another one that we did was a land study. I just remember I learned how to use the tax digest, and I was amazed at how many people owned the land and the portion some owned. I know it took a long time to collect the figures—about two years, more or less.

DANNY: We put together a brochure that went out. We were airing several segments, and we made up a little monthly calendar—sort of like a *TV Guide*—to send out to all the subscribers of the cable. That took most of our time [for a few weeks one quarter]. We didn't do many shows because we were really trying to get this prepared. We had a deadline to meet, and we saw what it was like to be rushed. We went through it all.

**ᐯᐯ**

MIKE: In doing cable programming, we finally got smart enough to put a timer up there to run the shows so I didn't have to drive up the mountain every day. We could go up and put a tape in the machine, and the timer would come on and run the tape without me having to be there. We changed the shows once a week. There was always and forever some sort of problem: the power would go off, or the timer would screw up. I'd always have to go up there and set the timer.

I am proud of the fact that through it all, the students were producing programming that went onto the cable. Then we discovered that we were spending an arm and a leg driving back and forth up to the studio. At the same time, the school decided that they were not going to allow two-hour blocks for classes anymore.

And we had begun to pick up many other things to do, like producing videos about what Foxfire students were doing aimed at teachers and students who were interested in doing similar things, and some weekly radio shows, so we backed away from cable programming. It is something I would like to start back with, but there were choices to be made. If you try to do a weekly radio show and video shows, produce stuff for other interested teachers and students, and produce a manual for teachers about what you do, you finally have to drop something. We dropped cable.

I started concentrating more on making sure that certain things were covered in the class rather than making the product the utmost aim of the program. Now we concentrate on what is called video literacy. Basically that means that when you come out of the classes, you have learned a little bit more about what makes a television show or a commercial work, and what makes them affect us the way they do. I guarantee you that once you have been through the course, you will watch TV in a different way. That is mainly what I want to happen. And, of course, you cannot do television without writing. We have begun to emphasize that skill more heavily.

Right now we are busiest producing tapes which will accompany the teacher's guides we are working on. Robbie Bailey is a Foxfire student right now and a rising twelfth-grader. He and Julie Hayman and Keri Gragg produced our first tape for teachers. It was about the Foxfire I class they were in at that time.

▼▼▼

ROBBIE BAILEY: I was in Foxfire I in ninth grade. I had just finished a project. Julie Hayman and Keri Gragg had just finished their projects, too. We were looking for something else to do. We went through a folder full of letters and we found a letter from the University of Georgia wanting to know a little more about Foxfire. We thought to ourselves, "What better way to tell somebody about something than on videotape?"

We went to the library and started to write down ideas about what we wanted to do. We wanted to cover basic information like how Foxfire started, what it was, and all that kind of stuff. We started taping stuff that went on in the classroom. Then the school year ended and the tape was sort of rough. Foxfire hired us during that summer to work on this videotape. We used part of the stuff off the tape we had, but we had to go back and shoot more footage. Sometimes we had to re-create and reshoot some of the classroom meetings to get it done—make it look like we were still in school.

At the end of the summer, we nearly had it done. One day after school started, we went to Atlanta to a professional post-production house to add music and make it real tight. When I walked in, what impressed me the most was that in this one room I saw all these guys with editing machines. When I looked on the screen, I saw that they were editing a show for ESPN. I watch that particular station sometimes. I was pretty much in awe about that, because here I was, a sixteen-year-old high school kid, with a bunch of professional editors. I hadn't really thought about people getting paid for that kind of work. It was too much fun.

I've still got my copy [of the Foxfire I tape] at home. I looked at it a couple of months ago. [Looking back,] it didn't feel so good all the times we had to start over and do stuff again, but that just comes with the territory. [When we did the first one,] we thought all you'd need was one day. We didn't think it would take—what, five months or six?

The next summer I worked on the video documentation of the process of putting *Foxfire: 25 Years* together. It was a good experience because the summer before I had learned to look for the things that you need to put a tape together. Mike was down here some and helped us figure out where we were making mistakes, but mainly it was up to us to figure it out.

MIKE: Robbie doesn't tell you that one person at the professional post-production house was so impressed with Robbie, Julie, and Keri that he has repeatedly offered to work out something to allow them to work with him if they want to do that. One professional producer has looked at the raw footage that Robbie and his assistants shot last summer and said that it looked great and that he had seen a lot of professionals who did not do as well.

The girls who are working this summer are carrying on in the same style. Evie Bessette, Beth Davis, and Alicia Brown are working on documenting the final steps in the production of *Foxfire: 25 Years*.

## B. Music and Radio

LYNETTE WILLIAMS ZOELLNER: I helped produce the first Foxfire record. It was a record of original country songs by Joyce Brookshire called *North Georgia Mountains*. The students met with Joyce, and we were around her the whole time she was here, which was probably about two or three weeks. Every night they were working, we would go down to the recording studio in Franklin, North Carolina, and we got to be right at the control panels if we wanted to. I didn't ever have the nerve to get on the control panel. I mainly just watched. We'd do stuff like carry the equipment in and do little errands. We would stay there until whenever they finished recording. Sometimes it was two and three o'clock in the morning. We thought it was big to go to a recording studio.

ᴡᴡ

RONNIE WELCH: I was in George's music class. The class was open, and everybody just kind of sat around together and taught one another what they had learned. It didn't necessarily matter which instrument, but George wanted us to learn how to play one song on it. We were all there to learn. So it wasn't like we was a bunch of wild Indians throwing paper and stuff like that. We wasn't. We was into what we was doing. It was a good class. I learned how to play the dulcimer and a little bit on the banjo and some on the guitar.

The class went to other schools to perform, but I just didn't ever get good enough to feel confident enough to do that. I just must not have a talent for music like I do other things. I did try, too. I wore I don't know how many blisters on my hands. Every evening when I'd get home from school, after I'd done my chores, I'd sit in my room and play.

One of the first Foxfire records featured Stanley Hicks telling snake stories to Boyd Queen.

Foxfire music class gave me an opportunity to learn some old music, and it got me involved. I went to some gigs with my uncle Red Jones playing bluegrass. Red's a funny banjo picker—he only plays with two fingers. But Foxfire music class got me involved with him. About that time there was quite a bit of music going on with the Foxfire String Band. I felt like I was one of them, whether I played with them or not.

▀▄▀

Tom Nixon: I got into Foxfire because I liked the bluegrass band I saw at the high school gym. Dean English and Gary Gottschalk, Mike Hamilton and Richard Hembree, they played just a few songs, and I thought, "I want to be up there. I want to play." My family was always musically oriented. I had played in front of people before. Everywhere I went, Daddy would set me up there and say, "Play something." About the middle of the fourth grade, I sort of tapered off and got interested in other things until I saw the Foxfire String Band.

Dean English, the banjo player for the band, lived in the Persimmon community, and he rode my bus. Along in the eighth grade, we got to talking on the bus, and I played him a tape of my cousin and me picking guitars. He said, "Well, that sounds pretty good there. You ought to just come down and pick with us during fifth period." It was the period I was in Georgia History class. I'd say, "Ms. Brown, I need to go the bathroom," you know, and I'd go out to the Foxfire music room. Ms. Brown asked me one day, "Tom, are you sick, son? You keep having to use the bathroom." I finally told her what I'd been doing. But she understood, and she got to where she'd let me go at the end of the period, and I'd come down and play and sing.

George also had a music performance class just getting started, and I took it and it was really a free-for-all. We'd come in there, and we'd pick up songs we wanted to do, and we would practice them, and play them, and perform in different elementary schools. But the string band itself worked both in and out of school. We practiced once a week on Thursday nights at George's house. I played the guitar most of the time, but the band said, "We need a mandolin player." So I just picked up the mandolin and began playing. George gave me some tablature, and I learned some songs that they were playing. I remember the first concert we played was an evening benefit performance at the yellow building at Clayton Elementary School. Of course I was nervous and everything. I got up and played with the band on three or four songs. We were also getting a few paying gigs here and there for $200 or $250. We thought that was big money then. I remember the first big trip we had was in Brunswick, Georgia.

Before we went to Brunswick, we played in the student council talent show. We won here at Rabun County High School, and we thought it was a big deal. When we went to district, we didn't think we would win, but we did! We were all excited. I remember after we'd won, they had a back room which was a bathroom, and we went back there and jumped up and down and screamed and hollered. It was a big thing.

The string band got a job playing at the 1982 World's Fair in Knoxville, Tennessee. That was a real experience, because we stayed two or three days, and it was nonstop music. We weren't used to that

As an eighth-grader, Tom Nixon, center, was already deeply involved in George's music classes.

at all. We were used to getting up and playing thirty minutes, and this was playing three times a day for over an hour for three days in a row. We were working side by side with other bands—real good bluegrass bands! We thought, "Lord, what are we going to do now!" Of course it was one big party, and we had a ball doing that. I guess I was thirteen or fourteen.

After we played the World's Fair, we started our first tape recording. The World's Fair was a way of getting ready for it. We really went through a lot of material, and we recorded at a studio in Franklin, North Carolina. It took our weekends, and as the time got closer for a deadline, we began to stay up during the week—stay up till three o'clock in the morning sometimes. I would leave Franklin in time to get to Persimmon and catch the bus and come to school, and it was really tiresome. I had George two or three times a day, and I would sleep during his class. Then at night we'd go back to work. It was real hard, but after we got through, everything was back to normal. We got to design our own label and be involved with all the marketing things that went on. George was kind of coaching us through everything, just like in the magazine and the books.

In 1983, the original Foxfire String Band went to the "Grand Ole Opry." Roy Acuff introduced us as "the Foxfire Boys," so we changed our name to the Foxfire Boys, and as a result the new bluegrass band at school became the Foxfire String Band. There are several different bands now. There are rock-and-roll bands, country bands, and there are a couple of gospel bands.

Barry Poss, the producer of Sugar Hill Records, helped get us on the "Grand Ole Opry." He knew Sonny Osborne pretty well, and Sonny is a veteran of bluegrass music and was on the board that screens new talent for the Opry. Well, Barry hyped up about how good we were and how we were young country boys. Barry asked someone at the Foxfire office to send him one of our tapes for Sonny to play for the Opry screening board. Well, Sonny handed it to them, and they

In one of their first big performances, the Foxfire String Band played at the Knoxville World's Fair. Left to right: Wayne Gipson, Steve McCall, Dean English, Tom Nixon, Richard Hembree, and Mike Hamilton.

opened it up and there was no tape in the box! They let us play on the "Grand Ole Opry" anyway, and they'd never heard us before.

I hadn't planned on it, but Mr. Acuff picked me out of the group to be the spokesman. Well, we got out there, and they came off a commercial, and here we were. I was in the middle, and of course I was the shortest one in the group. Roy Acuff puts his arm around me and says, "You look like a good man, why don't you be the spokesman?" I hadn't thought of anything to say, and I was real nervous. He introduced us and got us loosened up, though. He just joked around with us, and he had his arm around me, and he was asking these questions. He asked what we were going to play, and I told him. We played the first song. George said something about the *Foxfire* books and Foxfire, and we were going to play the second song. I'd done told Roy Acuff what we were going to play, but he asked me again, "What are you going to play?" and I said, " 'Grandfather's Clock,' I done told you one time." I shouldn't have said that. I'm all

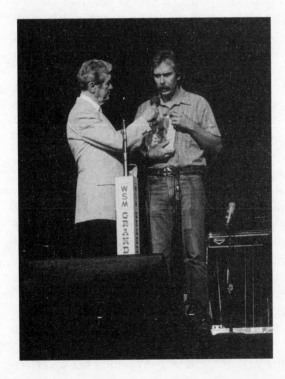

At the string band's performance on the "Grand Ole Opry," George Reynolds presented Roy Acuff with a set of *Foxfire* books.

the time saying stuff I shouldn't say. But he kept us on twelve and a half minutes on a half-hour show, and at the end of the show he said, "I wouldn't mind introducing them every Saturday night on the 'Grand Ole Opry,' because they are good and country."

It's an emotional high to perform. Playing at high schools and colleges is real fun, because when you get a good reception from somebody your own age—you know, people screaming and hollering—there's just nothing like it. The vibrations, I guess, are just going back and forth. When we played at the Opry, to hear that many people whistling and hollering and clapping, I just gasped and said, "Don't let me mess up now." There's nothing like it.

The band all sang and played together, and it became more like a family. It seems like we hung around together all the time. We had our families and, of course, all of our other friends we had in another circle. But I was younger. I remember I didn't hang out much with kids my own age because of the band. We played on weekends. I didn't go out and drag town. I kind of missed out on that scene, because the Foxfire Boys were playing somewhere. The other band I played with, the string band, was younger than I was, and there were all of the people that they hung around with. It ended up being a real healthy atmosphere—playing places, meeting new people, being in two different bands—just a wide circle and a broad range. Which is what Foxfire tends to do, to make you a well-rounded individual to survive in any kind of situation.

I worked one summer for Foxfire when we did the "Christian Harmony" recording and the magazine that accompanied it. We went to Canton, North Carolina, where I was exposed to Christian Harmony [shaped-note] singing. I learned how to edit and transcribe, and I did some taping, too. I remember I felt very inadequate editing, because my work was going to be published for thousands of people.

I had an experience being George's teacher's aide one year. As his aide, I would take half the class and he'd take half the class. Here I was, in the eleventh grade or twelfth grade, with seventh- and eighth-graders—oh, me! It was a real chore. We had a mixture of girls and boys in the class, but we had a particular group of girls one time that was something! They had their little bands, and they would play some country and some rock-and-roll, and they'd beat on the drums. Most of what they wanted to do, though, was have a big time, and George would get frustrated. George would try to work with all of them, but eventually, by the end of the period, I'd get stuck with the girls, and they were the hardest. The roughest group that I remember was that group of girls. They about drove us crazy, but they had talent, and several of them went on to do pretty well. One of them ended up in the string band, and one of them had a rock-and-roll band that went to the state talent competition and made their own video and everything.

The teaching/learning process was always a pretty interesting part of being an aide. The kids, as you know, can learn anything—and if they say, "Teach this to me," well, we've got to learn it first. It makes you more well rounded and gives you more experience. When you teach it to somebody after you have learned it, it just reinforces what you've already done. That's what Foxfire does, anyway. It's taught me that when you learn something and you tell somebody about it, you commit it to memory. You've altered the scheme in your brain. Maybe not altered it, but filled it in. That's how you learn.

I'd always thought about teaching, but the Foxfire experience shed more light on what I wanted to do. I learned a lot from George's playing and [from] watching him manuever people through what they wanted to do and what they didn't want to do. Usually in [most] classrooms it's: "Do this. This is what you're going to do. Do the questions at the end of the book, and you get graded, and you go home. And if you don't want to do that, I'll fail you." It was a big part to see him work with somebody, to get them motivated to want to do something. He'd say, "Well, you pick what you want. What's a song you like?" Everybody likes to sing the songs they like, and if you can perform it for somebody that's all the better. The radio shows, marketing the tapes, and all that comes with it. It was a big motivation. He'd get you to think about having fun doing something, or get you to think about why you want to do it.

It's hard to say whether teaching or performing is more satisfying. To see somebody do something that they weren't able to do before musically and to say, "Oh, I can do that. Boy, that sounds good!"— now that's a real good experience.

Church is a big part of my life, and it's the same with Wayne and Steve in the Foxfire Boys. We like to take songs that mean a lot to us in church and bring them back to the band. We get songs out of the old red-backed hymnal, we call it, and a lot of up-tempo numbers. The Boys are always on me to slow down—"Tom, you're playing too fast." But when we get to going and start singing a lot of times I tend to get faster and faster and faster. I guess I brought speed to the Foxfire Boys.

I teach Sunday School over there on occasion, and I guess my teaching is affected by Foxfire. We've got a Sunday School book we go by, and I can write out a lesson plan and do all that, but I like to get everybody's input and kind of center around the lesson by asking, "What do you think?" and "Why?" I like to get the kids to ask "Why?" One thing that Foxfire has showed me is if you are trying to get a point across and you believe in something, if you don't know why, then people aren't going to listen to you. You need to have some backup for what you are trying to say. If you don't, try not to talk a whole lot about it. When I was younger, I liked to argue; I like to discuss now. College and Foxfire have helped me to say, "Well, why?" and then come up with answers.

It's our sense of community and church that makes the band what it is. Benefits were the first concerts that Foxfire musicians did in the community, and we continue to play them in addition to commercial jobs. They're centered in different places around the community, and since all of us live spread out through the county we play for several different ones: "Come and play for my fire department"; "Come and play for our scholarship fund"; "So and so's sick up in the holler"; and so on. These kinds of jobs are important.

The school, the church, and the community are a circle. My sister and I were involved in Foxfire, of course, and the kids in my church were and still are involved in Foxfire. And the Foxfire bands play at churches. People out in different communities come in and sing also. I remember Arlene Rice and her daddy have a band that sings standard bluegrass music, and they came to our church one time. It's another circle of friends that you get to know. You make them a part of your life, and you become a part of their life. I guess that's what makes life interesting—trying to mix everything together and see how it comes out and yet stay separate. It's real interesting.

ᵂᵂ

DEAN ENGLISH: When I first saw George, he had some students on stage and they were playing. They were doing some kind of performance down at the gym. I talked to George and a few other people, and the more I found out about the class, the more I wanted to become a part of it. Once I got into George's class, I started learning all about the other Foxfire classes. That's when I started them. I really like the way the teachers run the classes. They don't push you into doing something. If you want to learn it, then you've got the opportunity to learn it. I like to have the opportunity to have the decision in what I do. Of all my Foxfire classes, I spent most time in music.

George's music class was where the Foxfire Boys bluegrass band all met. It took about a year or so for all of the members to get together the way the band is now. Our first real performance was for a school talent show. The first two songs we started were "Foggy Mountain Breakdown" and a song that Steven sings called "The Wreck of the Old Ninety-seven." We had to really practice to get those songs to come out smoothly. I think we won second place the first year.

When we first started together, we played music all the time. I'd get off the bus in the morning, and we'd pick before the bell rang. When I started driving, I'd play after school. I started taking banjo lessons from a guy named Freddy Webb. He's a good friend and a good teacher. The extra lessons helped me adjust when I was first getting started, because I wasn't going into class blank.

The first job we ever got paid for was the Miss RCHS contest. I usually save all our newspaper clippings, and I've got a picture of it. We had one microphone that we all stood around. We were scared to death. After that, we began to have people wanting us to play, and we kept on doing it.

Most people would say that the "Grand Ole Opry" was the biggest thing we've ever done. It was scary playing at the Opry, but they treated us real good. Before we knew it, it was time for us to go on stage. We just had to rush out there and do it. It was all real exciting and scary, but at the same time, we were just high on life. I think it really didn't hit all of us until we were off the stage and went into Roy Acuff's dressing room and talked to him. It took us about an hour to get settled down and realize what had just happened. We did pretty good for a bunch of scared people. You can't explain it until you do it. Everything goes through your mind. You're standing up there in front of a packed auditorium and everything you're doing, saying, or playing is going out over the radio all over the place. I was happy I was still standing.

We've made three recordings, and the idea of us doing albums was a good one. It was a big accomplishment and a lot of work. Now we're getting to where we are a professional band. If we want to go to a party and play for five hours, we're capable of doing it. The band has done all kinds of things. We've played everything from parties to churches, concerts to benefits. Benefits are fun to do. It's nice to do a benefit for someone that you know really needs the money. It makes you feel like a part of the family and the community.

I play bluegrass best, because that's what I've played the most. I can play guitar, banjo, a little bit of fiddle, and a little bit of piano. When you get into music and get the basics down, you can transfer what you've learned to a different instrument. If you can do something well, it kind of gives you a solid rock stand. People will say, "You're talented; you can do it," but it's not something just bred into me. Every now and then, I remember way back when I didn't play an instrument and wanted to—I thought I'd never be able to do it. When I got into the Foxfire class, I saw other people in the same shape, and when I saw them making progress, I realized it was something that could be done. After I did a little bit of it, I just couldn't get enough.

I feel we've really accomplished a lot when we practice hard and play on a stage in front of people who really enjoy it. Part of it is practice, and part of it just comes out of you. It doesn't matter where we are playing—if I get that kind of feeling, it's like I get chill bumps because I'm enjoying it so much. It's just always good. That's what I live for.

"The Foxfire Boys" today.

OHSOON SHROPSHIRE: When I was in the Foxfire String Band, audiences probably thought it was a little strange seeing a little Korean singing Appalachian folk songs. Most people thought it was as cute as a button. I don't know why, I guess it was kind of a novelty thing. I don't think the kids in the band really noticed, and it didn't matter.

String band was fun. It was a blast, and I wish I could do it again. I liked doing the work and going with the band to The Chicken Coop restaurant every week. Of course the The Chicken Coop crowd wasn't that big, but it was always fun. I always enjoyed listening to the band more than listening to myself. It was a good group—a very, very, very talented group.

I remember the crew was Brent Love, Jody Taylor, Tom Nixon, Arlene Rice, and I. Our trips back and forth to The Chicken Coop were pretty funny. The band itself was funny enough. You've got two girls, and all these guys, and George. I was a bit of a feminist at that point and still am today. You got these little country boys, who don't understand a woman's view. I think the thing I remember that stands out most is arguing with those men all the time. It never failed. Everywhere we went, they nagged me on. It was all in joking, though. A lot of kidding around.

I usually don't listen to country music, but I really learned to enjoy it. I especially loved working with Arlene. She's really talented, and it was a good experience being around her.

Performing is a good way to get hold of yourself. You gain a lot of confidence, and you have to know, or be confident in, what you're doing. I think most of all I felt privileged to work with people that were so talented. I feel like there are so many incredibly talented students, and so few have access to what Foxfire students have. It's a privilege to be included, even though everyone should be. It's nice to know that I had the opportunity and that I actually got to use it.

SIDNEY DENNIS: I had Foxfire music in eighth grade for thirty minutes a day during fifth period. Basically, what we did in that class was to use cans and stuff to make all kinds of musical instruments. It was really interesting, especially for a little eighth-grader, and it was neat to me because I'd never done anything like that before. For example, we had to make a percussion instrument that would beat and make noise. So I went home and took some lead shot. I put it into a container and shook it, and it sounded just like percussion. Another time, I made an instrument that was like a bamboo flute. It was simple to make. All I had to do was to drill about five holes. But even from this easy process, I learned so much about music. I learned about sound, pitch, and where the mouthpiece was.

I remember dipping tobacco in George's class. He really got upset, because we chose the days the principal and observers came around to check on our classes. Of course they found spit cups and stuff. Every time any observers came around, Bobby and I'd *always* be dipping, and George would get in trouble because of that. But I don't any more, and I don't smoke. I don't do any of that stuff.

No one is equal to George when it comes to teaching music—nobody. He'd really make you try. He was really involved in music, and he'd try to motivate you even if you weren't the most gifted person musically. Also, he knows his music very well. He knows anything from hard rock, to rap, to basic gospel.

▾▾▾

BETH LOVELL: I always liked to play music. My mother made me take piano for five or six years, and I dearly hated it. I got a chance to get one of these little plastic guitars at one time, and I really liked that, so once I got into George's class, I decided that that was the instrument I wanted to play. I learned how to play the banjo, mandolin, and bass, but the guitar was my main instrument. I played mostly bluegrass, because that was what I liked. Flatt and Scruggs were my heroes.

In the eighth grade we went out and played at the elementary schools. When I first got in there, I thought "Well, I want to make it to the string band." That was my goal at that time. I worked after school, and I worked hard during school practicing. I would always go over there to the music room during my ten-minute breaks, and I was always in George's room. If you ever needed to find me, that was where I would be.

I didn't think George even knew I could talk until I was in the tenth grade, but at the end of the ninth grade, George asked me if I would be in the string band. He was going to award the Foxfire belt buckle that year to the new string band people. I wasn't sure if I was ready to be in the string band at that time, and I told him that I would give him my answer along toward the end of school. On Awards Day, he handed me the award buckle, anyway, even though I hadn't even given him my answer. That was probably one of the most memorable things, for me, I think, getting that belt buckle.

■■■

BROOKS ADAMS: I first got involved in Foxfire music in the seventh grade, when we formed a music group called the Cat's Meow. Instead of bluegrass and country, we did fifties and sixties music. We were just kids having fun. Although we didn't have any major gigs, we did get to go to Atlanta a couple of times; we played for the Foxfire Mother's Day picnic, and we had one gig where we got lunch for free at a restaurant. Most of our things were just right here at the school.

Of course we'd be nervous when we'd go out at first, but after we'd been playing for a while, I decided, "Those people aren't nervous about hearing me, so why should I be nervous about playing to them." We probably messed up on some of the numbers when we went around to elementary schools two or three times a week. But it didn't matter. The most fun audience was the elementary school kids, because they were always excited. It's always exciting, having everybody looking at you. It's really cool to know that you're entertaining them and they're really enjoying it.

We've got a trophy in George's room for a talent show. We did two different versions of "Blue Moon" in the same song. I don't remember how it started, but somehow we decided to do "Blue Moon." There was this slow romantic version of "Blue Moon," but then there was this fast, fun kind of "Blue Moon." We didn't know which one we wanted to do, so we decided to do them both. As the last note faded out of the slow version, here came Lynn Morgan acting like a news reporter. She came up to Darren and Lori English, and they'd go through this little skit about how there had been reports of a streaker going through [based on the Ray Stevens song, "The Streak"]. Lori reported how she had seen the streaker: "He come running right by the cornflakes and down past the powdered eggs." Then she hollered, "Look out, Mumford!" and, "By then, it was too late. He'd done been mooned!" Then right after that, we started into the fast "Blue Moon" with the "ding, ding, ding, a-ding-a-dong ding . . ." I was the ding-dong man. I remember that well.

George had been approached by someone here at school asking if one of his groups could do a choral hymn for graduation ceremonies. We were the closest thing to a choir George had, so he came to us with his dilemma. First of all, there were only a few of us that could read music in the Cat's Meow. The way he wanted to teach us to read music was to use these shaped notes and teach us the name "do, re, mi," etc. of each note and let us be able to figure out where one pitch was in relation to others. We could pretty much sing in any key we wanted to, as long as we could feel that relation to one another. There were eight of us at that time, and we separated into four groups, one group for each harmony part. After we had learned our own parts separately, we would come together and sing all four parts at the same time, and it sounded good. Most of us were impressed with it and liked the way we did that, so we continued it and learned several songs with shaped notes. The song we sang that year at the baccalaureate service was "The Parting Hand." We decided at that time that, when we were seniors, we would get back together and sing it for our own baccalaureate service. And we did.

After the Cat's Meow, I got into the Foxfire String Band itself. Suzie Nixon and I were the only ones that carried over from the Cat's Meow to the string band. We did everything. [One of the things we started in music class was] the "Foxfire Radio Show." It started out as a fifteen-minute program, but in 1986 it expanded to thirty minutes. We would do different spots to be edited together as part of a show. I did a series of radio spots on old-time Georgia fiddle bands. I would play songs and give a little bit of background information that I got from the back of record covers or reference books. We would research the bands and write little five- to ten-minute spots. They were just a few paragraphs long, but it was really dense writing. We had to think about every word we would put on those spots, because, in radio, we were so pressed for time that we had to write everything as briefly and as meaningfully as possible. We would talk about the songs, introduce the musician(s), tell the audience what they were all about, and play songs that were good examples of the kind of style that that band had. If they had a real hot guitar picker or something, then we would play songs that featured that guitar picker. At the end of the song, we would add a little bit more, showing a different aspect of the band or something especially interesting. With a short little conclusion, that would usually take five to six minutes.

Suzie had a whole series on "The Carter Family." We also had another series—the kind of music that we didn't think Rabun County had been exposed to before. We featured people that were jazz, blues, or contemporary at that time. We always tried to write the programs so they would be educational and entertaining. We always enjoyed that series, because it was something new that we could really teach people about. We would feature people like Django Reinhardt.

George's music class was responsible for half of the normal weekly "Foxfire Radio Show," and Mike's radio students were responsible for the rest of it. They were responsible for editing the tape all together into a show. We would give them all these little spots on cassette tapes, give them a log of the tape, and tell them how to cue it up. They would put the different shows together.

The first summer I worked with Foxfire, we were doing a series on Rabun County musicians, and we interviewed Curtis Blackwell one afternoon at the auto parts store where he worked. We went in the back where they kept all the parts. It was raining, I remember, because they had a tin roof and you could hear the rain on the tape. Bud Carroll conducted the interview, and Suzie and I were technical support with the sound, pictures, and everything.

Suzie, George, and I had made the list of questions. We wanted to make the tape to use in a radio show which would include both our script and pieces of the interview itself. It was very different from the other Foxfire interviews, which are intended to be transcribed and edited—we wanted to use the actual sound of Curtis's voice. Because of that, we had to ask just the right questions to get the right kinds of answers. That was the first big step—we had to get him to say things we could use. Curtis had played with Bill Monroe and the Bluegrass Boys for a short while—not for too long, but for a few months. We sort of figured it would be the high point of his career. We asked him about that and [on the show we edited in some cuts] of him playing in Monroe's band. He played on the "Grand Ole Opry" back in the fifties, and we included a recording of that, too. We pretty much just let Curtis talk. We gave it an introduction, and maybe once in there we had Bud talking, and then we let Curtis talk some more and gave it a conclusion. After that, we used Bud's voice as the narrator.

One summer when George was putting together a course guide

for teachers, he wanted me to write a student's view of what happened. I had to go back and figure out why I had done everything and what I had gained from it. So the whole summer was spent writing part of the Foxfire Music/Language Arts course guide. After I had finished my first quarter at Georgia Tech, I saw George at Mr. B's one night. He asked me how school had been, and I told him, "It wasn't near as difficult as what I did working for you last summer." I think that blew his hat in the creek! What I did for George that summer was the hardest thing I'd ever done, because I was having to make something and to think it out all the way from start to finish. It had to be thought about and tumbled over. Not only did I have to say everything that had to be said, I had to say it in writing and use correct grammar. The grammar was the easy part of it. The piece went through at least five different drafts. At the end, Cynthia Powelson, our Foxfire teaching intern, gave me some really constructive criticism and helped me get that thing done. That piece took the whole summer to write.

The basic idea behind the radio project is to have students do research and use radio as the medium to reach the local audience with the final product. I didn't realize it when Suzie and I were doing radio for Foxfire that first summer, but in doing that, everything had an educational goal: everything that I was learning, gaining, and practicing that summer, everything from having to do the research about the topics, and writing down and taking notes, and turning information into script, and having to condense it into a spot that was short enough, using the right words in the right places. Not only did we have to pick out the right music as the example for a specific topic, but after that, we had to learn how to use the equipment, to set the levels, speak into a microphone, cue the tapes up to the right place, and keep track of all the recordings.

The radio equipment wasn't real hard to use. The heavy-duty technical stuff we would give to Mike's people to do, like editing the spots together into the whole radio shows. But what we did wasn't simple. We had a mixer, two or three tape decks, and a couple of record players.

We worked in the Audiovisual House on the Foxfire land. If I was going to record something with my voice, then Suzie would run the machine. She would be over there and push the button and give me the cue, and I could read my spiel. We couldn't hold our papers, because we would be shaking and making noise as we read them.

Everybody had to be perfectly quiet. We even had to turn off the overhead lights to keep the buzz off the tape.

Of course we didn't do it right the first time. When we first started making tapes, we would have to go with recordings, whether we liked them or not, just because we were running out of time. We just had to do it the best we could and shove it out. We got a lot better later. I bet if we went back and listened to a spot we did at the beginning of the summer, we could tell a difference in quality. We were practicing the whole summer, getting better as we went.

### C. Folklore, Environmental Science . . .

VAUGHN ROGERS: My first Foxfire class was Folklore with George Reynolds. Our first project was to go out and find old toys and old games that older people played before Mattel and all these other companies came out with toys. I did have a couple of games in the *Foxfire Book of Toys and Games.* My father played mumbles all the time when he was in elementary school, and that was one of the games that I came in with. You roll a knife off different points of your body like off your finger, or off your elbow.

We went out and got old stories like mysteries, ghost stories, legends, and stuff that people used to tell. For example, why is Screamer Mountain called Screamer Mountain? And how did Warwoman Road get its name? I do remember the stories about Warwoman. There are several different stories, but I think there was a white lady settler that got captured by the Indians. It's been documented several times in *Foxfire.* The projects I did really didn't involve interviews like the magazine class. We just did things as homework assignments, and we went out and asked our grandparents and parents about different stuff they did when they were young. We wrote them up and brought them back.

The folklore class was not a Foxfire writing class like Foxfire I or Foxfire II. Basically, we brought in the information, and we handed it over to the Foxfire I or Foxfire II class, and they wrote it up for the book. So basically, Folklore, I think, was just a study of the old ways, and different ways of doing things.

▀▀▀

SIDNEY DENNIS: I was in high school from 1980 to 1986; I took about everything Foxfire had to offer—magazine, music, video, environmental science. I joined Foxfire because I liked the people, and because it was *me*. It was the local culture, it was Rabun County people. I could be myself; that's what I like the most. You didn't have to be real smart; you just had to work. Another reason I joined was that Foxfire has so much to do with the outdoors. My brother and I loved the outdoors, and we hunted a lot.

Bob Bennett's environmental science class was the most interesting Foxfire class I ever took. We got a science credit for it. It dealt with nature, science, the different trees and plants, how to recognize the various species. We learned how to deal with the ropes course and shoot guns. We learned to work together as a team. We were all equal, and we had to rely on each other. At times it was hard work, but it was a real interesting class. There was always something interesting to do. When I had the class, there were thirty or more of us.

We went on a few field trips. One time the class went on a field trip to Joyce Kilmer National Park in North Carolina. Another time, we all went to Black Rock State Park, and yet another time we went to the fish hatchery. But at the time I had that class, the administration was getting really tight about field trips. There'd been a couple of wrecks at the high school, and they were worried. They didn't want anyone to leave campus, so the regulations got very, very tight.

I remember one time we were just getting back from a trip with Bob, and we witnessed somebody getting killed right there in that curve in the road before you get to the Rabun County High School. I'll never forget that. Bob and I went over to help the people. Some drunk had hit somebody, and a man died. It was so sad. That was really bad. I guess that's why they didn't want us to leave campus very much.

# The Land

## A. A Log House on Black Rock

WIG: When I first moved to Rabun County, I stayed out on Betty's Creek at the Jay Hambidge Art Foundation. It was run by a friend of our family's, and when I was thinking about going to Rabun Gap to teach, the woman in charge of the foundation, Mary Hambidge, said, "If you come here to teach, I'll let you live here on the place rent free."

She had a cabin that wasn't finished, and she said that if I finished it, I could live in it for as long as I wanted. I lived in one of the dorms at Rabun Gap as a houseparent, and then, after school and on weekends, I worked out there on the cabin with students who wanted to come along and help out. I got some experience in building and with involving students in construction.

I knew now I wanted my own place in Rabun. Through working on that cabin, I knew that I could build a house myself, and I knew that students would be willing to help me.

I also knew that Foxfire was growing as an organization, and it was beginning to accumulate artifacts. People would make things for us, which we would buy, even though there was nowhere to put them. In some cases, people who had things that they didn't want anymore, like liquor stills, would offer them to us. We had some of these artifacts stored in local barns on a temporary basis, but it was clear that they couldn't stay there forever.

So I began to look around for a piece of land of my own. About this time, around 1971, a piece of land came available in Mountain City. One of my former students, Kenneth Dailey, who knew that I was looking for property told me about it. I looked at it and liked it better than any I had seen so far. I couldn't buy all of it, though, because it was 110 acres and more money than I could handle alone. I bought the piece that was cheaper, and took an option on the adjoining piece, and asked the owner to give me six or eight months until I could have a meeting with the Board of Directors to decide if Foxfire could buy it or not. My idea at that point was to put cabins on Foxfire's piece to move our artifacts into. The board met and finally did decide to buy the other parcel. That's where the center is now.

Meanwhile on my piece, I picked out a place to put the house, and some former students who were bulldozer operators graded the road and carved out a place for it. Kenneth came up and laid off the footings and batter boards to get me started, and laid the cement blocks for the foundation.

Then I took over. I took my paycheck every month and used half to pay for personal expenses, then used the other half to go down to Blue Ridge Lumber and buy C- and D-grade pine lumber. Every weekend I would haul supplies up to the land in my pickup truck. Then I'd go to the Rabun Gap campus and pick up a truck load of kids who would be waiting there right after lunch, and we'd go there and work. At the end of the day, I would take all those kids down to a restaurant in town someplace. It was almost exclusively dorm students who helped. Some were from family situations that they didn't want to go back to, so it was fairly common on holidays for some to come and stay with me. We'd work for days. During summer vacations, dorm students would come spend a week or two at a time and pitch in with whatever was going on. I had students who were pretty handy with chainsaws—Gary Warfield and Carlton Young, for example—and they essentially dropped all the trees that we needed for logs, and I used some of the information we had learned from the log cabin interviews to build it. I never went in debt a penny on the house, and that's the way I like to do business. It took some scrounging around. For example, there was an outfit in town that basically sold junk, but they had furniture and building materials that had been scavenged from buildings that had been demolished. I got a set of plate-glass windows that had come out of an apartment building in Baltimore for five bucks apiece. The big chimney that's in the center was all built with rock that the kids and I picked up off the side of the mountain, and the poplar trees for the log walls didn't cost us anything. The student labor didn't cost me anything. They just

As the poplar trees were cut into logs for Wig's house, Gary Warfield, far right, led the team of students who carried them to the building site.

wanted something to do on the weekends. I paid them by buying them dinner, or having a cookout up on the land. A lot of the students who worked with me are still in touch, and we still talk to each other about that experience.

**WV**

BOB KUGEL: I don't know how long it took us to build Wig's house. I worked on it for about a year. I did the lower part, the logs, the chinking, and helped creosote the porch. I also did some roofing. I remember starting out chopping the logs that were on the land. It took a whole bunch of us kids to carry those logs. I remember driving the little nails between the logs to hold the cement.

Then I came back down there after school one summer, and the house was pretty much put together. The foundation and the logs were both already put up. He was working on the top part of the board and batten. I also remember carrying the toilet out of the back of his blue pickup. Wig's toilet!

Left to right: Gary, Mike Pignato, and Wig then slid the first big logs into place on the foundation.

As one group of students raised wall logs into place, another worked on the central chimney.

Going down there and working on his house is something I wouldn't normally have done—hanging out in those hills and mountains. It's one of those experiences in life that you will never forget.

◆◆◆

GARY WARFIELD [LETTERS FROM BERRY COLLEGE]: It sounds like you're keeping busy. Are there any other kids helping you? I wish I could. You don't know how much I liked working on your house. . . . The next time you take a load of corn, peas, beans, radishes, onions, tomatoes, okra, celery, lettuce, cabbage, rhubarb, watermelon, carrots, greens, peaches, and strawberries from your luscious garden to Suzy's and Harry's tell them hello for me. I miss seeing them.

—July 8, 1973

When the log walls were raised, students signed their names in the wet chinking. Bob Kugel signed his name twice: "Bob K."

I guess you're sealed up in your house by now. I wish I could have been there to help. I can hardly wait to see that chimney! I doubt if I'll be up your way this weekend, but maybe the next. I work twenty–twenty-five hours a week and my weekends are usually jammed. And I study like crazy. After this quarter, I'll have over forty quarter hours.

—October 16, 1973

I was thinking about you and wanted to write and wish you the *Best of Holidays!* I hope you get this before Christmas, but if you don't, I'll still be thinking of you roasting chestnuts on an open fire in your new fireplace. (Only kidding.)

—December 20, 1973

## B. The Foxfire Land and Cabins, and the Mountain City Property

WIG: While we were building my house, and before the Foxfire board met to vote whether or not to buy the adjoining piece of land, Aunt Arie mentioned a log building at the base of her driveway that had been a grist mill. We had gone past that building at least a hundred times but never knew what it was because it was completely covered in kudzu. When we left her house that afternoon, we stopped the car, and the kids and I went to the front of this wall of vines and shoved our way through it. We discovered an open door, pushed our way inside, and found all the works from this grist mill intact: wooden gears, hewed beams, the whole thing. Obviously, the person who owned it was going to let it rot, but it was valuable enough that it shouldn't be allowed to rot. So I tracked that person down to ask him if he would be willing to sell it. He said he would, so we bought the building from him for two thousand bucks. Then I hired a former student, Tommy Wilson, to be in charge of moving it. He measured the building and built a foundation for it on my property immediately adjacent to the lower tract I still held an option on.

I then went to a community person I knew, Millard Buchanan, to see if I could rent him and his truck for one day to go up there and let us load the building, and have him drive it up to the land. He had been interviewed several times before about logging, and his daughter, Emma Jean, had been involved in the program as one of my early students. A group of students from the school and Tommy then took the roof off, numbered the logs, took them apart, loaded them on Millard's truck, hauled them to the land, set it all back up again on its new foundation, and then added the works and gears. Then Tommy put new rafters and the new roof on it. Now we had a building to store some of the artifacts. That whole experience was so good that we began to think about the possibility of doing something similar with some of the other buildings that were out in the county just going to pieces.

Shortly after that, the board met and voted to buy the adjacent property, which opened up that whole lower piece. Millard, who had retired from logging and at that point was anxious to find something else to do, came up to me one day and said, "Do you want to get serious about moving some buildings up here, or do you want to talk about it for a few years?" We had some extra royalties money, and we decided to just jump in. I went ahead and hired him. He had contacts who knew people who knew where abandoned log buildings were, and the more we looked for buildings the more we found.

I gave Millard permission to go ahead and hire some community men to work with him, we put them on salary, and they began to do some serious work. One year they moved a dozen buildings. At the time, we weren't even sure what each building was for. We just knew that they were there and that we needed storage space. We also knew that the buildings themselves were artifacts, and in many cases were in danger. It made sense to do it. Or at least Millard and I thought it made sense.

That whole thing was just an amazing experience. I taught school all day, and when I'd finally get up there in the afternoon, I'd drive up into the midst of teams of men, some raising log walls, some building chimneys, some splitting shingles out of white oak to go on new roofs. It was like a circus. Millard was in the midst of all the noise shouting and laughing and pointing. In the summers, when we added students to the crews, it got even crazier. Some nights, Shirley, Millard's wife, would cook a big dinner, and Millard and I would sit up and talk—and this whole village just rose up around us.

At the same time, we had pretty much outgrown the office space up at Rabun Gap. I selected one cabin to be an office building, and we converted it with that in mind. We put studs on the inside, insulation, installed double-paned windows and fluorescent lights right from the start. We also knew we were about to hire a couple of staff people, both of whom had expressed an interest in living on the land.

The grist mill at the base of Aunt Arie's driveway as it looked before we moved it . . .

. . . being raised in its new location on the Foxfire land . . .

. . . and as it looks today.

Very early on, the buildings began to be split into three different functions. One was staff housing, one was office space, and the other was to house the collection of artifacts. The whole thing evolved from purchasing and moving that grist mill in 1972.

As we began to accumulate more buildings and more artifacts and as the word got out through the grapevine, people began to try to find it so they could see what was going on. In some cases they were community students' parents, family, and friends. That was fine, but then other people began coming into the area and trying to find the place also. But there wasn't any way we could deal with outside visitors. We didn't have much parking space up there, and I also wasn't sure that I wanted to hire folks just to give tours and pick up after people. Having the facility turn into a tourist attraction with people coming up there seven days a week just felt wrong.

But we were getting a lot of pressure from community organizations like the Chamber of Commerce, saying that we had a lot of people coming into this county who expected to see something of Foxfire because they'd purchased the books that had helped pay for the organization. And we had thought about the possibility of beginning some small businesses that might be run by former students. So we began to look around for a possible piece of property down on the main highway that we could use to give tourists something to see, and to perhaps offer them some products, the sale of which would support some small businesses in the county. In the early 1980s, a piece of land became available where the old Mountain City Hotel used to be years ago, and I got permission from the Board of Directors to buy it. Basically, it's most of one city block. One of the first things we did on that piece of property was to build our existing administrative and sales office.

The office building was designed by an architect who's a friend of mine in Atlanta named Paul Muldawer. It was built by a former student who became a contractor, Claude Rickman. It's a passive solar house, which serves not only a useful purpose as far as we're concerned, but also serves as a low-cost fuel-efficient model home for young couples to have a look at. Future plans for the whole block include some shops on the highway, a community historical center, an amphitheater for concerts, picnic areas, and some museum spaces. It's a long way from being finished right now, but I think that piece of property has a lot of potential. Robert Murray, our current buildings and grounds supervisor, and some students have since moved a couple of log houses and a grist mill down there, and over time I think we'll be really glad that we've got that piece of land. I think it's going to turn out to be one of the better decisions we've made.

But I'll bet we're ten years away from finishing it.

▃▃▃

EMMA BUCHANAN CHASTAIN AND SHIRLEY BUCHANAN, HER MOTHER:

EMMA: Daddy [Millard Buchanan] was a man who could do anything. It was especially amazing what he could do with his hands. He could whittle out anything with a knife. It was just unreal how he could whittle. He kept his knives razor-sharp. He always kept himself busy with his woodwork, and it was just normal for him to always be fiddling around with a lot of different ideas.

While he was working, Mother would sweep up the floor. She swept up more shavings than any woman I know.

Millard Buchanan: "I've worked all day many a day and not even got one log to the mill. Maybe take two days to get one log out pulling him all the way. Flat ground. Big logs was hard to move. Sometimes you'd walk up to one lying on the ground and it was all you could do to see over the top of it. They don't have nothing like that no more. When you go to moving one like that, you've got to *have* something. Now they've got equipment to move it with, but we didn't have nothing but cattle and horses. We had double and single and triple tackle blocks—blocks with rollers in them. Put two of them together, and sometimes put three of them together. Thread three into two and then on down into one. And then a few times I've had as high as twelve head of cattle to one log." (*Foxfire 4*) Millard died in 1989. His wife, Shirley, survives him.

SHIRLEY: The kids would pick up the shavings and play with them. You know, those shavings are real pretty.

EMMA: He used to sit there and make his own ax handles. He didn't buy handles. He made them.

One time, he was sitting on the living room floor whittling on a wagon wheel chandelier. He'd taken hammer handles and made this big old chandelier, and then he'd whittled out these hammer handles and put them on the chandelier. He made my children cane-bottom chairs, and I've got two rocking chairs he built. He's made a lot of homemade tables and furniture. He could do rock masonry. There just wasn't anything he couldn't do.

I feel that's the reason Wig came to Daddy. Wig knew Daddy could do it. He knew he could put those buildings up there, and he knew he would do a good job. He knew about Daddy's work, because Daddy had been interviewed before with his logging, and he knew that Daddy was knowledgeable about log cabins. So in 1973, he came to Daddy and asked if he'd go to work on the Foxfire property. Daddy decided to go up on the mountain and help. To start off, he picked out a crew of Claude Rickman and Doug James. They started the reconstruction in 1973. All the dwellings were up by 1978. They were all fixed, and they were all together. They were all in the same places they are currently.

I think that the Foxfire land was a definite landmark. There's no question about it. I also feel like it's a gift. It's just what is needed up here to preserve our heritage. I'm just real proud of the way it's doing that. It's a good place to store all those artifacts that are representative of those things we don't have anymore in this world. Think—if we don't preserve these things, our kids will never see them. I'm just really glad that Daddy could be a part of it all. We're real pleased that there's going to be a plaque up there in his memory.

▟▛▜

MIKE COOK: I remember that Wig said that he had some land in Mountain City. He told us where it was, and Paul Gillespie and I got in a jeep and drove up on the place. There were no roads or anything. It was pretty. I remember walking the boundaries of it. It's a long way around it.

I remember when we started moving the first building. Wig had hired Tommy Wilson to move the grist mill. Tommy had been real active in Foxfire, and he and I were real good friends. Tommy needed

One of the nearly thirty buildings on the Foxfire land is a small log church, the porch of which looks out over the whole complex and the mountains beyond.

a helper, and he asked Wig if they could hire me, so Tommy and I worked up there.

We started buying up buildings. Wig had stuff stored up all over the campus at Rabun Gap-Nacoochee School and in people's barns up on Wolffork. As the buildings began to get done up on the place, some of the artifacts came out of the barns and were [moved] up on the land. When it was first started, the idea was that it would be sort of a village. Then it turned out that we needed some office space and staff and guest housing.

It's continued to evolve, and now teachers come up there. We were just up there this morning doing a workshop with some teachers about how to use a videotape recorder and do projects in their school. It's changed into a working center.

**WW**

CLAUDE RICKMAN: [I remember working with Millard.] We'd go somewhere and take down a log building, and number all the logs, bring them up there, and put it up. And on rainy days up there, you'd take rocks and beat them in between the logs of the cabins. Then you'd take this red mud and lime and mortar mix and then fill in between them. We worked on a number of buildings, and I learned a lot about doing houses from that. I did that on and off for about two years. I'd come home in the summers from college and work. We were doing the fireplaces and doing the foundations.

The thing about that is you were learning. All a house is is a right triangle, so when you were sitting in a math class at school, all of a sudden one day you just looked up and you thought, "That is the same thing that I'm doing now." It is interrelated. If you knew your math real well you could build a house. A house is a right triangle. Put two of 'em together and you've a square or a rectangle, and if you know all those formulas that's all it is.

**WW**

Claude Rickman
and Millard made
several cabinets
together when the
weather kept
them from working
outdoors.

Claude, foreground,
was also involved in
reconstructing most
of the first buildings
moved to the Foxfire
land.

BIT CARVER KIMBALL AND KAYE CARVER COLLINS:

BIT: By the time we'd gotten to Rabun Gap School, they'd already purchased the Foxfire land. The main thing our class was involved in was deciding how it was going to be used. We voted on whether the land should be open for the public for tourists to come in, or whether it should be just for the community.

KAYE: One time when I went up on the land was when Harry and Marinda Brown had a loom put up in one of the cabins. A bunch of us were working one summer, and we all went up there, had a cookout, and watched them put the loom up.

BIT: I went up there when some students did an article on splitting boards, and I helped build the split-rail fence that goes around the barn. Another time, we had a party up there for the contacts.

RONNIE WELCH: I helped with a lot of the work up on the land. Course we had a crew of guys. That was several summers Foxfire hired me to work up there. That [Jackson County house without windows]—I call

Left to right: Anita Hamilton, Tom Carlton, and Bit Carver worked with Millard to build several fences out of old chestnut rails.

it the best-looking one. I redone the whole insides of it and tried to set it up as best we could as how it would have been whenever people were living in it. Aunt Arie's rope bed and all that, I set them up. I done a lot of that myself. Course you know how Wig is—he's real particular with everything—so we were under his care doing that.

And the shingles that are on top of it? They had a feller come in to teach us how to split shingles, and we done that and reroofed that building and the one beside it.

The biggest thing I was involved with was moving that little log building that sits beside the mill. Scott Shope was one of the students up there that summer, and his grandpa had built it and used it for a smokehouse and a canning house. [Then the land got sold, and Scott's family donated the building to Foxfire.]

Course we took pictures of how it was setting then, and we wrote down what they used it for. We dug a hole back into the bank there at the mill to set the foundation into. I laid some of the rocks for the base of it. We went and got the rock there off the property, and some of it I went on a Saturday and got out of a creek bank.

Then we moved it log for log, piece by piece, back up there and put it back up exactly how we took it down. Course we chinked it with red clay mud that was there on the land, and put new shingles on the roof. Each one of those things were things that we had learned from people.

So we brought it back up there and put it back together piece by piece, and put it back up right. Took us a pretty good while. Big job.

I remember we used to run into yellow jackets pretty regular. One day right after we got off dinner and started back to work, I was going through there with a sling blade working my tail off. I noticed them swarming around there. Really didn't think much about it, 'cause there was a bunch of them up there around that honeysuckle, and shoot, they got thicker and thicker. One of them hit me on the back of the neck, and by that time I'd done turned around they were behind me—flew up my shirt and just got all over me. I pulled off my shirt and ran down the hill hollering, and every one of them just a'dying laughing at me. I didn't think it was funny at the time, but when the hurt went away, it was funny.

They liked to eat me alive. Got stung twenty times in one day, I did. Twenty times that I could count. My head was numb. Got all in my hair. I couldn't get them beat out. I hate to say it now, but I didn't give Foxfire very much work the rest of the evening. I stayed up there with five gallons of gas and a damn shovel trying to beat them to death. I did. I dug them out. They tried to get me to come on away, and I wouldn't do it. I wasn't going to give up until I got them dug up out of there. I said, "That will be one nest that won't get me no more this year."

There was something going on all the time up there. [One time after he had sold his blacksmith shop to Foxfire and we had moved it and set it up,] Will Zoellner come up there. He was Ted's father-in-law, and he was heating up steel and beating on an anvil. There was a big crowd of people there, and I was one of them just standing around watching. I sure was young then. Later, I did do some steel in there one evening just playing around.

Another time Margie had a woman come up there on the land to show a bunch of students how to make soap. They made soap up there right down in front of the museum. I didn't know nothing about making lye soap, but I knew something about it by the time they was through. Some of it splashed up on me and burnt me.

[Sometimes the people who came up there were tourists who just wandered in.] And we would—not intentionally, I guess—well, maybe sometimes I got maybe a little bit over involved in trying to keep them out. Course we would dig drainage ditches across the road to keep the water from washing the road away, and I just had to dig them a little extra deep where the Cadillacs wouldn't make it up the hill. I might have been right or wrong. Well, Wig wasn't enthused with crowds coming up there and trying to get tours of the place and all. I guess he didn't mind them too bad, but he was pretty tied up with things going on. We were, too.

Although I did take some people around and show them the place and explain to them what everything was and how it worked and whatnot. It was good to know. It was good that I had the knowledge to tell them. I could say, "Right here is what I done, or me and our crew did." I wouldn't say "me." I'd say, "Here's what the maintenance crew has done this year." We did a lot of good work up there.

# Changing Schools

WIG: Rabun County High School wasn't big enough to hold all the high school students in the county, so 125 local students went to the Rabun Gap facility, a privately owned boarding school. The county school board and the trustees at Rabun Gap simply worked out an arrangement whereby the Rabun Gap facility was leased for a dollar a year, and during the school days, it was, in effect, a public school. The teachers who were on the campus by and large were state-paid teachers. But at three o'clock, when the community kids went home, there were another 120 kids left behind who were the boarding students. It was a unique arrangement in my experience.

Finally, the county was able to pass a bond referendum to build a brand-new high school big enough to hold all the public high school students, and it was critical that it happened because the high school in Clayton was in terrible shape. Between the time I arrived in Rabun County and the time they were able to pass the bond referendum, there had already been two major fires at the school, classrooms had been destroyed, the auditorium had been destroyed, they had classes meeting in the cafeteria, and it was a disaster.

The new school was going to open in 1977, and our big question was, "When all the public school students get pulled out of Rabun Gap, and the only students who are left are not from around here, can we continue to run a program like Foxfire, which is based on working with community people? Or should we move with the community students to the new school?"

In many ways, being at Rabun Gap was an advantage. It was a smaller school for one thing, and so you knew everyone. The school had built a new administration building after we'd started the program there, and they had turned over one whole end of the building to us so we had a darkroom and office spaces. Also, dorm kids were a captive audience, so when they had free time, which they often did, they would go up to the office and work, and it was common for these kids to be working in the evenings on transcribing, circulation, and articles. On weekends they were stuck on the campus and didn't have a lot to do, and so it was also common for that office to be full of kids on Saturdays and Sundays. A lot of them came from broken homes, and friendships with adults hadn't been very positive, and through us they were meeting people like Aunt Arie Carpenter and being blown away by the fact that there were adults that cared about them. In some cases, I think the dorm kids were being affected more by the whole experience than the community kids were.

So naturally, one of the big questions on the table was, "When they open the new high school, could we run one program at each school? Who runs each one?" It was very frustrating.

To try to make some progress, I went down to the Rabun County High School and asked permission to teach one English class of tenth-graders the year before the new school was to open. I said, "We're in the middle of trying to make this decision about what to do with Foxfire, and one of the ingredients in this decision is going to be whether or not you guys, when you open the new school, are even going to want us there at all. Another is whether or not your students would adopt this program. They might not want anything to do with it." If it turned out that they didn't want us at all, then the decision would be made.

I got permission from the principal to teach a class down there made up of twenty-five tenth-grade students. Because classrooms were in short supply, they gave me a room in a cement building without any windows. It had been one of the boiler rooms. It was like being in a little jail, but they gave me the students. I taught at Rabun Gap in the morning, and then went to the high school and taught that third-period class and had lunch down there, and then I turned around and drove back up to Rabun Gap and taught another class or two up there. I taught in both locations all that year, and at the end, the principal, Leland Dishman, made it clear that he would really like to have us at the new school. He said he had been keeping in touch with the students in the experimental class, had asked them what they thought, and they all unanimously wanted the program. One day he said to me, "If you agree to come down here, this will be the classroom we will give you," and the classroom he showed me at the new building was the one we are in now. I asked him if he'd let us build a darkroom in there, and he said, "As far as I'm concerned, this is your room, and you can do whatever you want to with it. Whatever you need, we'll provide."

We went through a series of staff meetings, and meetings with the students at Rabun Gap. When the time came to make the decision, we finally decided that the program really belonged to Rabun County and really belonged to Rabun County students. It was Rabun County people who had donated the money, and Rabun County elders who had provided the information the students had collected and printed, and we didn't have the staff resources to run the program in both schools; so with the formal invitation from the Rabun County High School, the decision was essentially made. Of the options we had, it seemed like the most logical, moral, responsible choice.

Coincidentally, about the time we decided to move the program, Millard was turning on the lights in that first office building up on our land, so the timing was perfect.

▼▼▼

SHAYNE BECK: It just came about that Foxfire was going to have a class there at the Rabun County High School. There was an offering in our tenth-grade registration packet to take a Foxfire course.

I really didn't know much about it, but I had heard a little bit, so I decided that I would take the course that year. Some kids didn't know what Foxfire was, so they didn't sign up for it, but the ones that did sign up had a real good time.

I was in that experimental class. Wig showed us how to lay out the book and how to interview people. We did a lot. Marty Henderson and I built a wooden lock for an article that wound up in *Foxfire 6*. We went to interview a man that built a muzzle-loader. We also interviewed Tombo's grandmother, Grannie Carrie, on some of the tales that she knew and some of the rough times that she had went through in her lifetime.

[By the end of the year, all twenty-five of us decided that we wanted to take another Foxfire course the next year in the new high school, and we all did. We just kept on going.]

▼▼▼

Kenny Runion visited the new class at Rabun County High School several times to be interviewed. Watching intently in the lower foreground is Shayne Beck.

Jeff Reeves, Kirk Patterson, Tombo Ramey, and Shayne Beck interviewed Tombo's Grannie Carrie McCurry as members of the experimental class.

LORIE RAMEY THOMPSON: We had always heard of Foxfire, but it was something at Rabun Gap School, not ours. I don't think anybody [really] understood what it was. We knew they wrote books and magazines. [However,] we didn't know what all was involved in the Foxfire curriculum.

Then Eliot Wigginton was starting a class at our high school. He was struggling. Rabun Gap was about to become a boarding school. He didn't know what to do, so he was going to teach at both schools to help make up his mind.

I wanted to be a part of that class very desperately. I didn't understand what all he was doing, and I certainly didn't know the basics of putting together a magazine, but I knew that [Foxfire] was something that I wanted to be a part of.

I think everyone at our school had a lot of questions about his class. The teachers thought we wasted a lot of time. They couldn't understand how Wig was actually teaching us. He was so unconventional in his teaching methods. [Foxfire] was something so new. At our school, it was strictly classrooms by the book, so there was a lot of teacher criticism toward him. I think now he has proven his point. He has received national recognition. There's no longer any doubt toward his teaching methods.

I had never had a teacher like him in any class I had experienced. [Other teachers] started with Lesson 10 on page 200, and you learned your grammar through English books. It was a very confined curriculum. Suddenly, Wig [began] teaching our tenth-grade class in a manner where we would go outside and learn [on our own]. Through that, he started making us notice things and to appreciate our surroundings. We started to notice how people talked, and their body language. We learned how to use a 35-mm camera. I was doing things I never thought I would be doing in relation to English. I never understood how I was learning out of those textbooks anyway. Now there was a relationship with the way I spoke, wrote, and communicated to how I lived.

Wig took a lot of his time to get us to the point to where we were recognizing what he was [actually] doing. We didn't know what we were learning [at first], but I learned more from Wig than from any other teacher I had. Sometime in that process, we started interviewing. I did an interview with my grandfather at this time. He would say that he didn't want to be interviewed, but he really did. I started to realize how much knowledge these older people had. It gave appreciation for your heritage through [interviewing]. It's so true. It opened up a lot of worlds for me. It did.

I also interviewed Amanda Turpin, whom I dearly loved. Wig was throwing out ideas one day in class for potential interviews and somehow her name was brought up. So Pam, Dawn, and I said we would interview her. I just fell in love with her. She was small, shy, and bashful. She had so much to share with us. She taught us how to make a special salve out of mutton tallow to put on burns and cuts. In Amanda's case, women of her age group valued family. Keep your family warm, raise your children right, teach them to love God, and you've made it.

We knew that we were helping Wig make up his mind about where to take Foxfire. Our class worked, and we made it work. We were so excited. Everyone wanted to be involved. We convinced him that [the public high school] is where he should be. We wanted it in our school. And it's because of us that it's there now.

Lorie Ramey, center, went on a Foxfire environmental field trip to the Georgia coast. At the far left is Margie Bennett.

My senior year, I was a Governor's Honors participant. I went in journalism. And I found I had more grammar skills and journalism skills than most of the other participants there.

ᵂᵂ

MORRIS BROWN: We at Rabun Gap-Nacoochee School realized why Foxfire had to move to Rabun County High School. When the new public high school was built, Rabun Gap became a private school available only to those who could pay the tuition. Only about thirty local boys and girls were able to do so; the rest went to Rabun County High School. With so few day students, who basically were the ones behind Foxfire, Wig's sources were practically dried up. So he needed to teach at a school with a greater enrollment. It was a matter of *having to*, if they expected to keep the Foxfire program alive. Also, it expanded Foxfire's horizons. There was access to more people in the county and community, to cousins, aunts, uncles, and friends who had stories to tell for the magazine.

So we understood from the beginning why the decision was made.

# The Publishing Continues

WIG: *Foxfire 2* went right onto the *New York Times* best-seller list just as the first one had.

At that point, Doubleday began to talk about doing a long-running series because it began to look as though a series was, in fact, what we had. For the next thirteen or fourteen years, we settled into a pattern where Foxfire was an elective English class in which students continued to produce the magazine on a quarterly basis, and periodically we collected that material into books. The Foxfire books themselves began to evolve into volumes that were focused on themes. For example, in *Foxfire 3*, a sequence of chapters has to do with handmade musical instruments. *Foxfire 5* starts with iron making and how that was done, and then goes to blacksmithing, to muzzleloading rifle making, and then to hunting. It makes a rather complete view of one aspect of mountain life. *Foxfire 7* is completely devoted to religion. *Foxfire 8* is almost completely devoted to traditional pottery making. Organizing them that way meant that we didn't have to wait until we had enough magazine articles done to fill a book. If we chose a theme like religion, we could move backward through all of the previous issues of the magazine over a ten-year period and pull all the interviews that had been done about religion, and then hire a group of students over the summer to do another series of interviews to fill the holes, and then deliver the manuscript at the end of the summer. In other words, students could continue to do articles for the magazine about any topic in which they were interested, and if we were going to put out a book about religion, we didn't have to force all of the students in the class for two years just to do magazine articles about religion so that we could make *Foxfire 7*. The way we chose the themes for the books, of course, would be dependent on looking through all the back issues and the material that hadn't found its way into books yet, getting an inventory of what themes were beginning to emerge, and once we established that, we could begin to go at the creation of another Foxfire book.

At the same time that we were putting new volumes together for Doubleday, we were also experimenting with the format of the magazine itself. People who have seen only the books don't realize that a substantial percentage of the contents of the magazines is devoted to issues that face us here in the mountains and to topics that are more current. So, for example, when the movie *Deliverance* came out, a group of the students became concerned about the fact that that movie portrays the Appalachian region in negative stereotypes. They interviewed a group of Rabun County people about how they felt about that film. They also interviewed some of the mountain people who had been portrayed in that film, who all turned out to be, in fact, people we had worked with in the past. So you see Mrs. Andy Webb, for example, in the film as a pathetic dirt-poor mountain woman. Mrs. Webb was, however, a woman whom the kids had interviewed at length some years earlier. She was a midwife who delivered over five hundred babies and was one of the most respected women in the community. That issue of *Foxfire* looked at that problem.

Another issue of the magazine was devoted to a profile of the Betty's Creek valley and how it has changed over time. That issue had interviews with a number of Betty's Creek families, genealogies of the more prominent residents, and insights into how and why the valley was changing. Several other issues were devoted to land use in the mountains and the need for zoning restrictions to keep developers from coming in and doing anything they want. Other magazines were devoted to one theme, and they eventually turned into books of their own. One, for example, was a cookbook.

Most of these special magazines, especially the ones having to do with current topics of concern, did not find their way into the book series itself because we felt that wasn't the kind of material readers of that series wanted. It's interesting, however, to think about putting together yet another book that is *just* made up of articles like that which show students wrestling with current issues. I don't know how widely accepted it would be, or how popular it would be, but it would certainly be interesting for those of us in this part of the country, anyway.

At some point, I guess the early eighties, the sales of the Foxfire books themselves began to slip, and there are several reasons for that. Just as a series of coincidences, each one feeding the next, generated an extraordinary demand for the early books, so, too, a similar set of coincidences reduced the sales of the later volumes. For example, reviewers themselves didn't know what else to say about the new volumes. They had already told the story, and all they could think of to say was, "Well, folks, here's another one!" Because the books weren't being widely reviewed, bookstores were reluctant to stock them in large numbers because they were afraid there wouldn't be much demand; and because they weren't stocking the books in large numbers, and because people weren't hearing about them, lots of potential customers didn't know the new volumes existed. So the whole thing began to become unraveled.

At that point, I found myself in the funny situation of being out somewhere speaking at a conference with a couple of students and having people come up to us and saying, "We really love the whole Foxfire series. We have all three of your books!" And this at a time when there were eight on the market. So the students and I made the decision that with the publication of *Foxfire 9*, we would stop the series and begin to look at some other projects that we might do together with Doubleday. In the introduction of *Foxfire 9*, I explained why that decision was made. Although Doubleday wanted to continue and would probably still publish a *Foxfire 10, 11*, and *12* if we were interested in doing that, our attention turned to what other kinds of books we might do that would be perhaps as interesting as, or even more interesting than, the Foxfire series itself. That's why the next books by Doubleday were *Sometimes a Shining Moment* and *A Foxfire Christmas*, and this book in celebration of the twenty-fifth birthday.

There was a new opportunity that came up, also, at about the same time as the last book in the series was published. Ending the series had nothing to do with this event. It's just another one of those happy accidents. John Dyson, the fraternity brother who had paid an attorney to draw up the incorporation papers for the Foxfire Fund, and who had remained on our board, called up one day and said, "I've got a surprise for you. I just bought E. P. Dutton, and I'd like to talk to you about our possibly doing some things together since I now own a publishing house. We can do just about whatever we want to."

That dovetailed perfectly with a plan that we had been playing with for a long time down here, which was to have our own publishing business. One of the reasons that we had been considering that was because, as an organization, we had wrestled off and on for years around strategies for our organization to be a catalyst to help start some new businesses in this area that could hire former students and bring them back home after college. Community economic development had turned into a theme that was running throughout staff discussions and class discussions for years. We just weren't quite sure how to get a handle on doing it. We had begun to collect information, for example, about community development corporations, and we had begun to collect examples of the kinds of small businesses that local people had started in other communities like ours. We were actively looking for possibilities.

When John called about his purchase of Dutton, it began to look as if we might be able to take one of those possibilities, which was having our own publishing company, and make it happen.

Earlier, as an experiment, we had published a couple of small books by ourselves. One was *Memories of a Mountain Shortline*, about the Tallulah Falls Railroad. We had written, designed, and distributed that book completely on our own as an experiment to see where the problems might be if we started our own publishing company. That experiment showed us that the single biggest problem we would have was in marketing and distribution. First of all, we just didn't know how to do it, and second of all, we didn't have the money for advertising and publicity.

So John and I began to talk about putting together several manuscripts down here, and having Dutton produce them as Foxfire Press titles. Dutton would market and distribute on a national scale, and would pay us royalties, and we would market and distribute those books to the extent we could and earn some income that way. Eventually, by being partners with Dutton, we could learn those lessons we needed about national distribution, and at some point maybe handle all the distribution ourselves.

John gave us a generous advance to allow us to hire some people full time to work with the students to put the new manuscripts together. The end result of that was that we produced the book about Aunt Arie, the first full-length portrait we had ever tried to do of one of the people the students were interviewing. We also took the cookbook the students had done as a special issue of the magazine and hired those same students and others to help us put together a much bigger volume called *The Foxfire Book of Appalachian Cookery*. We did a book about traditional toys and games, and we did a book about wine making.

Although the books were well received, especially the first two, sales never came close to the Foxfire Doubleday series. It began to look as though this thing might be in trouble. In retrospect, I think the major reason the Dutton series never took off was because Dutton itself, as a company under new ownership, lacked Doubleday's massive publicity and distribution system. The majority of the people I meet on the road still don't know today that that series of books from Dutton ever existed. Consequently, the books didn't sell very many copies, and they didn't come close to earning the kinds of revenues that they would need to earn to repay Dutton's advance. And consequently, those books were not reprinted, which doomed their sales. Eventually, not just because of this collaboration but because of a whole series of problems that the company ran into, John decided to sell Dutton to another group. The new owners didn't like the generous cooperative arrangement that John had worked out with us, and eventually we terminated that whole thing and abandoned the Foxfire Press idea. I've still got some hopes that at some point that initiative might be revived, but at the moment it really is on hold. Book publishing turns out to be a complicated and risky business. We don't have the sophistication or the capital to make it happen yet.

Luckily, this venture with Dutton didn't damage the relationship with Doubleday. Doubleday had been allowed to negotiate for those Foxfire Press books also, but they just couldn't come up with the kind of collaborative arrangement that John Dyson had offered us, so they understood why we undertook this venture with a different company. The doors were still open to future volumes that we wanted to bring to Doubleday, and that is what we're doing today.

The issue of community economic development, by the way, still continues to be something that we're interested in. Our research about small business development hasn't led us to be real hopeful, though, about our ever being able to have much of a major impact there. We can find very few of these things around the country that have been successful without inordinate amounts of outside funding. But one of the consultants we brought in to talk with us about economic development said something pretty interesting. After a visit of several days, he had a meeting with the staff, and he said, "I don't know why you guys are trying to get involved in this kind of thing at all because you are *already doing* community economic development without even realizing it. You've already got a company going that's got eight or nine employees, and you're already generating capital that's being returned back to the community. What do you want to try to start a bunch of brand-new businesses for? You already have one going that is having an impact in the local area and is making jobs available for students who want to come back from college and work full time here in Rabun County. Why try to do anything else? Just keep on doing what you're doing." So, that's basically what we have done.

From the early seventies up to the mid-eighties, while we were continuing to put out the magazine and experiment with new formats, continuing to put out the Doubleday series and experiment with new formats there, and doing the Foxfire Press books and the Dutton series and trying experiments there, we were also using the royalties income from the Foxfire series to add to the staff. There was so much going on that it was impossible for me to do it alone with the students, so I had begun to look around for adults to help out. One of the early people I hired was Suzie Angier, who had come down to Rabun County about the same time I had to work with a group of Vista volunteers. When Suzie's term with Vista was about to expire, and it looked as if she were going to go back home to Connecticut, she realized that she would enjoy staying around awhile longer. I wound up hiring Suzie before the first *Foxfire Book* was ever published, just because I had to have some help. During that first period that she spent with us, I just split my paycheck from the school system with her and supplemented it with some of the NEH grant that we had at that time, and told her that I couldn't promise much in terms of money or security, but that eventually, this thing might turn into something a little bigger. She signed on to help take students out on interviews and help do editing and almost immediately became indispensable. The kids loved her, and she had lots of energy and lots of smarts. In fact, it's Suzie who worked with a group of students herself to put together that Foxfire Press book about the Tallulah Falls Railroad. She did all kinds of special projects with students that I never would have had time to take on. Suzie wound up staying with us for, I guess, eleven or twelve years. Eventually, she did go back home to Connecticut.

Another person we hired who got deeply involved in the whole project was Margie Bennett. Margie's husband, Bob, had been hired by the Rabun Gap-Nacoochee School to work as the farm manager there. Margie was trained as a medical technologist. She wasn't sure if she wanted to commute to Clarkesville every day where she had been offered a job in that field. She came to my office one day and asked about the possibility of work with us. As it happened, Suzie and I were covered up at that point with projects, and the *Foxfire Book* was generating income, and so we added Margie also. Margie stayed with the organization for something like fifteen years, actually until just a couple of years ago when the Rabun Gap-Nacoochee School offered her a job designing and then running a new middle-school program. It was one of those offers that you can't refuse, so Margie took that on as a challenge, and that's where she still is.

We also hired Paul Gillespie, one of the best of the early group of students. Paul, with a group of students, put together *Foxfire 7* by himself. I didn't have anything at all to do with *Foxfire 7*. Paul had always wanted to get his law degree, and eventually he decided to go back to school and pursue law as a career. And there were lots of others. Mike Cook, for example, one of Paul's classmates, who came on at about the same time and is still with us. When you talk to former students, you'll find them talking about working with people like Suzie, Margie, and Paul constantly. That's how all that came about. If it hadn't been for the success of the Foxfire series, we would never have been able to do that. But because of the success of the series, and because of the income generated through royalties, and because the school basically trusted us and trusted what we were doing, we were able to add a number of projects and people to the work and affect in a pretty positive way a number of high school students whom I would never have been able to work with had it been just me and the regular classroom situation.

ᵂᵂᵂ

CLAUDE RICKMAN: I've got seven sisters and a brother. My two older sisters were in Foxfire, and they were bringing home the magazines and a lot of other stuff. [I looked at the articles and they were about] things I had known all my life, because that's the way I grew up. The older people that they were interviewing were guys that I had known [all my life]. Also, in school, I'd see Wig around and talk to him, so I started doing a good bit of stuff [for Foxfire] the last part of my sophomore year. Some of my friends were in Foxfire, like Gary Warfield, and because I knew where everybody lived, he and I would get out of class and go out on interviews. It was nice. I enjoyed seeing some of the older people, and I had a personal connection to the traditions that were being written about.

My grandfather built this house, for example. There was 196 acres here on the original farm, and when we were kids, we plowed everything you see out here in front with one mule. Had corn in every bit of that. You talk about working; our Saturdays wasn't quite like my nephews'. Daddy'd get us up at four-thirty, and we'd go milk the cows in that old barn right out there. Then he'd tell us we were getting our mind right. We'd sit there till daylight. Then when he left, you had so much to do during the day, and if you didn't have it done, it was a tough evening.

My grandfather, who I used to live with a good bit, and I used to go camping. We'd leave here in a mule and wagon and go down on

Gary Warfield interviewed Alex Stewart about making cedar buckets, tubs, and churns for *Foxfire 3*.

Claude Rickman was interviewed for this book by Chris Nix and Scott Cannon on the front porch of the house his grandfather built in the Wolffork Valley. His mother, Icie, still lives there.

Warwoman Road at Sandy Ford and Earl's Ford, and it would take us two days to get there. I was just a little kid. Go down there and camp for a week or two. He'd have hay in the bed of the wagon to sleep on, and as the week went on, the mule would eat up your hay and your bed would be gone. It got tougher. Then Momma and them would come see us on the weekend and bring some more hay, and things were better.

Grandpa only went through the third or fourth grade, but all through his life he had learned to do things. My bicycle would tear up, and he'd get out there and fix it. He'd never had a bicycle in his life. When something like that would tear up, he'd just sit down and look at it. He might look at it for an hour. What he was doing was tying all of that stuff he'd learned together from the times when he made liquor and the time he fixed other things. When he had it figured out, then he'd fix it. I think that's one of the big things today. If you could take your kids to work with you every day and they learned how to do all of these things, they might be better off. I know

I am. I look at some stuff today that is something I've never looked at before, and I see parts of other things I've worked on in it, and I know what to do to make it work.

I was familiar with the lifestyle Foxfire was researching, and it made me feel good about it. It was easy to relate to. My dad was fifty-three when I was born, and he was in his sixties when I was a little kid. I can still see him right out there in a chair under that big oak tree, and Hobe Beasley cutting his hair with some hand clippers. He'd come about every three weeks or so, and Daddy'd pay him a dollar, or a dollar and a half.

I can remember going up to John Conley's, the blacksmith, with Dad in an old '51 Chevrolet pickup. I've still got it. He'd make wagon wheels—charged Daddy twenty-five dollars a wheel. Or we'd take the blade off that old mule-drawn mower, and he had an old grinder that you pedaled back there in the back of his shop, and he'd sharpen that blade. Now you think about having to take that blade out, go up there, wait for somebody to grind it that way, and if there's somebody in front of you, you just stood around and waited. Then come back and put it in, and then a mule cutting something. If I was working for somebody now and I took that much time to go get something they'd fire me. It's a different time.

We gathered all of our corn with a mule and wagon, and you know corn shucks will cut you like a knife. You jerk that ear off there, and it's worse than a razor. When you cut your skin with one of those, it just doesn't heal. I used to think, "Man, if I can ever get out of this life, I'm gonna do something else!"

But you learned how to get something done, and one thing about this way of life was we did so much stuff together. Not planned. Not intentional. You didn't sit down and say, "We're now doing family stuff," but you did stuff together with your brothers and sisters. You'd be down there in the spring hoeing that corn, and many a day you'd run up on a copperhead or rattlesnake or something in the row. And then you're hauling the corn in, and then you're sitting out there freezing and shucking, and all that corn dust is in the air and you're breathing it in, and then you're at the mill with your Daddy, and then one winter day you're sitting there having corn bread and milk—like we did tonight—and it's a nice thing, and you remember the smells and the thoughts of it. And you know what it's like to have a job from start to finish. And you did stuff together, and it was there to do, and that could be a very boring job, or you could laugh and make it fun. I think I was real, real lucky to have had all of that.

"I think when God comes to get His church, He won't just get certain people. He wants all of those pure hearts; that's what He comes for and I think about that a lot. When God comes back and gets His children together, they'll be from everywhere—every church and nation. That's a glorious thing." (*Foxfire* 7) Beulah Perry, seated outside her home with Vivian Burrell.

◥◤◥

VIVIAN BURRELL MCCAY: My favorite contact was Beulah Perry. She was in her eighties when we interviewed her. She was the first black person we interviewed for *Foxfire.* I remember Beulah's grandfather was a slave. He was an overseer of a plantation. She told us that he had it a little better than most of the slaves because he had been educated by his owners. That always stuck in my mind. It seemed so amazing to know someone who had known a slave. She was just a real nice and pleasant lady. Beulah was always real tickled when we came to see her. She gave us vegetables from her garden to take home with us.

I helped some with the article on the effects the movie *Deliverance* had on Rabun County. I worked with Laurie Brunson, Barbara Taylor, and Mary Thomas on that. We went down to the river one day and were just interviewing people at random. I remember a lot of people saying they were really afraid to come to Rabun County after seeing that movie.

While I was in school, some of us did one whole issue of *Foxfire* on the Betty's Creek Valley. I was looking at it last night, and it had Maw and Paw, Grover Bradley, Jesse Rickman, Claude Darnell, Margaret Norton, Richard Norton—all these people are gone. The majority of the people on the cover are no longer with us.

The idea was to take a community and show the change that's gone on. That was 1975. I helped some with that, and of course they interviewed members of my family and even interviewed me. And it had both sides of my family tree on there, so it's one issue that's real important to me. It's part of my history right there. I learned a lot. At one time the Burrells and Hoppers owned a lot of Betty's Creek.

After they died, Pearl and Oscar [Martin's] place was divided up between the four girls. The youngest daughter got where they lived and some acreage around that. She lives in Highlands, and I guess they had no reason for wanting to keep it as far as moving down here or anything, so they sold that, and it went to a man from Atlanta. And I can understand. They wanted to stay in Highlands. I would have liked to have bought it, but I wasn't able to at the time. [The other three pieces are still in the family.]

So that issue really hits home with me. And in lots of the other valleys around here, the same thing was happening then and still is. A lot of the kids from Wolffork are no longer there anymore, I'm sure for the same reason I'm not on Betty's Creek. I can't afford to buy property up there. I'd love to. One little six-acre piece was left to my mom, and she's said that would go to me and Thad and Andrea [Burrell Potts] someday, but at one time there was hundreds of acres there in our family. Some of it was sold off when Grandpa was sick and they needed help with him. I would love to have had the property, but it wasn't mine to say anything about it, because I didn't do anything [to get] it.

This issue is really the main thing that I've got about the family. There's a family Bible and all, but it's not got what *this* has got in it. I mean this has got where my grandmaw Pearl's *talking*.

I don't get up there like I used to. I like it. Going up through there, I still get a really peaceful feeling—a real "going home" feeling that's never left me, and I haven't lived up there in twenty-three years.

⧊

Vivian Burrell McCay majored in photography and works today in advertising.

Vivian's mother, Stella Burrell, contributed a recipe for violet jelly to the Foxfire cookbook. On the left is Vivian's niece, Dawn Watson. Dawn and her brother and sister, David and DeeDee, were all part of the Foxfire program also, and are now in college. Their aunt, Andrea Burrell, helped us find Aunt Arie, and their parents, Varney and Linda Watson, have been good friends of the program since its beginning.

BIT CARVER KIMBALL AND KAYE CARVER COLLINS:

KAYE: I think what got me interested was the Foxfire students interviewing Daddy [Buck Carver]. You know, Daddy was interviewed a zillion times for Foxfire. So he thought Foxfire was the very thing. He especially admired Wig.

BIT: He was also interviewed by Bruce Dale from *National Geographic*, who'd written a book on gypsies. Bruce was gonna do one like it on the Appalachian people. It sure was a big deal. It gives you a sense of pride to see your own daddy being interviewed, even though you aren't a part of it or doing the interviewing yourself. It's an ego boost just to see somebody pay that much attention to your own daddy.

Buck Carver built a miniature liquor still for the Foxfire collection. He also taught us how to find and raise ginseng: "And another thing—old-timers used to go a'courting, and they were nearly always ashamed to eat dinner with their girls and so forth, you know. And their intestines would get to growling because they'd get empty. They'd always carry a little piece of sang in their pocket and chew them a little piece of that sang and they'd stop that. They called it guts growling. And it'd stop them things from growling, too, I mean. It's embarrassing. [A friend of mine] said he guessed he'd eat a pound of it to keep them from growling in front of his girl." (*Foxfire 4*) Buck died in 1985. He is survived by his wife, Leona; their daughter, Kaye Carver Collins, now works for Foxfire.

Robbie Bailey interviewed Leona Carver, his great-aunt, for *Foxfire*. Currently a high school senior, Robbie was one of the editors of this book.

Later it was so neat seeing my parents in the Foxfire books. I might skim through the rest of the material, but things that Daddy or Mama said, I would read them word for word. And now that he's dead, we've got those interviews to go back to. And now, Robbie Bailey has been interviewing Mama. It's neat to see it continuing on.

If we hadn't been involved in Foxfire, we wouldn't have been able to do the smallest part of what we actually did at that period of our lives. Foxfire was an outlet for our accomplishments, and I'm sure our parents recognized this.

Aside from our folks, I guess my favorite contacts would have to be Lawton and Florence Brooks. He was good friends with our father for years and years, so it was easy to go interview him. it was just like we were one of his kids. Lawton impressed me because he was just a fun-loving guy.

KAYE: I remember one time when we interviewed him about pranks he'd played. I'll never forget the time he told us about taking a wagon apart and putting it back together on top of a barn when he was serenading at Christmastime. And you'd never ever hear Lawton say anything bad about a person. He's always got something good to say.

Florence and Lawton Brooks have been interviewed nearly as many times as Aunt Arie. Florence died in 1984. Lawton is still well and active: "They's as much difference in people now as they is in day an' night. People don't care for people no more like they used to. Used t'be if anybody got sick in th'community, why people'd go see about'em, not just pass'em by. If you lived in our community, even if you was seven or eight mile away, when we heard you was sick, we'd go see about you. If you had a crop, we'd go and see about it. See about crops, take care of your animals, get you out of th'rut while you was sick. Then when you get up, maybe I might get sick, and then you'd help, come in with wagons and mules, gather corn, haul hay . . . anything I'd need would be done for me, just like you'd do it for yourself. And nowadays you can get sick and people ain't gonna go see about you t'ask how y'are, let alone do anything for you. You'd freeze t'death 'cause they ain't gonna get you no wood." (*Foxfire 3*)

I remember after the Annie Perry article was published, a letter came from someone who was high up in the state government saying what a great article it was and how great a person she was. It just made me feel wonderful that I'd been able to get that across in that article.

BIT: Sometimes you left an impression that you hadn't even realized you were leaving. You'd do something without even thinking about it, and then they'd write this big long letter about this little bitty thing. So you knew you made a difference, and it really meant a lot.

It was a lot harder doing the magazine than the books because to

Annie Perry: "When you live in the country, you can have a garden and you can go pick fresh vegetables when you want'em, and they don't cost you so much. God gives you the strength and if you use what He gave you, you might not make a bountiful crop, but you can make some. If you've lived long enough and nobody won't hire you and you're able to work, you *can* make you something to eat" (*Foxfire* 4). Annie died in 1990.

produce the magazine, you had to start from scratch. With the book, you had everything right there in front of you. All you had to do was pick and choose. But it was still great when it came out. It made me feel real proud.

And by the time we had been involved for a year or two, we were certified to do it all. Somebody had taught us how to use the darkroom, how to do a layout, how to use the camera, and how to use the tape recorder, and we did everything from the beginning to the end.

KAYE: We knew what was expected of us, and we knew we had to do it because there was nobody else to do it. Every bit of it. We carried the responsibility of the magazine 100 percent. But it was worth it because it was so much fun and so rewarding. Everything that you did saw immediate results.

And each time a new student came into Foxfire, they normally tried to team them with seniors to, you know, sort of break them in and help them learn what they were doing.

BIT: This did involve helping and teaching each other, and it made you feel important to teach the younger kids. The real experience in teaching, however, was when we went out to other places to try to get new magazines started. It was so hard even trying to teach those kids the Foxfire concept, much less the details of it. We did, though.

KAYE: We were involved in every aspect of the operation, even when there were problems with the use of our name. One time, for instance, there was a group of log-cabin builders in Macon County who wanted to call themselves "Foxfire Log Homes." This was an illegal use of our trademark name, and we had to sue them in order to get them stopped.

BIT: These people sold [prefabricated log home kits]. You know, Foxfire didn't want to associate with something like that [and mislead buyers into thinking they were getting something authentic]. Foxfire, I felt, had built a reputation as having some integrity, with one of its missions to protect mountain people, their heritage and their way of life.

Another time, there was this restaurant down at Tallulah Falls that wanted to use the magazine covers for their menus. We stopped that, too. [We didn't want our magazine associated with a barbecue joint for tourists.]

ᵂ

LYNN BUTLER: I came to Rabun Gap-Nacoochee School in 1973 from a small town in upstate New York, not too different from Clayton or Rabun Gap. I liked school when I came to Rabun Gap, but before that time, I was really turned off to school in general. When I was thirteen, in seventh grade, I was put in the dumb class because I had failed math the last year. It was really shameful to be put in that class. Also, drugs were getting big at my high school, and both of my parents worked. I was also having many problems with my family.

My grandmother was living in Atlanta at that time, and she sent for me to go to Rabun Gap School because she knew I wanted to get away.

One of the main reasons I came to Rabun Gap School was to get involved in the Foxfire program. My first year at Rabun Gap was very difficult. It took a lot of adjustment for me. I had many personality conflicts with the other students. I was shy; I guess you would say I was an introvert. We used to have devotions at nighttime right after supper, and one time during my junior year, during devotion, Wig had to stand up and talk. One of the things he said was, "Lynn Butler is someone I want you to notice because she's very sensitive." Later, when I had planned to go on an interview for Foxfire, I got sick and I decided I didn't want to go because I didn't want to get the contact sick. This was the first time that it occurred to me that I *was* sensitive.

It actually wasn't until the end of my sophomore year that I got involved in *Foxfire*. That was when I got close to Margie Bennett, and she took me on my first interview, with Millard Buchanan. Once I was in the magazine class, I got really involved. I even earned a little card that said, "Editor" on it. It's still in my wallet.

Early on, I began a series of interviews with black Appalachian people. I was basically the only student in Foxfire at that time who really wanted to do that. I wasn't out to do some kind of exposé on racism in Appalachia. I just wanted to find out what was different about the black experience, and I felt comfortable doing it, partly because of my background. I lived for nine years in Westchester, and my parents were ardent supporters of the Civil Rights movement, and I really felt blacks should be more widely represented in the books. I worked on the project alone except, of course, for Margie, who sat right beside me most of the time.

All the people I interviewed for this project really stand out in my mind. I came in contact with them in various ways. I met Bruce Mosley working at the Dillard House, and I interviewed him. Then I met his wife, Selma. That interview is one I really pushed for, and it was published in *Foxfire 7*, the book about religion in the mountains, and Selma represented the black Baptists. She was not on the official list of contacts because she was not indigenous to the area, but when I was interviewing Bruce, I really got to talking with her. I wanted to go back and interview her because she was just so fascinating and such a great talker. She sat down at the piano singing gospel and just blew me away. So I asked Margie if I could do the interview, and she said, "If you really want to, you can."

One of the interviews we conducted with Lynn for this book took place while she was visiting Rabun County in the summer of 1989. While she was here, she and Selma Mosely got together again, and we tape recorded part of their reunion:

Selma: It's very pleasant seeing you again. It's been a long time.

Lynn: It has been a long time. It's been more than ten years.

Selma: I probably wouldn't of knowed [recognized] you no more.

Lynn: I look different now than when I was in high school.

Selma: You know, after the book came out, and I got to reading it, I didn't know I could talk that much! [There was a] lesson from the book. There was a boy called me from California which I didn't know [the boy]. [He] called me early one Saturday [morning], and he said, "Mrs. Mosley?"

I said, "Yes, this is she."

He said, "I'm calling from California. I picked up the *Foxfire* 7 and read your conversion in there. [It] did something for me. I'm on the edge of disaster."

When he said that, I mean it just looked like the Lord put the words in my mouth [to] talk to this young man. So, I said, "Well, how did you get my number?"

He said, "I got it through the operator." He [had] called the white set of Mosleys 'cause there's a white set of them here, and he was asking for Selma Mosley. They told him how to reach me.

Of course that phone call was a thrill. I had never had nothing to happen like that. This young man was seemingly about to do something to hisself, but he said when he picked up that book, and he read my conversion, that is what stopped him, and he wanted to talk to me personally. That made me feel good.

I told them in church, and I called my son in Charleston [South Carolina], and I told him about it. "You know, I have never had nothing like that happen to me in my life."

He said, "Mamma, you never know, you might see that young man [one day] face to face."

This experience has increased my faith very much so. I try to do by going to my Heavenly Father. I do try to grow in His faith, and I ask Him for more faith each and every day.

Lynn: I think that when you were talking about your religious experience and working in the church, I identified so strongly with that in a way that I had not before as a young person. Religion to me was something I was saving for when I got older, but I really felt like after talking to you I saw that your faith was such a day-to-day experience. That really had an effect on me.

Selma: May God bless your heart.

One of Lynn Butler's favorite people was Anna Tutt: "I recall one time when a man was hanged. I was about seven or eight years old. We children woke up and heard our father walking about the house in the dark. We said, 'Pa, what's the matter?'

"He said, 'They're hanging someone over there.' It was about a mile there, I guess, across a creek. And it seems like it was a white-looking oak tree. I think they used to say a hanging tree never had any leaves on it.

"He said, 'Y'all be quiet because if they come and ask me to help take him down, I'll have to go.' Naturally we were frightened but that was all that was said. He felt he was compelled to go if they came and asked him to help take the body down." (*Foxfire 8*)

Then Bruce told me about Harley Penland, and his neighbor introduced me to him. And I met a woman who was involved in the Meals on Wheels program, and she knew Anna Tutt, and she introduced me to her. I guess she was my favorite. She was the first one I interviewed who was really expansive and frank and open when it came to racial issues. The others didn't feel comfortable talking about it. Many people in that area wouldn't even admit that there *were* racial issues, but there were. A couple of students did criticize my project, and I had to defend myself, but I also had some support. Those interviews, except for Selma's, were all published in *Foxfire 8*. The one that scared me was the one with Carrie Stewart. She lived in

Franklin, North Carolina, and she was almost a hundred years old. I spent a great deal of time with her. At one point, it looked like the interview might go right into *Foxfire 8* without being published in the magazine first. I had a fit! I exclaimed, "She's ninety-eight years old. She'll die before you get the book printed!" I don't remember whether that fit had any effect at all. The interview did get in the book, however, and Carrie lived to see it.

Johnny Scruggs interviewed "Po Boy" Jenkins, the mule swapper, in the general store across the street from his apartment in Danielsville and in the courthouse square: "Back in '34 and in '35, I guess I sold a hundred mules to Farm Security. . . . The [farmers] would be down and out, you know, and the Government would loan 'em five or six hundred dollars to make a crop with. . . . Buy 'em a mule and a few farming tools. And some of 'em made good and some of 'em—the Government lost it.

". . . The intention of it was *fine*. But it was the most abused of any programs I nearly ever knew. All Government programs are abused. You know that. I hate to say it, but a big percent of the people think that when they beat the Government out of some money, that's all right. 'Let'em lose it. We'll stick 'em.' But then I know another fellow right up the road here about a mile out of town—they bought him a farm and he went out and went to work and made cotton and paid for it in three or four years. Paid it all back. Says, 'I didn't owe nobody a nickel.' " (*Foxfire 8*) "Po Boy" died in the mid-1980s.

JOHNNY SCRUGGS: A couple of friends and myself did three stories. All of them got printed in the quarterly magazine. We did one in Dahlonega with Bill and Amy Trammell. He was a gold miner. He was one of the original guys who got the gold and took it by wagon to the state capitol in Atlanta for the dome. We also did one with a guy that lives in Clayton. He was Ben Chappell. He always rode around in a horse and buggy. He never drove a car. We did basically a personality interview about his background and about his childhood.

We also did one with "Po Boy" Jenkins, who lived in Danielsville. It's just outside of Athens. He was a mule trader. I remember that we interviewed him out by a Civil War monument in the center of the town where there was a courthouse, just like all of the old towns. We interviewed him there. It was Wig, Clay Smith, and me. I remember that after the interview we went to a Dolly Parton concert. It was the first concert I had ever been to.

TOMBO RAMEY: I started by thinking of people that I could interview and do articles on and the first one that came to my mind was my granny. I got a couple of my cousins and one of my best friends, Shayne Beck, and we went and did a couple of articles on her. I think the interviews turned out real well. She was eighty-eight years old at the time we were doing them, and boy, was she a ball of fire back then. She lived for ten more years, and I wish I had done more with her. She did her own thing and she had her own ways. For instance, she still drew her water out of a well when she always had the opportunity to be on city water. When I was young, she still cooked on a wood stove, and she could have had an electric one. She was set in her ways.

When Grannie Carrie and everybody saw my article, they were real excited. Grannie was tickled to death to see her picture in there.

I wish I could have done more with Foxfire. I always thought of things I wanted to do, and I still do today. I just don't seem to take time out to do all the things that I would like to do. Like after my granny died, we did research on our family tree and found she was part Cherokee, and part of her family left on the Trail of Tears. That was something I wish I could have gotten before she died.

Grannie Carrie McCurry: "I used to go up there to the old people's meeting but I quit that thing. I come in there one time and this woman sat down and she said, 'Do you believe there is a God?'

"I said, 'Yes, I do.'

"She said, 'No, there ain't no such thing as a God.' She says, 'There won't be no end to this world.'

" 'Well,' I says, 'you're crazy.' And there was another woman sitting beside me and she said, 'Just get up and leave.'

" 'Well,' I says, 'she can talk till her tongue goes dry. I won't believe what she says nohow.' " (*Foxfire*, Summer 1977)

Grannie Carrie died in 1985. Her house stands abandoned in Tiger, Georgia.


JOHN SINGLETON: I don't think you join things like Foxfire to learn about the culture. You already think you know everything about the culture, and it's only after you get involved that you realize that you're more distant than you thought [you were] from it. I joined because it seemed like an interesting thing to do. To be able to go out and interview people, and to know that maybe what I was doing would be a valuable thing to put in a book, was really exciting. It was different than just rote grammar skills.

My parents liked it. My mother and father both taught at the school, and Dad taught right across from the Foxfire room. They thought it was a really neat program. Mom really looked up to Wig. They thought it was a really positive thing. They were excited to see that I could actually do something for a while and stay with it.

And my folks were so excited about the article I did on my grandfather. They loved to talk about it at the family reunions.

I was involved specifically in *Foxfire 6* and *9*. The chapter I did for *6* was about Ben Ward, and the one I did in *Foxfire 9* was about my family, the Moores. The Ben Ward article was basically just interviews with Ben Ward's son, Ray. It was really fascinating because Ben was a genius, but he was living in the middle of nowhere. He put all of his genius into building a dam, a hydroelectric plant, and a water-powered sawmill—all from scrap. He invented all kinds of gadgets to make it all work. Some are even patented. Probably what's most

On one interview, John Singleton and Darryl Garland walked across the dam Ben Ward built. Ben: "It takes a bit of an idiot, a bit of genius to begin some jobs. An idiot to start, a genius to finish it. I built my cement dam in 1963–64. It was almost too much for me. Delerium [sic] set in during the winter but let up in the spring." (*Foxfire 6*)

162 FOXFIRE: 25 YEARS

interesting about that is that today, the dam that he built on the Watauga River still functions. The power company in North Carolina purchases power that that dam generates. This is quite a reminder of the man's intelligence.

I was impressed by his eccentricities as much as his inventions. He had played softball for the Watauga team, and the team lost one of ten years that he played and they blamed him. That made him mad, and so what he did was he took a bulldozer, and this was in the forties, and he scraped off the top of one of the mountains that he owned and built a baseball field that overlooked the Watauga Valley. Then he went out and he equipped his own team, and he came back a few years later and beat the Watauga league in baseball. He had been accused of being such a bad player, but was still pitching at the age of sixty, so I was impressed by that.

Ray Ward, Ben's son, showed Darryl and John how to operate Ben's water-powered sawmill, still in use today. Ray: "Another thing I often heard him say was that if he was setting up an ideal government and he was the ruler, he would feel like he had as just and as fair a country as possible if he could go into even the most humble home and spend a comfortable night and have a good meal. 'Then,' he would say, 'we could boast of being on the threshold of civilization.' " (*Foxfire 6*)

Later, Ben killed himself. He ran a hose into his car from the exhaust pipe and committed suicide. The man was brilliant, way beyond his years, but when his health began to break down, he knew he was going to pass away, and he just didn't want to pass away slowly.

I'll never forget what Ben was able to accomplish back there in the hills. This man was so brilliant. [He had the] baseball field, he had a perpetual motion machine he was working on, he had a library of two thousand books, all of which he had read and made notes in, he had the dam that he had built which brought electricity first to that part of the country, and he was known around the community. There are bunches and bunches of Wards still up there. He was just one of them, and I was struck with how much one man can accomplish in a whole community, and yet at the same time just be one small part of it.

And I think his son was really, really concerned about his father and about doing justice to him. I think that was the single thing on his mind. I don't think he was fascinated by us being interested at all. He just wanted to get the story right. We threw a baseball with his son, and played around the river. It was a funny experience. On the one hand, you're a kid throwing a baseball, and chasing their dog, and then on the other hand you're an adult interviewing and talking to these people trying to get and shape information so that it makes sense to other people.

My favorite, of course, was the article about my grandfather. I remember it still, and I'm so proud about that article. There's so much weight on you when you do an interview with a stranger, but with this interview, I knew everybody, so I had to be careful not to lead the interview to only the things I wanted to talk about because that would have been, in a sense, like editing. I remember being really worried about the way I was involved in that situation. You feel more connected to it when you're interviewing your own family because you're the person doing the interview, and you're also *part* of what's being interviewed.

My grandfather was so excited about the interview. He was so touched about being a part of it because he had read all the Foxfire books and he had tinkered with everything in them. I think we still have a pair of ox harnesses that he tried to make using directions from *Foxfire*. So Grandpa had a real sense of purpose for what he was doing. He wanted to get down the things that his father had held,

Frank C. Moore went through scores of letters and documents with his grandson, John: "Now years and years from now, people that you'd heard about from all of my generation won't amount to anything if somebody doesn't keep a record of it for your children. Someone's gotta keep it alive.

"I love to preserve history. It means so much to me now. All my childhood life—without preserving it—it's gone. I'm living in a new age. I'm living in a age now where I'm nearly a stranger in my own county. People's moving in here by the hundreds, and not twenty or thirty years ago I knew everybody in Clay County by name. Used to serve on the school board and every committee that's ever been in the county. Sold goods for twenty years right here and round about. But now I go out and I'm a stranger.

"Without this history, you're losing out. If someone doesn't keep a record of it, you'll know nothing. These things have to be passed down or you lose out." (Foxfire 9)

and that his father had held before him, so he had a direction that he was going in, and I guess I couldn't have changed it if I had tried.

I worship my grandfather. I always did. He was actually a young adult in the Depression. I think what Grandpa admired more than anything was just firmness. He didn't dream, really. He wanted an education for his kids, and very few people sent their kids to school at that time, but he sent all four of his children through college. And my grandfather was so much a part of the land that it didn't occur to him to describe it. He'd been there in that valley all his life, as well as generations before him. When I think of my grandfather, I think of him as part of the landscape, as a part of everything that was there. He wasn't someone living on the land. My grandfather was part of the land.

The things that I learned from my grandfather I've never been able to practice. Probably the best one is that he was so firm, but he was so gentle. He was such a strong, quiet figure, and I'm just the opposite. It was a couple of years later that he passed away. During that time, he saw his community changing. His family had been a part of the beginnings of Hayesville, and in the end he saw the roads filling up and all the cars with out-of-town tags going up roads that were never traveled before.

He was really good to me. He loved his family. He was really a central figure. So many Sundays I remember going to my grandfather's house. For me, he was a sense of direction.

▀▀▀

KIM HAMILTON MCKAY, DANA HOLCOMB ADAMS, AND ROSANNE CHASTAIN WEBB:

KIM: When we were in Foxfire, our biggest project was putting together the cookbook. Wig and Margie had talked about doing something different from just the magazine, and the three of us wanted to try. One of the ideas was a children's book. Then Dana wanted to do a book of ghost stories because we'd just done interviews about haint tales, and there's a lot of them in Rabun, but we were afraid people weren't interested in books like that and we didn't think it would sell. Besides, we wanted to get it done during the summer, so we decided to go with a cookbook. We thought that would be easier because we could pull a lot of back articles and old recipes from issues of *Foxfire* and have the bulk of our information pulled together fast. We started by pulling articles that had recipes in them and interviewing our families.

DANA: The more we interviewed, though, and the more we looked at the information we were getting from the magazines, the more we realized what we weren't getting, and that we really didn't have as much as we thought we did.

KIM: I don't think we actually realized what we were doing when we started. We probably would have had second thoughts if we had known! Rosanne had this little MG and I can remember riding—all three of us piled in that little car. You ought to have seen the three of us packed in there with cameras and tape recorders and equipment.

Our first interview for the cookbook was with Jake and Bertha Waldroop. It was up in North Carolina—a big field with a two-story house and a barn out behind it. She was a short lady with real white hair. He wore overalls and took us out back to show us the different stuff in the barn.

ROSANNE: Margie took us, and Bertha was in the kitchen cooking trout.

Bertha Waldroop: "Instead of having to grease and flour my cake pans every time before I pour my cake batter into them, I cut out some circles of waxed paper and have them on hand to line my pans with. . . . I rub some Crisco around the edges of the pan where the paper touches the sides. The cake will come right out without coming apart." (*The Foxfire Book of Appalachian Cookery*)

KIM: It was nothing unusual for her to be in the kitchen cooking. We were real concerned about how to make biscuits on a wood stove, and that's all we could think about then, and she said biscuits were the least of our worries, and boy, was she right. We didn't realize until later that the real trick was being able to keep five things going at once.

DANA: Do you remember Harriet Echols telling that recipe about how to catch a husband out of one of her cookbooks, and at that time we were all interested in dating and courting? We were determined to put that in the cookbook.

ROSANNE: The interview I liked best was with Aunt Addie Norton. She was just always smiling and real perky, and she was so excited to

Addie Norton: "I made a lot of mistakes before I learned how to cook. I sure did; I made a many a one. I put in hours of piddling—come up by myself and nobody to tell me how to do noth-ing. But I tell you one thing, if you learn it by yourself, if you have to get down and dig for it, it never gets out of you. It stays there as long as you live because you had to dig it out of the mud before you knowed what it was." (*The Foxfire Book of Appalachian Cookery*) Addie died in 1986.

see us. She was always talking about how when she changed from a wood stove to a gas stove, she always burned everything because it cooked so fast, and she was used to it taking a while. And she would talk about how she didn't trust her gas stove because she was afraid she would burn herself up, or burn the house down. She would go in there and open her stove and there would be this little shriveled up black potato, and she'd say, "I leave food in there and turn it on and it just cooks." She was so funny and sweet.

DANA: The oldest person we talked to and one I really enjoyed, was Granny Cabe. She was the one who wore the little bonnet around her head and the apron with a long dress.

KIM: We walked in and she had her quilting stuff laid out in the living room—the different little patches of different colors laid out already cut out, and the quilting frame hanging from the ceiling—and she apologized every time we turned around about the house being such a mess, but it wasn't. They all did that. You'd walk into their house and the first thing they started doing was apologizing for their house being in a mess.

Every time we would try to get a picture of Granny Cabe at her wood stove, she would freeze like a statue. It wouldn't be the pose or

Granny Mary Cabe: "I bake what I call an oven pie. I put fruit in the bottom of the pan. Then I make up my dough and put it on top of my fruit. I cook it on top of the stove till the stuff gets to boiling. Then I set it in the oven and bake it." (*The Foxfire Book of Appalachian Cookery*) Mary died in 1983.

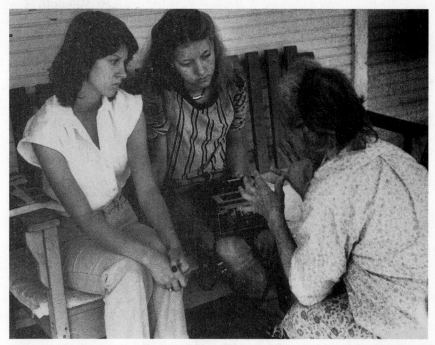

Rosanne Chastain and Dana Holcomb spent hours with Arizona Dickerson. Arizona Dickerson: "My mother always cooked her beans in a iron pot on the fireplace. They're not good if you don't cook down to the grease. A lot of people don't know how to cook beans. They leave water on them. I cook mine down to the grease, but not burned." (*The Foxfire Book of Appalachian Cookery*) Arizona died in 1987.

the picture we'd want, and we would try to get her moving to show us something else, and I mean she would move an inch and then turn around and look and just smile. A lot of them didn't want you to take pictures, and they were real uncomfortable at first. Then after you talked to them and cut up and joked, and they'd go on to the next thing, you could take out the camera and they didn't even know it was going on. Then they'd like it.

We took some pictures back to Arizona and Mimi and Terry Dickerson and they had a fit over the pictures because it had been so long since they had had any pictures of themselves, and I mean some of them were not what I considered good pictures, but they still said, "Oh, that's me," and "That looks good. I like that one." And usually it was because one of us was in it with them.

DANA: Arizona and Mimi have died now, but I still go by and visit Terry.

KIM: At first they were real quiet and timid, and we thought we'd never get them to talk, and then finally they did. Especially Terry. He would laugh and cut up and joke and go on with us.

ROSANNE: When we'd visit, they would meet us out on the porch. All of 'em. Come out to the front porch and wave while we got out of the car. And Terry would just about bounce, he was so excited to see us.

DANA: Mrs. Dickerson had an old cookbook there, and as we flipped the pages, you could tell her favorite recipes because they had the most splatter marks on them, or she'd put a little star or something beside them.

ROSANNE: You know, it's so funny because I couldn't even cook when we were doing all that. I mean peanut butter and jelly was as far as I could go, and they were telling about all these recipes, and making pickles, and I had no idea what they were talking about. That was an education in itself.

KIM: Then we went up to Granny Burrell's, and she was one of the ones that still cooked on a wood stove. We went during the summer, and I remember how hot it was. She hadn't even started cooking a meal yet! As far as I know, she still cooks on a wood stove.

We talked to my granny, Mrs. Underwood, and one thing that Granny liked cooking with best was iron skillets. All of them swore by their skillets and their cast-iron pans. That was what made their cooking so good—that, and cooking it slow. Those were the two things we heard over and over again.

ROSANNE: I interviewed my grandmother. I had saved her until the last, and because it was my grandmother I went in bebopping around and not taking it real seriously. My grandmother is kind of a laid-back, quiet woman, who never puts her foot down, and finally, after about two hours of me messing around, she says, "Are we going to do this interview or not?"

"Well, if you want me to."

She said, "I do. Let's sit down and do it." She was really anticipating being interviewed, and I didn't think it was a big deal to her, but apparently it was because she sat me down and said, "Now turn on that tape recorder."

I was thrilled when we did this book because my grandmother lived out in the country and made pickles and baked her own cookies, and until we did that book, I thought nobody else had a granny who did all of that, so I thought she was sort of different. And it was so nice to meet other people that still did stuff the way she did because it kind of reinforced that she was all right.

KIM: Then we had to try all the recipes out. If it hadn't been for Margie and Ann [Moore] helping, we would have been up the creek. And you had to translate how much a pinch was, and a sprinkle. We got "a pinch" so many times it was pitiful. And when you tried to pin them down, they'd say, "Just however you want it to taste." You'd ask about sixty questions to finally find out they meant about a quarter of a teaspoon.

Dana Holcomb also interviewed her grandfather, D. B. Dayton. D. B. Dayton: "People was a whole lot healthier then than they are now. We never was sick, hardly. When we needed medicine, we had turpentine, castor oil, and salts. I didn't like castor oil—Lord, no! Just as sure as you started taking a bad cold, that's when they give you some. They said castor oil and salts would work colds out of you. If somebody got cut and was bleeding bad, they would reach up in the back of the chimney to get some soot and put on it. We called the soot in the chimney 'cobweb.' They used hog lard for burns and catnip tea for babies to break the hives out on them. When your stomach is out of shape, your lips are cracked, or you have fever blisters, dig up yellow root and chew it." (*Foxfire 9*) D. B. Dayton died in 1986.

KIM: Finally, when we were putting it all together, since school had started, we had to do it after school. Part of it would be at Dana's and another part would be at work. We'd have it all over the dining room table at one person's house, and in her bedroom, too! It was wild. And we still had to do our homework and stuff. I didn't realize how much work was involved. By the time we got to the end of it, we were burned. I see things now I would have changed, but we were about to get burned out and we just wanted it finished. I thought we did pretty good.

DANA: And I think the interviews gave a lot of these people who didn't have their families coming regularly something to look forward to. And what I got out of this whole thing was a real respect for the older generation. In high school, you're not in a position to see a lot of old people. You're around your grandma and grandpa, when you come home from school, but that's not anything like what we got into.

ᴧᴧᴧ

VAUGHN ROGERS: I first joined Foxfire, like many other students, because it seemed to be an easier way to get English credit. It was the hardest class to get into, and so I wanted to get in and see what it was like and what the noise was all about. Then it turned out to be real interesting. You end up discovering a different process of learning, and I think after everybody's first class with Foxfire, they get involved and wanted to do more with it.

My first article was the one with Furman Arvey. My topic originally was on how to preserve fruits other than freezing them, because back in the early days they didn't have freezers and stuff. Someone told us about him, and I'd not done an interview yet, so Wig asked if I wanted to take that one. I said, "Fine, let's do it." So Wig and I went up and interviewed Mr. Arvey. I'd never interviewed anybody, and I was kind of nervous, and I just threw in a few questions here and there, so Wig helped out with the questions. I assume that's the way it is with everybody's first article.

I'd have to say Mr. Moore, who is John Singleton's grandfather, was probably the most interesting interview I did. John did most of the interviewing. I ended up just helping him on it with the research. He had already interviewed his grandfather the first time, and we went back for a second interview. It was interesting to see that he

Vaughn Rogers interviewed Furman Arvey in his shop: "I think everybody [around here] made a mistake to ever sell their land. There's some good people coming in here, [but lots of people here left themselves with nothing]. We made a mistake selling our land. Once the money's gone, it's all gone, and what is there left? Just like that little heifer out yonder. A fellow offered me $500 for her. I said, 'I can see the heifer, but if I had the money, I wouldn't see it very long. I'll just keep her a while.' Money ain't worth nothing. A man's gotta have *some* of it, ain't he? But when you sell off all you have to get it, [you make a mistake]. It don't last long. It sure don't." (*Foxfire*, Spring 1980)

had saved everything. It was like he was in his early life and was preparing for that particular interview, like he knew it was going to happen. His family had saved all of the letters and pictures from when family members were in the Civil War and had gone off to fight. They had a complete family tree from the time the family moved to the United States from Ireland. It was amazing to see the detailed records that they had kept over the years, and continued to keep as they added new births to the family tree and kept up with what everybody was doing.

The main thing you learn in these interviews is that there was a different life before our generation. A more self-sufficient life. Also that there is a lot to learn from our ancestors—our grandparents— and that they're really smarter and have a lot more knowledge than

Wesley Taylor and Mitch Whitmire documented the entire process for *Foxfire 6* as Leonard Webb made a banjo out of a long-necked gourd. Leonard died in 1982.

we thought. That is not captured without these interviews, and I think that it's great that this organization started early enough to capture these special moments and times. There's so much of heritage that is lost because things are not written down and saved. I guess every Foxfire student will tell you the same thing.

▼▼▼

WESLEY TAYLOR: The main thing I did in magazine production was [an article about] Leonard Webb on making a gourd banjo. It was published in *Foxfire 6*. We were on the cover of the issue of *Foxfire* that it appeared in first. I had about four interviews with him. He was a great character. He'd only work on those banjos for around ten hours a week. Sometimes it would be a month [before he'd finish a banjo].

My grandmother, Clyde English, was also pretty active [in Foxfire]. She was interviewed a long time ago [and featured in] some of the early books. Through the Depression, she and my grandfather lived hard, and they learned to stetch a dollar for miles. I think that's why she was interviewed so much.

▼▼▼

DONNA BRADSHAW SPEED: I was involved in Foxfire from 1979 to 1983. I joined Foxfire mainly because of my mom. She and Foxfire had always been in touch with each other, and we'd always read the Foxfire books in our family. Foxfire uses her a lot as a reference to find contacts. Working at the Georgia Mountain Arts Craft Co-op, she knows all the people in the area. She makes corn-shuck dolls, and she's shown on the JFG coffee commercials that Foxfire helped with making a corn-shuck doll.

Donna Bradshaw and Julie Bradshaw interviewed Lester Addis. Lester Addis: "They tell me [a spreading adder is] a awful poisonous snake, but I never knowed'em t'bite me 'r' an'thing. I *have* killed a few of 'em around here. They got a blunt tail an' a fat head. Most all snakes that got a blunt tail is poisonous." (*The Foxfire Book*)

The hardest interview I ever did was with Lester Addis. He was a very old neighbor of ours who lived over on Persimmon. He would mumble; you couldn't hear what he said. He wouldn't go inside for the interview, so we had to do it outside. It was windy, and he was splitting wood.

When we tried to transcribe the tape, we could only hear little bits and pieces. Everything we got we had to drag out of him. But Lester knew about everything. He made all of his own farm equipment, and he didn't go to the store at all. His sister had a grist mill, so he grew corn and took it down there to grind it for cornmeal. He lived in an old house with no electricity, and he had his own well.

The prices of things just blew his mind. He just couldn't understand why they're so high. That's why he'd never buy anything. One time he had a power bill of twenty-eight dollars and he about freaked. He just thought that was an ungodly price to pay for power.

Another time he had to buy a wheelbarrow, and my brother went to pick it up for him. They showed it to him, and he said it was the very thing he wanted. Then they showed him the bill, and he thought they were lying. He thought it was way too much to pay.

ᵂᵂ

RONNIE WELCH: When I first met Wig—well, it was, seems like, twenty years ago, but it ain't been. A bunch [of water gone under the bridge since then].

When my daddy was alive, I used to live down in Clarkesville. When he died, I was seven years old, and we moved back up to Rabun County. Mama and I lived then with Granny until I was thirteen, and it was while we were living with her that I met him. I was going up on the Foxfire land a couple of years before I went to high school.

We lived in an old house across the road from the beer joints. Didn't have no bathroom—had an outhouse. Didn't have no bathtub. We would take baths in a—I called it a pot—a washtub. I used to wear clothes to school that my pants were way up high on my legs and sometimes dirty. And I was doing nothing but going to school—didn't know very much at all. I didn't do nothing but just go to school and come home and bust wood and get it in; and I was running errands back and forth across the road, buying Granny and everybody cigarettes and stuff. Didn't have nothing to do. Wig—you know how he is; he's just easygoing—I just picked up with him, you know? He kinda took me under his wing, I guess. I didn't have anybody to lean on or to help me. He told me to come on up and see the [Foxfire] land. So I headed out one day up there—walked up there from the house 'cause I didn't have no driver's license—and he took me around and showed me everything, and I guess it was one of the biggest things that had ever hit me. It was real interesting to me, and I'd go up there from time to time during that summer fooling around, helping him work in the garden or helping with whatever was going on. It didn't matter to me. I thought it was something special.

As the summer went along, I got more involved in the things that was going on, and I got to know all the people up there, including George, Bob, Margie, and all of them, and I thought that was home away from home. Everybody up there has always been good to me. And Wig explained to me what Foxfire was all about in the school, and asked me would I be interested, and I told him, "Yeah."

The first year I started high school, which was seventh grade, Wig got me into his class, and then I don't know. Seemed like right about that time was the start of whenever everything started coming to-gether—or I really started paying attention to things in the world, I guess you could say, because I really hadn't before. Whenever I hit the seventh grade was when it really started clicking in my mind as far as life in general, because whenever I was staying down at Granny's, why, I didn't see nothing but school. Like I said, I'd come home and didn't get out and get to see nothing. Didn't know nothing. What I learned, I just learned on my own. [Then] I stayed with Foxfire all the way until I graduated, and I guess you could say I was involved with just a little bit of probably everything that I could get my hands into. A lot of students stuck with music the whole time, a lot of students stuck with photography. That wasn't me. I got my hands into a little bit of all that I could. And as I got older and better at what I was doing, I probably helped a lot of other students from time to time, just like Foxfire taught me. As a matter of fact, I know I did. Hell, I could do an article up by myself at that time and get it ready to go.

Once I got in Wig's class, I interviewed Mr. Plott on Plott hound dogs. That's mostly what you could hear on the tape was them dogs. And I started to interview my granny one time and couldn't get nothing out of her. She was one person that *did* know the damn recorder was there and wouldn't say nothing. I tried and tried to get her to talk, but I couldn't. But when that tape recorder wasn't around, she'd tell me tales.

We also interviewed Clyde and Kenny Runion on some of their little toys. They both had toys they called "My trick toys." You know, the ones where you have to try and figure out how to get them apart. Kenny'd hand us one while he was talking there and tell us to be figuring this out while he was talking the whole time. He'd just get a kick out of us 'cause we couldn't figure them out. They were so simple to him. Things like that stuck with me. I had a lot of things that stuck with me.

Clyde Runion has taught us how to make chairs out of mountain laurel, and make wooden-wheeled wagons and whirleygigs: "These windmills have been around for a long time in the mountains. I just build them for a hobby thing, myself. I just like to see them run, you know.

"I made [a windmill] once with a man riding a horse. Every time it would turn, the horse would go. I just had one on it. It didn't work too good, though. You had to have it all hooked up together to where as the horse went one way, the man went backward. You had to bend one crank down and the other up 'cause one pulled the horse down and at the same time, the other one pushed the man backward. It's real complicated to make one of them. And when it got wet, it wouldn't work.

"I used to make them with lights on them with a generator. When the wind blows, it would light up, you know. The generator would put out, and the lights would come on. It's pretty to have different kinds of bulbs in there. And when the wind would blow, it would light up." (*Foxfire 6*) Clyde and his wife, Ethel, are still favorite contacts. Many of their children have been in the Foxfire program. The youngest, Wally, died in 1989.

And we interviewed Willard Watson up in North Carolina. He made toys, too, out of wood—wagons and people and churns. I've still got one of his puzzles.

I remember his black hat and his scruffy beard. In the morning time from about eight in the morning to about twelve, he'd wear sandals, and then he'd put on some old—I don't know what you'd call them—Pinocchio shoes. He'd made them hisself. They were pretty wild looking. I asked him one day why. He said, "Well, the sandals are comfortable, but when they get tired on my feet, my old shoes are comfortabler than them."

He sat up underneath a shade tree late one evening after we thought we was through interviewing, and he got off on some of his best stuff telling about when he was a kid and how he got started.

Dan Melton and Ronnie Welch spent two days with Willard Watson in Deep Gap, N.C. Willard Watson: "I ain't gonna leave home no more. I told the undertakers up here some few days ago, I said, 'Boys, when you come down to get this old carcass, don't put no necktie on my neck. I don't want it. I want my shirttail to be unbuttoned just like I've always wore it.' When it gets cold enough to make me button my shirt up and cover my ears, it's time to go to the house! I was hatched out about a mile from here on the mountain on June 1, 1905, and I've been back here thirty years and I'm gonna wind it up here. I'm gonna take my final sleep—my last night—up at the house. The old lady, she differs with me a little. She don't want them to bring her home from the funeral home. But I do. I want to spend my last night right here with my children at home. So that's it." (*Foxfire 6*).

You know how a lot of things will just come out in conversation, and sometimes if they were telling it just how it was, later they would show you. After that tape recorder was off, they would get up and go to walking over here: "Let me show you this, let me show you that."

It wasn't all gravy train. It wasn't all easy. You had to go back into the class and put the interview into book perspective, which ain't an easy task for anybody, or it didn't seem like it was to *me* at the time. I had to do my own photographs for the magazine, and Wig showed me how. It all had to be done right. You might have to go over the article time and time again; but as far as dealing with the people, I never really had a hard time 'cause they were all caring people and didn't mind us being there at all. They enjoyed telling stories.

And I got a lot of knowledge from that. How to hew a log to build my own home. I could probably build my own log home right now. Everything from making soap to planting a garden—turning your onion buds upside down to make them get stronger for whenever they do get out into the world. That's what Papaw told me. I kept on telling Wig that. I don't know if he was aggravating me or not, but he acted like he really didn't believe me. I helped him plant his garden every year. He dug it with a shovel instead of a tiller. Tried to get him to let me bring the tiller up there but he wouldn't listen. We planted three rows my way and three rows his way, and mine were bigger and stronger than his. He'll tell you today they were. He didn't believe me, but now he believes me. Plant them upside down so they will have a hard time getting out, and they will be strong by the time they do get out, so supposedly they do better. I ain't meaning strong as far as taste—just meaning strong as far as plant. I don't reckon they tasted any stronger. Mine tasted good. Wig will tell you that, too. He probably didn't get to eat very many of his.

Papaw was something else. He used to have a logging truck, and I'd have to help maintain it. I guess that's how I first got started right there with my mechanical ability was with Papaw. I had just started going up to Foxfire.

One time, we had been down on Warwoman [Road], I guess, about ten hours. As the day went on, he was sipping a little liquor here and there.

We'd been down there working all day long. I guess I was somewhere around fourteen, and I was doing most of the work, and he was getting drunker and drunker as the time went on. Well, I thought I was doing most of the work, but he was just smart in his old age and could do as much as I could do by talking. He felt he could.

We got ready to go home, and he was drunk as a big monkey and couldn't drive. I had to help him get up in the truck. He got over there in the passenger's side and told me to get up underneath the steering wheel.

I said, "Papaw, I can't drive."

"Yeah, you can, too. We ain't staying out here all night." So he told me to get under the steering wheel and drive—so I did.

I'd drove around up at the house before—just pulled his car around for him, or drove up to the gas station and got him some gas. And so just as soon as we pulled out on the highway, I just turned the truck like a car. The whole ass end of it, and it loaded with logs, went off in a big ditch there. He said, "Now hold her down!" We cleaned out Warwoman's ditches that day all the way down to the house. Didn't get caught or nothing. Him just a'dying laughing the whole time. I didn't know how to drive an old straight shift or nothing else. Me fourteen years old and never had drove a damn logging truck. We made it home. I don't know how, but we did. I guess with his drunkness and hardheadness and me scared to death, we made it, but I was in every ditch from Warwoman to the house.

I wasn't ever scared of him whenever he was sober. I guess whenever he got drunk, his voice just got a little rougher and deeper and I done whatever he said. He taught me a lot.

That's another thing about *Foxfire*. I did get an opportunity to do an interview on him. That meant a lot to me. That just goes to show you right there that a lot of other people's kids and grandkids thank Foxfire for doing that—for keeping all the knowledge that [older people have] gained over the years. Especially after they're gone. It means a lot.

Papaw was a miner. Actually, he was a dynamite man is what he called himself. He said, "I'm a dynamite man. One of the best in the country," he said. And I believe him. He helped do Black Rock Road, and all up in Hiawassee. Anywhere there was a lot of heavy rock to be blasted, he said they all called on him.

One time he was down in a mine, and there was eight of them. Said him and another man was the only two chewing tobacco, and eventually six of them died and him and the other man didn't. He said it was on account of he was spitting out all that dust.

He was a pretty amazing fellow. He'd chew tobacco and smoke cigarettes at the same time. Try to spit on all the grass to kill it; he didn't like grass—had no use for grass. It just took up his yard. I guess I can set here and tell you about small things like that for quite a while. But he taught me a lot. And a lot of the things was things that you can't learn today. The things that he told me while I was doing the interview were things that he come upon just while we doing it, but he might not have come across if we hadn't been there doing the interview. Just on a normal everyday basis talking with Papaw, he would talk about old times, but he just really wouldn't go into detail. I was probing him that day for a purpose. He brung out a lot of stuff then that helped me. All in general, in my eyes, he was just a hell of a man. Not because he was my papaw, like I said, but just

John Welch: "They used to be a dance hall right around that bend right there till that cyclone come through there. It nearly killed old man Jim Stancil—didn't kill Jim dead, but killed Sary Jane *dead.* That was his wife. Blowed his house plumb away. Blowed Cory Bell and Clary Zell about 250 feet into a field but it didn't hurt them young'uns a bit, and how in the world *that* couldn'a happened I don't know. But it did. It twisted hickory trees off three and four foot through just like you'd take a match stem and twist it off. A lot of people say that she won't come through here, but I know it did and they's lots of othern's know it did. Blowed Verner Coleman away and Fate Wilburn—all he had—away. House and all. Miss Stancil had us younguns' pictures, and one of these Speeds from Warwoman found one of them right on top of the Georgia Bald. Took that picture back to my daddy. Shore did." (*Foxfire,* Winter 1979) John died in 1982.

his old hardheaded ways. That's all. It's the only way to put it. He's just my papaw, but no one thing lingers in my mind all the time. Everything about my papaw does.

A lot of things stick in my head. I guess each one of the people I interviewed had their own thing that stuck in my head, and that is what I was there interviewing them about. Like I said, I have a lot of respect for old people, and they all do different than people do today. They have a whole different way of going about it. Talking with their hands—telling you about this big old rock up on the side of the hill, making motions—just things like that stick in my head. I can still see them telling the stories. It's like they were still there and doing it.

And now I try to stick, right or wrong, to a lot of the old-timey ways because I feel that they're right. Like today, if a lot more people had stuck to the way it used to be, then we might be a lot better off. Like all these damn new drugs, and the ozone eat up—none of that stuff wouldn't be happening.

While I was in school, Wig also got me started on stamp collecting. Whenever he was young, him and his dad used to collect stamps together. We just got started talking about it, and I got interested in that and have been stamp collecting for a long time, since then. I got a bunch of them. I don't know how many thousands. Whole big bags full of ones I still ain't got put into books. I got a bunch of them when I went to different places like Washington. When we was on these trips, if I had time, I went to the Smithsonian Institute, and I got some stamps from there. They had these bags full of stamps, like two hundred and fifty in there, that you could get for five dollars. Stamps from across the world. I thought they was all right. I had to buy me a couple of bags while I was there. Ann [Foxfire's circulation manager] helped me a lot with my stamp collection. She would save her stamps for me. I had a big box that I had them in laid out and all. Right before school got out, probably my last year, twelfth grade, the last thing I done was I ran back up there where Ann worked. She always had an envelope hanging up there—"Ronnie's stamps" wrote on it— and I got that off there with the pin still stuck in it. I guess it was four or five months ago I was digging through my stamps and all, and I pulled out that packet, and it had "Ronnie's stamps" wrote on it. I recognized Ann's handwriting. It was kind of neat. I never had even pulled the stamps out of the sack, but I did then.

▼▼▼

Allison Adams: I sometimes wonder if the students in Foxfire now are as dedicated as the early people were. I think much of the dedication on the part of the early students came from the fact that they started it; it was their baby. What the Foxfire students have to work with now—even what we had when I came to Foxfire—is something that somebody else began. You have to think, "Hey, the magazine, so what? What can I do to make a difference in it? What can I do to add my own personality to it? We are a very different people from those kids in the sixties. We are children of the eighties; we have to do something new and exciting!" [When I was in Foxfire, some of us tried to do that.]

Since I grew up in Rabun County, I had been hearing about Foxfire all my life. When I was in the fourth grade in Girl Scouts, my mother, our troop leader, arranged to have Paul Gillespie take all of us on a tour of the Foxfire land. We were able to see all the cabins, mills, and other restored buildings, and I really enjoyed it.

I really became involved in Foxfire, however, in the tenth grade. I first took a music class with George, and then after that I took Foxfire I, the introductory course. From there on out, I took the magazine class. I had a wonderful time. I worked for Foxfire in the summer each year and then came back to the class in the fall.

My parents really loved Foxfire. They encouraged me in everything that I did. Mama would let me stay late after school for Foxfire, and before I learned to drive, she would come and pick me up even though we lived far away in Rabun Gap. Later, when I could drive, she always understood when I needed to take the car to school so I could stay late and work afterward. Even though my brother, Brooks, and I have both graduated from high school and are no longer in Foxfire, my family has still maintained a close relationship with the organization. My father is now a member of Foxfire's Community Advisory Board. He and George Reynolds, Foxfire's music instructor, often go fishing together.

One of the biggest projects I was involved in was when we did *Foxfire 9*. It was fun working on *Foxfire 9* in the summer because I got along well with the other students. That was probably one of the best groups of people I've ever worked with in my life—I believe it was Kyle Conway, Chet Welch, Cheryl Wall, Kelly Shropshire, Greg Darnell, and Al Edwards. We worked well together; we also worked well with Wig.

Nola Campbell: "I personally don't hold nothin' against the white people 'cause my mother was white. I love the white people, and I love the Indians. I'll fight for the Indians quicker than I'll fight for the white people, though. If somebody stands up there and cusses the ol' black Indians, then they're gonna have me to whip if I can fight 'em, and I'll try! I've got in more fusses about [the mistreatment of the Indians] than anything in the world. I might get whipped, but somebody will know I was there." (*Foxfire 9*)

At one point, we went to New York to see the editor, Loretta Barrett, to discuss the contents of the book. That was fun, we sat in her office in a huge high-rise. We also had a few phone calls with her. We didn't need to see her too much, however, because we basically knew what to do in terms of format and content.

There was some existing material, so a lot of what we did that summer was to go on very long intensive interviews to fill gaps. Cheryl and I went to Rock Hill, South Carolina, and spent many hours with Nola Campbell. We went up there to interview Nola because she is half Catawba Indian and makes Catawba Indian pottery. She ended up giving us hours and hours of material on life as a Catawba Indian and some of the difficulties she faced, and a lot of childhood stories. That turned out to be a great interview because we came back with about five or six tapes about her entire life and society and environment, and a lot of pictures. That interview was so long that we would interview her for about two hours at a time, and then we'd go outside and walk around.

Of all the people I met during the five or six years I spent working with Foxfire, probably the one who meant the most to me and had the most personal impact on me was Carolyn Stradley. We interviewed her for *Foxfire 9*. She was a fascinating person—as a matter of fact, there was an article on the front page of the business section of yesterday's *Atlanta Constitution* about her. She was invited to the White House to visit President Bush as a reward for being one of the outstanding business people of the United States.

She was born and raised in Youngcane, Georgia. When she was a small child, her mother died, and her father moved to Atlanta and abandoned her and her brother. They basically fended for themselves for the rest of their lives. She did a pretty good job of raising herself! She stayed in school, she worked like a dog, she maintained a lot of personality. When she was fifteen, she moved to Atlanta. She entered high school and graduated with honors; then she went to Tech, and she had to take care of her husband, who was on kidney dialysis. After her husband died, she climbed her way up through different jobs and ended up owning her own paving company and paving some of the runways at Hartsfield International Airport. Today she's an extremely successful person. Her story is one of those amazing stories of people defying the mountain stereotypes.

Seeing someone with that kind of determination to escape poverty and escape the stereotype and make something of herself; and seeing

Carolyn Stradley: "My mother died on Sunday, she was buried on Tuesday, and the following weekend my father was remarried. He chose to live in the Atlanta area with his new wife. [He left my brother and me in our little house in Youngcane to look after ourselves.]

"The winters get sort of severe over there and I can remember waking up sometimes and I'd have ice frozen across my face from the condensation of my breath. I think being cold was one of the things I remember most. It would be dark by the time the school bus got me home. Some mornings I didn't properly cover the coals in the fireplace before I left for school and I would come in by myself in the evening and [the fire would be completely out and I'd] not have kerosene to start a new fire.

"There were times I could almost literally leave my body, and it was like [the cold, the hunger, the troubles] were happening to someone else. I could just step aside and I wasn't cold anymore. I wasn't hungry. The Japanese have this theory that one can drink tea from an empty cup. That's the way I think I got." (*Foxfire 9*) Carolyn is regularly cited by various business publications as one of the most outstanding businesswomen in Georgia.

someone who was able to still believe in herself, even though she had been dumped on so many times by the people who should have been taking care of her—well, that is something nobody should be asked to do, but it is amazing that she was able to do it.

I had a vague idea about what I wanted to do with the rest of my life before I interviewed her, but after I met her, I realized that I ought to start setting goals then in order to achieve things. Interviewing her made me sit down and really think about what I wanted to do, and that's how I was able to get into Agnes Scott and get a job before I graduated. I set these goals for myself early as a result of realizing what she had done. She was really determined early on in terms of what she was going to do, and she fought for it. That was a very strong, emotional interview. She was in tears at one point, and we were all in tears ourselves. She's someone who inspires me and should inspire any woman who ever had any ambition.

The summer after I graduated from high school, I was hired back to work on the wine making book for E. P. Dutton. Those summers were special to me. I remember Joyce Colborn, Wig's administrative assistant, used to bring in her little boy, John, to work. He was about five or six then, and John had a crush on me. I'd be working upstairs in the main office, and John would sit downstairs. I'd be working up there, and all of a sudden I'd see this paper airplane land next to me. I'd open it up, and he'd written love notes to me. He didn't remember that when I asked him at the Mother's Day picnic. He said, "I remember you, but I don't remember being in love with you!"

There was one day on the land [I remember, even though I wasn't there and had to hear about it secondhand]. I was in New York City with Wig. It was the summer after I had graduated, and for some reason there was no one on the land but Kelly Shropshire and Chet Welch. Chet was working in the main office. Kelly was down below working in the other office. Chet was playing around on the phones, and he managed, at one point, to get down to Kelly's office and mess up all the phone buttons. Then he got back up to the upper office and he called down to the second number, and Kelly answered, "Good morning, Foxfire. Can I help you?"

Chet said, "Hey, this is Zell Miller. Is Wig there?"

Kelly said, "Oh no, Wig's not here."

"Well, is Margie there?" They went through the whole thing. Nobody was there. It was just the two of them, and so finally he said, "Well, is my good ol' boy Chet Welch there? I would just love to talk to my old buddy Chet."

She goes, "Yes, Chet's here, " and she was trying to put him on, but Chet had switched the buttons so she couldn't get the right button. She was afraid that she was going to hang up on old Zell, our lieutenant governor. So she ended up putting the phone down, running up to the other cabin, got up there, and told Chet, "Zell Miller is on the phone and he wants to talk to you!"

Chet picked up the phone like it was a big joke and shouted, "Hey, Zell!" She was sure Chet hadn't believed it was Zell Miller on the phone and was making a total fool of himself, and she has never lived that down. We still harass her about that till this day. It wasn't until a week later that we told her what was going on.

One of the times I remember most was when Kelly and I worked together on writing introductions. Wig felt that introductions had been reduced to little half-paragraphs of biographical material that really weren't very meaningful to anyone, so he began emphasizing them again in his teaching. We went through the whole process of discussing what they should be like and how they should be written. We covered such questions as: in what order should you put the ideas together? How long should they be? What's the purpose of an introduction in the first place?

As a result of all this discussion we turned out some five- and six-page introductions, and I thought they included some quite touching material. We each contributed to part of the process, and we learned from each other. I taught Kelly the basic process of introduction writing; she taught me how to put myself into it—how to express the emotions I was feeling as I contacted these people. For example, we wrote the Carolyn Stradley introduction together. I was able to see first how I wanted it to be formed, what style to use, what order to put the information in, and what was most and least important. She, on the other hand, was able to help me with the emotional side of the process. "Allison," she reminded me, "don't forget how you felt!" She would not let me forget how special this meeting with Carolyn Stradley had been to me. It was very important for us to work together like that, and I think some good material resulted.

Though of course I loved Foxfire, there were a few things that troubled me about it from time to time. For one thing, I was very dedicated to Foxfire, and I took a great deal of responsibility in everything. I would work long hours after school, have jobs in the summer, make presentations on trips, and do lots and lots of articles. Because I worked so hard, I would hate it when people dropped their Foxfire responsibilities the minute they stepped out of the classroom.

I also hated it when people would come into the classroom and say to themselves, "Well, I really don't want to work today. I think I'll just sit here and read something."

There was another thing that bothered me, and this one is harder to describe and define. You see, Eliot Wigginton is a gifted and dedicated man, but he has so many demands on his time. The same is true of all the other staff members. Sometimes I would feel that all the staff members had so much going on in their lives that they would forget I was there. It was always so hard to get their attention and to say, "Listen and slow down for a second. I need your help! I need to talk to you!" They just couldn't see that I really was in need of a conversation. Sometimes it was hardest to draw attention to myself when I needed it the most.

Also, Wig and Margie always expected such excellence (as I'm sure they still do) and I would always get so discouraged with myself because I didn't feel like I was meeting their standards. I would spend four hours working on something and then they would say, "You have to do this over again. It's got problems." It was always so frustrating when that happened. When I look back at it, however, I appreciate it because I know they were demanding excellence of me. Now, as a result, I always demand excellence of myself. Everything that I do I try to do to the very best of my ability. I don't take things lightly; I take them very seriously.

ᴡᴡ

OhSoon Shropshire: I remember when Wig got Teacher of the Year. Everybody was real happy. When you work for Foxfire, you take it for granted since you have the class every day and do it so often. We all knew that Wig was an excellent teacher, but we took that for granted also. Then for someone else to recognize him—well, it was a comment on *everyone,* and not just him. He's got to have good students to be a good teacher, so that was actually also a really big honor for *us.*

ᴡᴡ

Kyle Conway: I had a summer job with Foxfire in 1984. The first thing I started working on was getting the magazine out—the plain old late issue that didn't get finished up at school. Every year that happens. That is the first thing we did. The rest of that summer was mainly getting major interviews that hadn't been gotten around to yet for the book because the people lived so far away.

Everybody gets their own project, but it was interesting how we worked together. Roy Roberts happened to be my project, but I wasn't the only one who worked on it. Everybody has a hand in everything, but you adopt one that becomes *your* project. That's what happened with Roy. There were three interviews that went into that.

How we met him was bizarre. We were taking Monroe Ledford up to North Carolina to track down some of his relatives that he hadn't seen in years. We were in Wig's car way out in nowhere in North Carolina, and we had stopped for lunch at this café. It was the weirdest thing. We were sitting there eating, and one of the customers said, "You're Eliot Wigginton of the Foxfire books, aren't you?"

Wig said, "Yeah."

He said, "Well, there's somebody you ought to meet."

We're kinda, "Yeah, we'll meet him."

He goes and gets this guy, and it was Roy Roberts. He sat down and we start talking, and we find out he used to make charcoal. Wig's always interested in something. He had never heard about how it was done, and he had been curious about it for years. It turns out that Roy had *done* all these things. We just whipped out a tape recorder right there in this café, right there on the table, and started right up with him.

I don't know how long we talked with him that first time, but it was enough to say, "Hey, we gotta go back." We left and we went on and met these people that were relatives of Monroe, but the whole trip was really a success because we met Roy. We came back and called up Roy and said, "We want to come up and spend some time and interview you again."

He said, "Sure, great." So we set that up. Wig and I and Al Edwards and Chet Welch went up there, and we spent two days with him.

That first day had been a long, *long* day, talking to him and hearing about his experiences. We were all worn out. It had been a long drive up there, and then we sat there and talked, and walked around with him. He had made about five or six toys for us—squirt guns and pop guns out of elder branches, and so on. He had also showed us how to walk on stilts. He had them there for the kids who would come with their parents and stay in his tourist cabins.

He had also pulled a few jokes on us. While we were walking around, for example, he was throwing rocks with a sling. He got to

Roy Roberts: "Skunks like them old eggs best. It was funny how they would break an egg. They would catch it in their front feet and they'd throw it behind them between their back legs. If it didn't hit something behind them and break, they'd turn around and throw it in a different direction. They'd keep on until they heard a crack. If they missed several times, they'd get impatient, and boy they'd get in a hurry then." (*Foxfire 9*)

where he was bragging a little bit, so I questioned him on his accuracy. He said that he could take a rock off the top of my head. He stood me right there on a stump and put a rock on my head and stepped back, and had his sling all ready; I jumped down and yanked the rock off my head. He said, "See, it works every time!" He was *always* doing stuff like that. By then it was dark, maybe ten-thirty or something. At that point he was whittling away, trying to make a whistle, but he couldn't get the stick that he needed. We were all sitting there when, BOOM, there he goes. Takes off into the woods to find the stick that he wanted. Here we are kinda looking at each other dumbfounded, going, "Well, should somebody go with him? What if he falls in the dark or something?"

But we just sat there not knowing what to do. Here he comes back running down the bank from the woods, had his stick and was carving away. He went on to show us how to make a whistle.

The next morning we got up pretty early, but of course Roy was already up. Had been up for hours. He had already made three more toys. We drag outta bed, and he's spry and up and at 'em. Another day. That was the day that he showed us all his old land where his general store used to be and the charcoal kilns he had built. He would just take off, and we would be left in the dust trying to catch up with him. We were so tired. If you look at the pictures, this eighty-two-year-old man is in front and everyone else is about three paces behind. He was always out in front trucking along. We were always going, "How did he get up there?"

The image of Roy that I remember the best is a picture that Al took. It made the cover of the magazine. This was when Al was really getting into experimenting with photography. We were standing in front of the door of the kiln, the light was flooding in, and we were silhouetted against the door. That's the most vivid image that I remember, and it was captured by Al.

You just can't capture everything with a camera or tape recorder, though. That's why I had a hard time with the introduction because I wanted the reader to know the personalities behind the photographs. I think that is what a good introduction should have in it. I thought, "How can I *really* help the readers to share this with us?" and hopefully I did that. What I tried to do was step back from the interview and take a look around and try to absorb everything. That helps a bit when you're writing something, not necessarily for *Foxfire*, but for other things you do later on.

I remember working with Wig forever on that introduction, writing version after version after draft after draft. I had to keep honing and polishing and changing little things. I was really pleased with the final product. With something like that, you work on it and work on it and just throw your hands up in frustration and walk away. But then, something clicks. You sit in calmness, and all of a sudden you say, "Hey! This is it! This is good!" After it's over, you can stop and look back and say, "Hey! That was all right." That's what happens. That's how it goes.

The other challenge in writing magazine articles is how to fit things together. When you're editing, you are wondering, "Where does everything go? How does everything fit together?" Roy, he had so many things that he did that really didn't fit together. How do you fit raising skunks into running a general store and making charcoal? That gets tough. I wrestled with that Roy Roberts thing for weeks. After it was transcribed and everything, it was spread all over this entire floor for days that summer. I was *still* trying to put that together during the school year in class.

But it came out really well. One of the biggest lessons I learned from that interview is you're never too old. I hope I'm half as active as him when I get that old. And he's still that way today, seven years later. Now, because of the article, he and his wife are friends of Foxfire.

It was another year or so after we finished *Foxfire 9* before the book actually came out. It was like that with Wig's book, *Sometimes a Shining Moment.* I remember Wig needed a lot of photographs developed. Joseph Fowler and I locked ourselves into the darkroom down at school for about seven hours straight. We just cranked out pictures, one right after another. We went to New York with Wig to Doubleday, and actually worked in a conference room there. We just took it over, spread everything out, mounted pictures, coded the plates to the text, wrote captions, and just put it all together. I also did a couple of diagrams of the classroom for it. And that thing didn't come out till two or three *years* later.

But it's worth it. In Foxfire, you've got something to do, and it's not going to get done unless you do it. It still amazes me what I can do. Foxfire was just the beginning of that. You're going up to Doubleday and you're walking in with all these editors and stuff and working side by side with them. It's like, "Wow! Here I am, a high school student, doing that." It always amazed me. For Wig, it's no big deal. He knows what high school kids are capable of doing. But every once in a while he still gets surprised, too, at what they can do. He's sitting there pushing you to do it. You're always saying, "This is pretty neat; look what I did." You learn that, and anything is possible. A little hard work never hurt anybody. You learn how to present yourself in front of a group of people that you've never seen before and organize your thoughts so they can understand what you're trying to say. Here I was, fifteen years old, talking to a bunch of teachers and telling them how to teach their classes. It was a kick for me showing them how to do things.

On top of the ridge behind Roy Roberts's row of tourist cabins, Al Edwards and Kyle Conway discovered a checker table Roy had built for the amusement of his guests.

I showed a teacher I had at the Air Force Academy my chapter in *Foxfire 9*, and he was really impressed. He said, "When did you write that?"

I said, "Oh, about five years ago." He asked questions about it, and [I had] kind of forgotten things. Maybe you don't really appreciate it until you're eighty-two years old, like Roy, and you can sit back and have time to remember it all.

▀▄▀

AL EDWARDS: [The summer after my sophomore year I worked for *Foxfire*, and one of the interviews I really remember was with Roy Roberts.] I do remember we got pretty hog wild with the camera. Either we just got hog wild or didn't bring enough film, because the last three fourths of the last day, we only had twelve exposures left and that was it, so every single picture had to be something we could use. When you go through the article, every single picture that was in that last half a roll was used in it. That was probably one of the biggest jumps in a condensed period of time that I'd ever made in terms of ability, and to me that was the high point of the whole interview. It certainly was an experience to have, and you accumulate these experiences, and they all just distill out at some point.

What I really got involved with through Foxfire was photography. When I took the Foxfire I class, everybody learned how to use the single lens reflex camera. Actually, I had been taught how to use a camera twice before, but I forgot both times immediately because somebody just sat there and told us, "This is how you use a camera." Then you [would] play with it for a few minutes, and they'd take it somewhere and hide it so you really didn't get a real grasp on it.

Then I got in Foxfire and started *doing* it. At the same time, the county had gotten a state grant to rebuild houses that were falling down and nearly uninhabitable. As a Foxfire project, Mark Turpen and I did a series of before and after shots of these houses for their report to the state, and we printed the pictures after school.

About that time I went on a Scout trip outing in South Carolina. I took a photograph of a lighthouse and ended up entering it in a competition and won a national Scholastic Art Award. I don't think it ever got published, but it was on exhibit in New York City where they exhibited all the national award winners. I got a big plaque and a couple of certificates. That was a good, positive encouragement at the time, and it was also helpful in getting into college.

After that, I really got sort of hooked on photography. That winter, I wanted access to a darkroom in the evenings, so Foxfire let me use the one on the Foxfire land. I had it all to myself. When I worked was at night. After Mom got home from work, I'd grab the car and come rolling up the hill, and I just came and went as I pleased. That was pretty fun because I didn't realize that the heat in the darkroom worked, so I never turned the heat on. On real cold days all my chemicals were really cold. The hydroquinine in your developer neutralizes below fifty-eight degrees Fahrenheit. I would come in and all my chemicals would be fifty degrees Fahrenheit, so I would get all these bizarre prints [that were] really trashed out. I'd stay some nights till midnight, stagger home, go to sleep, and go to school the next day.

My senior year, I even tried to make my own chemicals. I was in Mr. Croom's physics class, and he had an old book of chemistry exercises, and it had a recipe for making emulsions for paper, and making a developer solution and a hypo solution. Then I found some

Al's lighthouse photograph.

other recipes for the same stuff, and he gave me the key to the room where he stashed all the chemicals, so when everyone would go off to pep rallies, I would sneak off to the chemistry room.

During that year, I also spent a lot of time in the Foxfire darkroom printing up my portfolio to send with my applications to college. One of the places I applied was the Rhode Island School of Design. I had actually been on the campus before because the first summer I worked for Foxfire, Wig and I had gone there to speak at a conference of state arts educators. We were there for a couple of days, so we had time to roam around the campus. At that point, I had no intention of really pursuing photography. Then when I really got into it, I remembered the place and decided I wanted to go back. They accepted me, and so I went there for a year. Then I took a year off to work and save some cash to go back. Then I went back and did some part-time studies for another year. Now, I'm off again. It's on a year, off a year.

LAURA LEE: I was a junior when I first got involved in Foxfire. I didn't take Foxfire I; I took Appalachian Literature first. It was the first quarter they ever offered it; it was a trial run, an experiment just to see if it worked. There were only six people in our class. I read *River of Earth* and a couple of poetry books by James Still. That led to the James Still issue of the magazine, which was the main project I did for Foxfire. It was a huge undertaking. It took almost two years to get finished. I was involved in conducting the interviews, editing and organizing the quotes, writing the introduction, and so forth, both in class during the school year and in summer jobs I had with Foxfire both before and after I graduated.

The project involved a series of interviews with James Still, both here in our classroom and at his home in Kentucky, and the catchy anecdotes and sayings he had heard mountain people use over the years and had written down in his journals. [A collection of them was published first in *Foxfire*, and then the majority of them were accepted by University of Kentucky Press for a book they plan to publish in fall 1991.]

I remember one trip to Hindman, Kentucky, to interview him and to take pictures of his house. It was in April of 1987. The people involved were Wig, OhSoon Shropshire, Sheri Thurmond, and myself. We set out late and stopped on the way at Kingsport, Tennessee, to spend the night. During the night it snowed over a foot, and it was still snowing hard the next morning, so we couldn't get to Kentucky. Wig called ahead and they said, "Don't even try it. All the power lines are down, and the roads are closed." We tried to go back home, and we got partway back, but then we couldn't get any further. We were stuck for three or four days at the Holiday Inn in Newport, Tennessee. State troopers had closed the interstates down completely. By the end of the four days, OhSoon and Sheri and I were getting so bored that we were leaving dumb notes around for future guests to find, making tents out of the beds, taking pictures of the curtains, and things like

James Still: "Now and then I still hear remnants of the language spoken by Chaucer and the Elizabethans, such as 'sass' for vegetables, 'hit' for it or 'fit' for fight. People here are more likely to express themselves in an original manner than any place I know. I think it is something to celebrate. I don't want or expect Appalachian speech to be like any other. It has its own individuality, its own syntax. To be unlettered is not necessarily to be unintelligent. It's a rare day when I'm out and about that I fail to hear something linguistically interesting. I go to the post office and I'll hear somebody say something that's of interest to me. That has a lot to do with why I live here. Of course, there are other reasons. I've travelled a bit yet I keep coming back like iron filings to a magnet. Here, we are more conscious of the individual. Everybody is somebody." (*Foxfire*, Fall 1988) The book Laura helped edit, *Wolfpen Notebooks*, will be published by the University of Kentucky Press in 1991.

that. The hotel was all filled up. They could only give us one room, so Wig slept on a lounge chair in the Holidome out by the pool.

Later, we did make it to Kentucky. James Still was modest and unpretentious. Imagine, here's this famous author, eighty years old, and he's been famous for I don't know how long. His books are known all over the world. But he's just like your grandpa; he's sweet and modest about the whole thing. He loves writing just for the sake of writing; he doesn't care about the money he makes or the fame he receives.

When I look back at the beginning of the article, when I was rearranging excerpts from interviews, I had no idea what it would turn into later on. James Still would send in typewritten pages with the sayings on them. I didn't know how to use the computer at that time, and I didn't want to learn how to use it, so I'd take the sayings and cut them apart one by one and paste them down in categories by themes on long sheets of paper. I spent a couple of months doing that. Then they said I had to use the computer, so all that work I'd done was for nothing. The computer came pretty easily to me, though, once I had my hands on it, and it made my task much simpler.

Every now and then, one of those quotes just pops across my head, and I get to thinking, "Where did that come from?"

Then I remember, "Oh, yeah. It came from the James Still notebooks."

I guess the one that comes the most often is, "God must have sent the strongest people to live in the mountains; otherwise they couldn't have survived it."

Other people tell me that, after reading the sayings *Foxfire* published, one will stick in their minds. My sister remembers the quote,"Hello, snakebrains," and she even uses it sometimes.

I mostly tended to work by myself. I wasn't very good at working on a team. Especially on the James Still project, I tried to do everything myself, and that was my big mistake. I guess that's what doing that project taught me—sometimes you have to work with other people.

▰▰▰

ALLYN STOCKTON: I remember Momma told me, "Allyn, you're not going to major in Foxfire in high school." I did take a lot of Foxfire courses, but I also took chemistry and algebra and all that, and I was on the football team, but Foxfire was all that I was interested in. You could take Folklore as a Social Studies, Foxfire I and II counted as Englishes, outdoor education as a P.E., and then you could take video and radio production.

Over the years, we met a lot of people in the Foxfire classroom. They ought to keep a guest list of all the people who have come in. It was somebody different about every week. One time it was a group of Navaho Indians. They were trying to start something like Foxfire. There were groups all the time. Always something going on.

Wig had a cookout at his house for our graduation present. He cooked steak and we ate watermelon. We kicked back on his porch. We had never seen the foxfire moss that glows. Wig said, "I want to show you guys something." We went out into the woods and knocked a stump over, and what I saw was the neatest thing. It was glowing.

TONIA KELLY: I worked on the Ellison Dendy personality portrait. I did it with a couple of other girls. He was my preacher's father. I had seen him in their yard, but I had never really talked to him until we went and interviewed him. I still go see him now and speak. He still knows who I am and remembers doing the article. He was ninety-three or ninety-four when we did it and he's still doing real well. I was surprised at how clear his mind was. He could remember things he'd done when he was three or four years old, like the trouble he'd gotten into, and I can't remember things like that. It was really amazing.

My eleventh-grade year, I did an article about horses with Conway Watkins. I did that one mostly by myself. It was something I enjoyed because I enjoy working with horses and Conway opened up a whole new aspect of the subject for me. Both he and his wife are really nice people, and he knew what he was talking about. If I didn't understand something, he didn't mind explaining it better until I understood it. On some things, I'm like, "Wait a minute, what are you talking about?"

At the annual Mother's Day Foxfire picnics that I went to, I helped people when they came. I would greet them at their cars and walk them in and find them a place to sit down. I helped with making sure everyone had a name tag, and I helped where I was needed. The people I would meet and talk to were really proud to have somebody meet them. They really liked that, especially the ones I had talked to and worked with. I had a lot of family there, too, because most of my

Ellison Dendy: "I met the only girl I ever went with in 1920. That was Delsie Gibson. I'd been on a logging job out in Haywood County and was going up to Goldmine. She was coming down the trail and we met [for the first time]. I gave her my picture and I went on home but I told her I'd come back down to see her. [When we met later,] and she gave me my picture, you know what she told me? She said, 'You can put your slippers under my bed anytime you want to!' [Laughter] You know that's what I done! I married her—the only woman I ever went with in my whole life. On April 7, 1921, we got married in Franklin. All my wedding cost me was ten dollars for the license and the blood test and I gave the preacher seventy-five cents." (*Foxfire*, Summer 1987)

family have been contacts. Aunt Arie was. My great-aunts and -uncles were. Interviewing them you learned things that you never would have learned, like some of the things my granddad and my grandma have done. I think it's interesting how little we do know of the ones who are really close to us.

MARY SUE RAAF: The Dendy interview was my first. We were all real nervous about it because when we first got there, he opened the door, and there was this really old man, and the first thing he did was greet each of us in a different language. We're going, "Oh my gosh!"

We were all sitting there listening to him, and it was sort of a disaster because we got there and the batteries for the tape recorder didn't work, and we didn't have a plug in. The lady had to go next door and borrow her neighbor's tape recorder. Later on the power went out. I learned everything that you should not do on that interview.

I loved Margie. I really think that in many ways, Margie was the one running things. She was always very helpful because when Wig was out of town, you didn't have to worry about it. If Margie told you

Tonia Kelly interviewed Conway Watkins. Conway Watkins: "My daddy never would make liquor, but I tried it myself. Buck Carver and me got caught one time up there on the Highlands Mountain. It was above the old rock quarry up there. We had [our liquor] in thirty-six fifty-five gallon barrels. We were running a pretty good-sized place. That ol' federal man said, 'Didn't you know you couldn't come up here in North Carolina and make liquor?'

"I said, 'Didn't figure it would last forever.' [Laughter]

"About the next thing he said was, 'Where did all this sugar come from?'

" 'It's been a long time ago but when I went to school, history taught that the majority of it came from Cuba.' " (*Foxfire*, Winter 1987)

how to do something, you knew it would be right. Margie always knew what Wig wanted. I miss her. She was always willing to sit down there and help you transcribe. If you couldn't type, she would sit there and type your article while you read it out to her. She was always willing to go on interviews with you if you were afraid to go by yourself or if you didn't know what to do. I was upset when I found out that she was leaving. I didn't want her to go.

And we always had fun on trips with her. We used to get mad because we thought that Margie didn't get enough recognition. We thought Margie should get to go off on some of the big trips, but he always sent her to Athens, and we thought she should get to go to somewhere good.

When I was in the eleventh grade, the staff experimented with another way of getting students involved in decisions that affected the organization. Up until then, the decisions that needed to be made were carried to the classes but sometimes staff members would forget to poll their classes, or the discussion would get postponed. Since the staff met in the classroom every Tuesday after school, someone suggested that maybe representatives from the various classes might attend the staff meetings and try deciding things that way. It was called the A Team. I think originally we were supposed to vote to choose somebody to go, but it ended up being whoever wanted to go could. There were a lot of us who went at first, and then it started tapering off. I thought it was really good, and I really enjoyed it because we got so much more involved in the actual decisions of everything.

I liked it especially because Wig started letting us talk about the trips and help decide who was going to go. It seemed a lot more fair with the A Team. What we did was look at what Foxfire classes students had been in, what they had done, and what their skills were. Then, we would go through their résumés and choose two or three who would be good. Next, we would give Wig the people we chose and he would choose from there.

I also remember the year that Wig got the Teacher of the Year Award. I was not really surprised because I thought he deserved that. We were all excited about it, but Wig was saying, "Oh no! I don't want that. I don't want to win. I can't win," because he knew he'd be expected to be on the road even more. He didn't make a big deal of it in class, but the year was hectic. We would walk in the classroom and there would be all kinds of cameras and lights. It was an exciting time because a lot of people came into the class talking to us. They would say, "Oh, what is it like to have the Teacher of the Year for your teacher?" I would say, "I don't know; he's just Wig!" But it was sort of amazing. I got interviewed, and my mom's boyfriend who lives in Chicago called her and said, "I just saw Mary Sue on TV!"

# Aunt Arie on Broadway

WIG: Susan Cooper, the author of a wonderful series of adolescent books like *The Grey King* and *The Dark Is Rising*, was asked by Hume Cronyn and Jessica Tandy to put together an hour-long television special called "The Many Faces of Love," which would be readings that Hume and Jessie would do about all different kinds of love: love of a brother for a sister, love of a good friend for another good friend, love of a husband for a wife—all illustrated by passages from literature that expressed each beautifully. Susan was researching for them and finding passages they could weave into this hour-long television show.

The show was almost finished, and Hume called Susan up and said, "We're four minutes short. We need a four-minute piece." Susan had seen *The Foxfire Book*, and had read the chapter about Aunt Arie, and she had been captivated by her. She sent to Hume, along with some other material, a copy of that *Foxfire Book* with the Aunt Arie chapter clipped. Hume and Jessie read that and they got excited.

What eventually happened was that they could not use Aunt Arie in the show, but they kept that *Foxfire Book*, and they kept thinking about a play based on readings from the interviews with the people who were portrayed in it. Susan got in touch with us to say that an idea was beginning to evolve and asked if we had sold the dramatic rights to anyone. We said they were available, and we asked, "What have you got in mind?"

After she told us, we said, "Well, that sounds interesting. If you want to do something like that, what you have to do is come down to Rabun County and present the idea to the students and let them question you until they're satisfied. Then the students will vote as to whether or not to get involved."

One day Hume and Susan arrived. The students didn't have any idea who Hume Cronyn was. They didn't know anything about his reputation. As far as they were concerned, he was just another person in a long line of people trying to use their work. It was summer, and we were all up on the land. I gathered all the students together who we had hired that summer, and the staff members. We all met in one of the offices up there, and the kids grilled Hume and Susan for, I guess, an hour or more. "Are you going to put 'Foxfire' in the title? If you are, we've got to make sure the contents of the play are exactly right because if people connect the play with Foxfire, we want it to be accurate. We don't want something that's going to make fun of mountain people. We want it to be clean." The kids said that if they saw something in the script that needed to come out, they had to be allowed to demand that it be taken out. Slowly but surely they got all the issues out on the table, and then they asked Hume and Susan to leave and walk around outside for a while. The kids shut the door and continued the discussion for an hour or an hour and a half about whether to proceed.

Hume tells the story well in an interview done with him during the filming of the play for a Hallmark Hall of Fame special: "Everybody sat on the floor [in the office] except Susan Cooper and me. We sat in the only two chairs, and they fired questions at us, and then they let us know that we could leave the room while they debated what they wanted to do, and we went out and walked up the side of a hillside pasture and walked around and around, and waited and waited and waited, and finally one of the students came out and said, 'I guess y'all can come back now.'

"And we said, 'How did we do?' and he said, 'Well, we think maybe you're all right.' "

I think the students were intrigued by the possibility of working with Hume and Susan because *Deliverance* had come out by then, and lots of local residents had reacted pretty violently to the way *Deliverance* portrayed mountain people. The kids thought that they might be able to make a contribution, through this play, that would tell a truer side of the mountain story. Besides, they trusted these two.

With the agreement that the students would be able to participate in the process, and could have scenes taken out and changes made if necessary, we proceeded. It really was to the kids' credit that the issue here was not selling the dramatic rights and making a lot of money. I think the students sold the rights for something like $2,500. Profit was not one of the considerations. The big consideration was making a positive contribution to the public image of Appalachia instead of a negative one.

Hume and Susan began to develop a script, and every time they would get a version ready, they would share it with the students for comments. In some of the early versions of the play itself, I would have students there, and sometimes the students would insist that certain pieces be taken out. It was lucky that we had that in the contract because I can remember scenes that really did need to come out. For example, there was one scene where a former student has come back to Rabun Gap to teach, and she has a big argument with one of the community people about land development. The argument takes place in a bar, and the two of them are knocking back shots of bourbon. The kids said, "You got to take that whole thing out of there. There's no way that a schoolteacher—much less a first-year female teacher—would be seen in a bar with somebody drinking. She would be fired."

It was to Hume and Susan's credit that they agreed, and that they all stayed true to the contract. It's an example of the kinds of professionals they are. We're still friends today because of that relationship, which was kept honest from the beginning.

Jessica decided very quickly that she was going to base her character on Aunt Arie. In the play, she's dressed exactly like Aunt Arie, and she tells a number of the stories Aunt Arie told us. In one of the scenes, she's trying to get the eyeballs out of a hog's head. The plot of the play is not Aunt Arie's life, but there are a lot of similarities between Aunt Arie's actual life and the character that Jessica Tandy creates.

The play ran first in the Stratford Festival in Ontario, Canada, and then they went into rewrites. Next, it was done at the Guthrie in Minneapolis for a whole season. I took a group of students up to see it. When we got back, we sat around a table and the students discussed the play piece by piece—the setting, costumes. characterizations and accents, and plot. They taped the discussions and sent those tapes off to Hume and Jessie with suggestions. Then I got plane tickets for the entire staff and sent them up there to see it and to react. Finally, it went on the road, after another year's worth of

Hume Cronyn and Jessica Tandy in a publicity photo for the Guthrie production of *Foxfire*.

rewrites, to various cities like Boston, on its way to Broadway. On opening night in New York, we were given a block of tickets so that we could invite our board members and our editors from Doubleday. Students and staff members were there. It was a popular play; it ran for almost a year. When it had been at the Guthrie in Minneapolis, it got a standing ovation every single night that it ran, and on Broadway, opening night, a standing ovation.

Later, Hallmark decided to turn it into one of their television specials. The play survived virtually intact in that Hallmark version, except that, instead of Keith Carradine, John Denver played the part of the son in the Hallmark special. It was filmed here, and one of the nice things was having people like John Denver around. He did a couple of benefit concerts for people in the area—a kid, for example, who needed a transplant. He asked the Foxfire Boys to start the concert, and then he did a set and they backed him up, and then they did a number of songs together on stage. It was great. A lot of the students who were in the program at that time are in the Hallmark film.

The whole thing was a good experience, I think primarily because the students were involved in it right from the beginning. That, combined with the fact that Susan and Hume and Jessie are just consummate professionals who completely defy yet another stereotype—that of the whining, demanding, self-centered, ego-ridden Hollywood actor. The kids' instinct that they could be trusted paid off in spades. That was another one of those rewarding experiences for me as a teacher. It taught me some lessons I won't soon forget.

ᐱᐱ

BIT CARVER KIMBALL: [Several years before Hume and Susan came to us about doing a play,] we were involved in turning away a movie about the area that [some other people] wanted to film here. The script was really bad. They didn't know their butt from a hole in the ground when it came to mountain ways and people, but they didn't want to change the script.

They went ahead and made the movie someplace else in the mountains, and a group of us went to watch that film in Atlanta, and it was the biggest joke that ever was. If you'd read any of the *Foxfire* articles at all, you'd know that what they were doing was impossible. It was so strange. They had new potatoes coming out of the ground in February and March—all kinds of crazy stuff.

What I'm glad of is that we didn't have anything to do with it. The main reason we didn't was that they'd wanted to use the Foxfire name, and we didn't want the name to be put with something like that. There were kids in our classes who felt really strongly about this. We didn't take no guff off nobody. I would have loved to have a movie at that time, but not the way those people wanted to do it. They couldn't come up to our standards, and so we just said, "Forget it."

ᐱᐱ

VAUGHN ROGERS: After the decision was made to go ahead with the play, I remember doing voice tapes for it. Basically, they'd set up a recorder and have us read certain things so that the actresses and actors could pick up our accents.

My inner feelings on the script were that it pretty much told the story of Rabun County and this part of the country. The early, bigger families had a number of kids, and most of them have moved away and left the parents on the land alone. Then one parent dies and leaves the other, in this case Annie, alone. There's not a lot of interest among the kids in dividing up the land among them because there would be too many disputes between brothers and sisters wanting certain pieces and arguing over them, and none of them want to move back anyway, so what they usually end up doing is selling it and splitting up the money.

[That problem the play presents] is real. That's really what's happening. The play gives the feeling that outsiders are taking over, and you do get that feeling in this area. It's a real problem, but what do you do? I went away to college, and when I graduated I came back, but the only way I could afford to come back was to be involved in my family's business, which is building supply, or in real estate. [Or I could have worked in one of the local factories.] Although I like to maintain things in their natural state, I realize now, being in business, that the only way you can stay in business is for the area to grow.

In the play, I got frustrated with the outsiders, and it angered me that that land developer would bebop in to Annie's house and try to take advantage of her circumstances and fast talk her into selling what had always been hers. [But what was she going to do?]

That's pretty much how I felt after seeing the play.

**WW**

DONNA BRADSHAW SPEED: I remember going to see the premiere of the Foxfire play at the Guthrie Theater. My mama was out of town, and before the trip, I wasn't even sure whether I wanted to go. I was just so scared of flying, and I'd never been out of Clayton before.

But it was fun when we got there. Everybody was so nice, and they treated you like an important person. That was the first time I ever realized how big Foxfire was. That's something that's hard to realize until you get out of school, go places, and see and talk to other people.

I was in drama at the high school at that time, but that big theater just blew my mind! It was a huge, huge place. I was able to meet Jessica Tandy and Hume Cronyn. The play was great. Kim and I watched it twice, and we both just boohooed through the whole performance. Later, Jessica and Hume took us to our first French restaurant.

Another thing we did on that trip was to go to a school and give speeches. We also signed autographs at a bookstore.

It was great to have people make you feel like you were somebody. The people really liked *Foxfire*, too. I loved every bit of it.

There was a world of difference between the play and the Hallmark movie. I liked the movie, but I loved the play.

ᴡ

KIM HAMILTON MCKAY: Donna Bradshaw and I went to the Guthrie Theater. I've still got a blue T-shirt with "The Guthrie" on it.

I remember when they were doing the play and they took out the hog's head. Everybody in the audience started dying laughing.

Donna and I were crying at one point. They made it that realistic. It was at the end when Annie knew she was going to live with her son and was going to sell the farm. At that time, everybody was having bitter feelings about real estate people down in Rabun.

I've still got pictures of where we were in the dressing room with Jessica and Hume. [Jessica and Hume] were real nice. We went out to supper that night, and you could tell that they were a close couple. It tickled you to sit and eat with them. They were equals, and they respected each other because they had been together a long time. One of them wasn't more powerful than the other one, and they were both real polite. I remember Hume smoked a pipe. You know, you wonder if some actors are putting on a front. [Jessica and Hume] weren't.

ᴡ

OHSOON SHROPSHIRE: When they were going to do a production of the play at the Alliance Theater in Atlanta, the producers came up and toured the land and picked out artifacts like a wagon that they wanted to use in the set. I remember Wig asked a bunch of students to help load the things in a truck and get them ready to take down there. [Then a group of us] went to see the Atlanta production. It was real neat, with all the stage props borrowed from Foxfire.

It was a very well-written play. Rural land is so precious these days and there isn't much of it left. I resent the developers that come in. I understand that there is an increased need for housing—houses on the lake, apartments, and condos. But there's so few people left who own the original land that they were born on, and that's something special that you should preserve.

Every big town and every little town has its own personality. You have to maintain the individual heritage of every town. It's like Rabun County. There is only one Mountain City and one Clayton.

You can tear down the condominiums, but you've already ruined the land, and the people that lived there have already moved on and died. Often land is irreplaceable. A lot of people don't think about that. Change is good, but sometimes I don't feel like the price is worth it.

TONIA KELLY: My mom, grandparents, and I went to the play when it was brought to Highlands. [Foxfire had fixed it so that a whole group of Rabun County people could go, including lots of the older people.] It was good. I really liked it. It was sad because it was so true. Aunt Arie's land had to be sold when she died. There weren't any children to take it over.

[When they decided to make the play into a Hallmark movie and film it down here,] I met the producer and took her to show her the Foxfire property.

BROOKS ADAMS: I remember a good bit about the Hallmark movie. I actually got to be in it, so that was fun. I remember when they came and showed us their script. I remember looking over it and suggesting some changes. I remember having correspondence with them back and forth and all that. When it actually came time to make it, I took a day off from school and went up to Highlands to try out for a speaking part. I went with Suzie Nixon and Darren Volk. We got to be in the music scene with John Denver at the Mountain City Play House.

Being able to be behind the scenes and see how everything was put together, and how all the different people worked with each other to get every little thing done to make it all work and look natural, was real interesting.

At a reception for the cast of the Hallmark production of *Foxfire* at the home of Ed and Nancy West, John Denver and the Foxfire Boys became friends.

TOM NIXON: The filming of the Foxfire play was a big experience for us. It's when John Denver was in town, and we got to back him up on stage. We were playing a benefit for a kid who needed a liver transplant, and John had been asked by the promoters to do a guest performance. We had played at a reception for the movie stars, and he had talked about having us play with him, but we didn't think much about it.

The concert was at the stadium at the high school. John Denver wasn't there yet. We played a set to start things off. It was getting late, and a rock-and-roll band from Franklin was playing. Our banjo player, Dean, and his girlfriend were going back to Atlanta, and they had left. Well, here we are, and here comes John Denver in a helicopter from another concert he had had to do that evening. In the time he's getting ready, Dean's down the road, but had to turn around and come back because his girlfriend had left something in somebody's car. Just then there's an announcement on the PA: "Are the Foxfire Boys still here?" It just so happened that Dean was there, thank goodness, and we got to play with John Denver.

We were also asked to play in a barn dance during the movie when Jessica Tandy was dancing. We were on the set and got paid like everybody else. I had to look like I was playing the fiddle, and, of course, we were dressed up and had our makeup on. But it was a real important Foxfire experience to participate in the making of the whole thing.

A film crew also interviewed my great-aunt, Gertrude Keener, about the Foxfire play when they were making the Hallmark program. [She was filmed for a half-hour television special called "The Making of *Foxfire*."] Her situation is very similar to that of Annie in the play. She is a big landowner, and she is a widow, and she has a son who lives down in Florida who sells real estate, except she's not moving. She's not going anywhere. She's held on to her land. She hasn't just sold it all. It means a lot to her to preserve it. It was the home place that she and my grandmother and all of their folks were raised on. She is eighty-six years old, but she'll get right out there and feed her cows and go on all day long. She and her family had to work in the fields, and everything had to be like clockwork from daylight till dark. They couldn't go in and sit down and watch TV and expect to turn on the dishwasher and washing machine. All that was done by hand. It took all day. They grew all of their food, and all the money they made was labor—splitting rails, and selling tan bark. A lot of my uncles made liquor as they got older, just to make money. Values that make a person have self-discipline, honesty, and teamwork are values that Gertrude holds true to, and her religious beliefs are as big a part of her as anything.

▀▀▀▀▀▀▀▀▀▀▀▀▀▀▀▀▀▀▀▀▀▀▀▀▀▀▀▀▀▀▀▀▀▀▀▀▀▀▀▀▀▀▀▀▀▀▀▀▀▀

# On the Road

---

WIG: One of the first times I can remember taking a group of students with me out of town for an overnight trip was when I took Mike Cook, Paul Gillespie, and David Wilson with me to Atlanta where the magazine was going to be given an award by the Georgia Writers' Association. We drove to Atlanta, rented a couple of rooms in a hotel, and received the award the next day. It was then, for the first time, that I realized how important a trip like that could be to students. I had never realized, for example, that a lot of the things I had taken for granted were things that the students had never been exposed to before. One of those students on that trip had never ridden in an elevator, or been in a hotel, or left a wake-up call. It just blew them away.

It also turned out to be valuable because the recognition that they received was brought back home and shared with other students, and there was an energy there that raised the level of intensity a little as they shared their experiences. Most of the students in those kinds of situations had also never given speeches, and you could see the growing confidence as they gave their speeches and answered questions. When they were asked questions, they were really thinking about what they were doing and about the purpose of our work in a way that they hadn't thought about it before. People would come up to students, for example, and ask questions like: "Where do you think this whole operation is going to be in five years?" or "Are you looking at other cultures in the country and appreciating them more because of what you've been doing in Georgia?" It was stuff that students hadn't really thought about seriously. They were coming back, then, and making questions like that part of the class discussions that were going on, and lots of times, those questions would point us toward new activities that we hadn't done before in class.

For all those reasons and more, it became increasingly apparent that some of those kinds of experiences might be just as important, if not more important in some ways, than the specific projects that they were working on in Rabun County. I made up my mind early on, primarily because of that Atlanta trip, that whenever I was asked to come someplace and give a talk about the work, I would insist that I be allowed to bring a student or two along, and that the organization that invited us pay the travel expenses for those students, also. That evolved into a policy where if an organization did not agree to bring students and pay for their transportation, hotel, and meals, then I just wouldn't accept the invitation unless it was a very special kind of situation where the organization just couldn't, and it would be such an intriguing opportunity for students that Foxfire would pay the student expenses—which was the case on a recent trip to Australia. In these cases, we tap a special Foxfire account which is made up of

The high point of any Foxfire presentation comes when students in the program speak about their work. In 1990, for example, Beth Davis and Shay Daniel spoke at the Appalachian Studies Conference, held at Unicoi State Park, near Helen, Georgia.

any honoraria we are paid for presentations above and beyond expenses.

What happens, of course, every single time that we go someplace and give a speech is that although the organization might have been nervous in the beginning about having students there, once they hear the students speak, unanimously the reaction is, "I see now the wisdom of having kids along. Hearing the students talk about the program gives it a kind of authenticity and a reality that just hearing you talk about it doesn't have at all. Having the opportunity to take a couple of students into a separate room and really ask them hard questions about the work is something that for many of the conference participants was the highlight of their visit here. Thanks for educating us to this possibility that we hadn't thought about before. From now on, we're going to see if there aren't some ways that we can involve students in these conference presentations every year." I think it has been a win-win situation for everybody. And by and large, a lot of the really vivid memories that students who have been through the program have are of times when we were on the road together, and things that happened to us while we were gone which, for many of those students, were the first such events in their lives. Those trips help them grow in their awareness of the outside world and other people, in their awareness of the importance of the work we do here in Georgia, and in their own self-confidence and self-esteem. That's become a permanent feature of our program, and I hope it always will be.

ᵂᵂᵂ

MIKE COOK: It was the first real trip we had ever gone on. We went to the Georgia Writers' Association, which was giving us a big award for being one of the best magazines in the Southeast.

The women's club where the meeting was being held was right in the vicinity of Fourteenth and Peachtree. During that time, it was the hippy district in Atlanta. That's where all the strange people with flowers in their hair were. You'd go down there and walk on the streets and you'd see all of these weird people. Then we walked into this building where they were having the GWA meeting and there were all of these older, gray-haired ladies dressed in their formal dresses. It was as if you had walked out of one world into another.

It was a first for a lot of us. Wig remembers David as never having been on an elevator, for example. I didn't know what a wake-up call was.

There was one thing from this trip that I will never forget. I was used to eating chicken with my fingers. But we got into this banquet situation, and there were all of these formal utensils to use. They had chicken, and I was supposed to eat it with my knife and fork. I didn't know how to do that. I was looking around trying to figure out what was going on. I felt real good when finally I got some meat off of the bone. We've made fun of David Wilson a thousand times for this little incident, but David couldn't get any meat off of his chicken. So as not to look stupid, he got the skin off of it and threw it in his mouth. He got that skin over his windpipe, and every time he breathed out it would inflate, and when he breathed in it would collapse, and he couldn't get any air. He finally hit himself on the side of his head and knocked it sideways and swallowed it.

This trip was a big deal because we got the first award *Foxfire* received. To get statewide recognition when you're first getting started was a real nice thing. We just had a good time and I was glad to be in on it.

☗

JAN BROWN BONNER: One of the things I disliked about my experience with Foxfire was public speaking. I hated giving speeches and I still hate it. I loved going on the trips, but I didn't want to do a lot of speaking because I'm not good at it.

One summer when I was in college and working for Foxfire, Mary Garth and I went to Philadelphia alone to speak at a conference on Southern culture. We had been on other trips and were old enough to travel alone, so Wig sent us. You talk about two country people lost in the city. We flew up there—I think it was the first time I had flown, or the second—but the flight didn't bother me. When we got to the airport, we had to take a taxi to an elite hotel downtown because that's where the convention was.

I remember our biggest problem was we couldn't find anything affordable to eat. The restaurant in the hotel was exclusive and expensive. We walked down the street, and I'll never forget this; it's probably the most embarrassing thing that has ever happened to me. Finally, we found this cellar restaurant. We decided we'd try it. We went in and there was not a thing on the menu we could afford.

Nothing. And there was a bar in the middle with a movie star we recognized there.

We had already been seated, and we were so naive we didn't know whether we should get up and walk out or what. Finally the waitress came over, and she was kind enough to make us a salad. We had gone with the intention of getting a good meal and we ended up with this tiny little salad. We ate it, paid, and then we walked out, and it seemed everybody was looking. We learned not to walk into places like that again without knowing where we were going.

▾▾▾

GENELLE BROWN [JAN'S MOTHER]: Wig felt sure that they could travel alone. That gave them more confidence. I know he sent Jan and another girl to Philadelphia once, to a meeting to report on Foxfire. He let them get on the plane, get their hotel, do the whole bit. Here are two kids who had never been anywhere, but he assumed that they could do it and they did it. He just put a lot of confidence in them.

I was worried. I thought, "I don't know whether this child can go to Philadelphia and look after herself for two or three days, find the right hotel, get to the right place for the meeting, and be able to stand before a crowd and give a report on Foxfire." I worried a lot. But they did it.

▾▾▾

CLAUDE RICKMAN: I was twelve and I had always wanted to fly. I had a cow named Cindy, and I sold her and bought a plane ticket and flew to Virginia and back just to fly, but other than that I hadn't traveled much. We used to think it was a big deal to go to Tallulah Falls on Sunday. My sister was in school down there, and we had an old '48 Chevrolet. We'd go down there on Sunday, and I used to think like that was the end of the world. That was only twenty miles away, but of course the roads were a little different then.

The first trip I went on with Wig was to Washington to the National Trust for Historic Preservation. We walked in there, and I had on a pair of blue jeans and a little shirt. There was these ladies decked out with this jewelry and stuff and like three hundred people sitting in the auditorium. It was so fancy I looked out there and I was nervous. That night before, we were out at dinner and I said, "Let's plan what we're going to talk about," and Wig said, "No, you'll do fine. Just tell them what you think and what you feel. There's no pretense." I said, "Well, I don't want any, but let's kind of get a plan of what we're gonna do." We didn't anyway, and Wig got up there and like in two minutes after he started talking to those ladies, we could've got up there and spit on the floor and they would have clapped. I mean he just had them captivated, and I just sat there. All of a sudden it was my turn to talk and it was easy.

After *The Foxfire Book* came out, Paul Gillespie and I were on the "Today" show. Frank McGee, who is dead now, talked to us for a while afterward. You were sitting there and they probably had ten or twelve cameras and you could look at yourself and see yourself ten or twelve times. You could see the front of your head, the back of your head, the side of your head, but it didn't make much difference to me. It was a good experience.

Wig and Paul and I went out to dinner the night after we did the "Today" show and they wouldn't let us go into the restaurant 'cause we didn't have jackets on, which at the time I thought was foolish. Anyway, we rented us some there for a quarter. We looked like a bunch of fools. We'd have been better off if they would've let us in in the first place. Wig was sitting there in his jacket, and it looked awful. It must have been from the thirties. It was a kind of a plaid-looking jacket. I had one on that was so tight that I couldn't bend my arms. Paul had on one that was too big. I mean it was pitiful, and we had to pay a quarter apiece to wear them.

**W**

KAYE CARVER COLLINS: My very first trip I ever went on was to Chicago, Illinois. The school superintendent took us out to this real ritzy restaurant, you know, where you have five forks and four spoons. It was real confusing, and I was going, "Oh, gosh, what do I do now?"

That was the first time I ever gave a speech to a really big group. We went to an elementary school, and they had an auditorium full of people. I hate to give speeches in front of even a small group of people, and I was petrified. I remember I was so nervous my voice was quivering. Then I started talking about Annie Perry, and I looked out into the audience and saw this little white-haired lady. I thought, "Well, that little white-haired lady is just like Annie Perry." From then on, I knew it was going to be all right.

**W**

BIT CARVER KIMBALL: We went to Atlanta a few times on little trips. One time Anita Jenkins and I went down. It was [a Rabun Gap School fund-raising luncheon] in conjunction with the women's guilds, and it was at this big, fancy, ritzy house with tennis courts and a swimming pool in the backyard. We had never seen anything before like that in our lives. They were having a fashion show there, and as I look back, Anita and I should have felt funny in our high-top Converses and jeans and big slouchy shirts. We didn't, though. We just fit right in because we were with Foxfire. We didn't care.

On another trip to Atlanta, we had to give a speech at a church. When it was my turn to speak, I didn't pay any attention to what the audience was listening to. I just talked about how my daddy was a moonshiner and that through *Foxfire* I got to understand that moonshining was a fine art. When I said that in front of all those church people, they just burst out laughing. That was a total shock to me because I didn't expect anybody to laugh at that. I wasn't trying to be funny. After the speech, everybody came up to us and asked for our autographs.

▚▚

LYNN BUTLER: The first Foxfire trip I went on was to Waycross, Georgia, down near the Okefenokee Swamp in south Georgia. We flew down from Toccoa in a little twin-engine Cessna with this pilot whose radio name was Snow White. He had half of a dollar bill, and an old friend down there who lived south of Savannah had the other half, and they were going to put the two together and party. It looked to me like he was more focused on that party that was coming up and not his job, so I was scared to death. I said to myself, "Oh, God, I'm not gonna live through this!"

When I first set out on this trip, I didn't realize that Wig was going to make us speak. I was just going along for the ride! Then, when he got there, he talked to us right before the meeting, and he said, "I want you to talk about your first interview."

"Why do you want us to talk about this?" I said. "I'm not gonna talk to these people. These are teachers; these are adults. What am I gonna say to them?"

When the meeting started and all the teachers were there, however, I did get up, and I stumbled through five minutes of something because I didn't want to disappoint Wig. I probably would not have gone on the trip if I had known I was going to have to speak.

The second trip I made was to Samford College in Alabama. This time, I knew I'd have to speak, and I think I carried myself a little bit better than before. My third trip was to Abilene, Texas, and that was the most fun of all for me because I was able to meet other kids who were working on a project. When we talked, we weren't just talking to the teachers; we were talking to the kids as well. That was certainly a lot more pleasant to me, and it had more impact on me overall. I remember that after we got through with the presentation, the kids had a party, and we went over to somebody's house. That trip was my first time west of the Mississippi, and before that I'd thought everyone in Texas wore cowboy boots and drove big cars, and I was impressed to find out they were just normal folks.

⋎⋎⋎

JOHNNY SCRUGGS: Wig, Clay Smith, and I went to Monterey, California, to speak at an Association of Experiential Education Conference. I'd never seen the ocean. It was my first commercial airline flight. We gave a speech to a group of teachers on Foxfire, basically our experience from the time we left Atlanta, and our observations of the conference itself. We told them what went on at the different seminars that we had been to there. It was a great trip. To be seventeen years old and get to go to California was a great experience.

We went on Delta Airlines on a big L-1011. I picked up the *Sky* magazine, and there was an article in there about Foxfire with pictures and everything. Wig hadn't even seen it yet. Here it was my first commercial flight, and they had an article about us in the airline's magazine.

It's ironic that we went to Monterey, California, because three years later I was stationed there in the service. I was telling Wig the other day that there sure were a lot of coincidences on that trip.

⋎⋎⋎

JOHN SINGLETON: I went to a national student journalism conference in St. Louis with Darrell Edwards to accept a national award for *Foxfire*. We were selected by the students to go, and we went by ourselves. That was my most memorable speech probably because it was my worst. The fellow that got up to introduce us gave a twenty-five-minute speech. It looked as if he had read my notes. He just covered everything I intended to say. I intended to talk about Wig and how he started the program, and his interaction with the students, and how we had been asked to take on adult roles. I just listened to him and I said, "Oh no!" because he just continually said everything I was going to say. When he got through, in essence he had taken care of all of my speech. I had to speak, since someone had to say something, so I just went up and said, "Thank you," and that we appreciated it, and that was that. I didn't know what else to do.

When I looked out in the audience, there were at least a thousand faces out there. Many of them were students just like myself. Many of them were there to attend workshops. I think we were in the unique position of being some of the only students there actually conducting a workshop. [That was separate from the speech.] You don't have time to go into depth, so we just talked about the little things, like setting up a recorder, that you can cover in a workshop. We answered their questions more than anything. Everyone was curious about how high school students put out a book, so generally we answered questions about that.

But it was fun to see people your own age and be telling them things from the point of view of a teacher, yet you are also a student like them. A lot of times as students we're treated as students. Then there are situations where even adults are looking at you as an adult to teach them. I think it really puts you in a different shoe when you have responsibility like that.

In some ways, that was a bad trip. The money we had been sent with wasn't enough to pay the bill. As Darrell was trying to check out, I was up in the room and the phone rang, and I answered it. It was Darrell, and his voice was really quivering, and he said, "John, they're not going to let us leave!" He said that until we gave them the money for the room they wouldn't let us check out. I couldn't get in touch with the people who were looking after us. It was just Darrell and me. No one from the staff had gone with us. We were out of money.

But it worked itself out when I called Foxfire. I'll never forget; Margie Bennett answered the phone, and when I told her the story, she just started laughing. We were pretty nervous, but that sort of broke the ice!

ᴡᴧᴧ

ROSANNE CHASTAIN WEBB: When *Foxfire 6* was published, Carol Rogers and I got to go to New York to be on the "Today" show. Carol took the cover photograph for the hardcover edition, and I was the first runner-up. That's why we were there. She was the first student to ever take the cover photograph for one of the Foxfire books.

The night before, Doubleday took us to Rockefeller Center where NBC is, and we sat in this lady's office that was being renovated. Her desk was like in this closet, and she sat on the floor and she said, "Okay, this is what Tom Brokaw's probably going to ask you tomorrow," and then she gets right in our faces and starts shooting questions at us real hard. "What do you think about so and so?" Carol and I are just sitting there with our mouths open, and then she crosses her arms and says to Wig, "If they're going to do this tomorrow, they can't go on. You'll have to go by yourself."

Wig said, "Well, if they don't go, I don't go."

"Well," she said, "they can't act like this tomorrow. They have to be able to answer these questions." And Carol and I kind of looked at each other. Wig told us afterward, "You are going to have to think about these questions, you know, and be prepared to answer them, but Brokaw's going to be much smoother and more tactful than that."

[We thought about the questions that night at the hotel,] and the next morning I was so scared. Then they took us into the makeup room and did our makeup. We were sitting in there and we kept hearing this commotion out in the hall, and Carol Rogers went and stuck her head out the door, and Steve Martin was out in the hall posing for pictures with the crew. She waved at him, and he waved back. I said, "What are you doing?" She turned like real red in the face, and she couldn't talk.

She said, "Come here," and I went and stuck my head out the door and there he was. He's a little bitty short guy. It seems like he's real tall, but I guess that's just Hollywood magic. But he seems real sweet. He smiled at us and waved.

[Then they called us in and Brokaw did the interview. Carol's picture was blown up behind us as a background, and we had some of the toys with us that are featured in the book, and we showed how they worked.] I don't really remember all he asked us, but it must have gone okay. The thing I remember the most is the very last comment. He kind of sprang it on us. It was, "Well, now, when you guys go to college, your professors are going to be real impressed because you've already got all this experience." We never thought about that before, so we kind of looked at each other and sat there and went "Dahhh." There was like this silence where he's waiting for a response, and we just sort of laughed, didn't know what to say. That was kind of uncomfortable.

Trips like that were neat, though, because we always did neat stuff. Like in New York, we went to see the Broadway show *The Elephant Man*, starring David Bowie. A few months after that, the movie *The Elephant Man* came out, and people were like, "You want to go see the movie?"

"Nah. I saw the Broadway show."

▚▚

VAUGHN ROGERS: One time Darryl Garland and I went to Philadelphia. That was neat. We got to see the historic area of Philadelphia. They had a lot of museums and stuff there. We stayed in a Williamsburg-type bed-and-breakfast place. It was like walking into somebody's house. You went up the steps and down the hall, and Darryl and I had one bedroom, and Wig had another bedroom. That was pretty neat. I've still got brochures on it on my desk at home. That was my first speech, and there were over five hundred English teachers. I was so nervous. I remember standing behind the podium with my knees shaking. Wig said, "Draw up an outline of things you want to talk about—just key points that will help you remember," and every speech I've done since then, that's how I've done it.

▚▚

WESLEY TAYLOR: Traveling was one of the favorite things we did. Man, I traveled all over the place. I went to New York twice, Washington, D.C., three times, went to St. Louis, Lexington, Cincinnati, Memphis. I was not well traveled before—I had been out West one time when I was twelve—but to get to go to New York and hobnob around was just great. We did some really interesting things that were fun and they were learning experiences that were probably the most valuable things I remember.

When you travel, there's a lot of things you don't know until you do it: how to find the airport and get around, how to get your tickets and get your boarding passes, and actually board a plane, and things like that. When you get to the hotel, you learn how to tip and what to tip for. And a lot of the times when you go on a trip, they will joke you about your accent. Me being from Rabun County, when I would go to Washington or New York, they would just love to hear me talk. That was neat.

One of the most memorable times was when we went to New York just before *Foxfire 5* came out. We stayed at the Biltmore Hotel. You remember in *The Great Gatsby* where they meet under the clock at the Biltmore? Well, that's where we were. Bill Strachan, our editor, wanted me to see New York at night, so we went down to the World Trade Towers where there was a restaurant on top called the Windows on the World. Wig had on corduroy jeans, and I had on denim jeans, and we got in the elevator and rode all the way to the top to the restaurant and the guy says, "You can't come in, you don't meet the dress code."

So we had to go back down the elevator, get a taxi, and drive about thirty blocks back across Manhattan to Bill's house. He happened to wear the same size pants I did, so I borrowed a pair of his, and we went back across town, back up the elevator to the one hundred and seventh floor to the restaurant. It was a perfectly clear night, and you could see fireworks going off and everything. It was beautiful. It was another one of those weird adventures.

**W**

DONNA BRADSHAW SPEED: I went to Canada with some other Foxfire students. They sent us there on an exchange, and that was a great experience, even though I didn't want to go at first.

In this program, we had it arranged so that first the students from Canada would come and stay with our families, and then people in Foxfire would go and stay with their families. I remember one student came to stay with me. Her name was Kim Bitty. Then it was our turn to go up, but I wasn't planning to go.

But then my mom found out they were sending Rabun County students away, so she called Wig to see if I could go. I called Kim, the girl who'd stayed with me, to see if I could stay with her, and this plan worked out. It was an experience I'll never forget.

It was a two-week stay, and I remember that at first I was really homesick. They set the seven of us kids out by ourselves at the airport because, of course, one of Foxfire's goals is to get you to learn how to do everything yourself. We'd never done anything like that before. We had to get on the plane, and once we got to Canada, we had to rent a van to take us for two more hours to get where we were going. We were like lost puppies until we got there and found the people.

We went to school where our hosts went, and we discovered that in some ways their schools were really different from our schools here. They didn't paddle people; they were shocked when we told them about being paddled. They had computers in every classroom, and they had thirteen years of school instead of twelve. The students were allowed to get up any time in the middle of class and just leave. They didn't have to have an excuse or anything. I'd like that myself. Of course, I'd probably never graduate because I would have gotten up and left a lot.

But it wasn't just school. *Everything* about Canada was really different. We did lots of fun things. We were able to go cross-country skiing; I'd never done that before. That was real fun. The people talked funny, and of course they all liked the way we talked. You'd be having a conversation with somebody, and then you'd turn around and find everybody staring at you. You'd think, "Oh no, what did I do?" but they were just wanting to listen to you talk.

▼▼▼

DEAN ENGLISH: One time I went on a trip with Wig out to San Diego. It was a good trip. The people really care when you go on these trips. Usually you do something like that, and they treat you like a king.

On that trip to San Diego, I had an expensive Stelling banjo with me. The guy who made my banjo and his shop was out there. While I was out there, I thought I could let him adjust it. After we gave our speeches, some of the teachers at the conference offered to drive me out to his shop. He met me there, showed me around the workshop, took my banjo apart and cleaned it and adjusted it, and then we spent a couple of hours visiting and playing music. He had the serial numbers for every banjo he'd ever made, and he told me the history of my banjo.

On the way back, we got to the airport and started to get on the plane and the man at the desk said we'd have to check the banjo— that we couldn't carry it on. Well, we had carried it on the plane *to* California and no one said anything. Wig explained that, and told the guy that it had just been taken apart and tuned and all, but he wouldn't budge. Well, Wig was like a father, you know, and he pitched a fit. The guy went and got his supervisor, and *that* guy finally said the only way we could take it on the plane was to buy a ticket for it and strap it in a seat. So Wig ended up buying a whole plane ticket just for my banjo. There was no way he was going to let them throw it into that baggage compartment under the plane. It rode all the way back strapped in the seat beside me with a seatbelt.

The whole thing was real fun. I can't think of anything we've done with Foxfire that was real dull. We've always had a good time.

▼▲▼

RONNIE WELCH: I went off on a couple of trips, and that really got me fired up. I was ready to go, then. They were good for me. They taught me a lot.

None of my family knew what in the world to think about them. I liked to never got them convinced to let me go. They just never had thought of me going off as young as I was. It took just as long for them to understand what Foxfire was about as it did me. They was real skeptical about me going, but after I made one or two trips, they were convinced that it was a good thing.

What it amounted to was that everybody had heard about us over the country, and they wanted to hear more about how it worked. What we did in school was so much different, and I guess what a lot of people felt was that it was a way to get the stuff across in school that you would normally learn, but in a much better and freewheeling way. You know, you'd be out with normal people teaching you things that they'd learned over the years—traditions, folklore—and then you'd go back in the classroom and put it into book form; and by doing that, you would learn everything that you would have learned in your grammar class, and more. That's what everybody had heard about, and lots of them wanted to try and get something like that started because of the fact that it was teaching kids in a real different, good way.

And after we'd get there, we'd help teachers, and I didn't even realize exactly what I was doing then. Like I said, I still thought it was all in fun, you know? It was just normal. But I was getting used to being around different people and being able to talk to them and tell them about it because I enjoyed telling them about it. I thought it was all right. As I got on up a little bit older, I really started to understand and put everything together.

One of my biggest and favorite trips was the last one. We went to

Togiak, Alaska. Wig had a friend up there who was a teacher, and we stayed in her house. It was a long flight up there and back. We was give out.

Going into Togiak, we flew in a chartered plane—little bitty twin-engine white and blue airplane. It had just enough room up in the cockpit for two people, and barely enough room in the back for two people, and then your luggage behind the seat. That's all it was. I got up there in front with the pilot, and Wig got in back. Partway there, the pilot told me to put my hand on the wheel. I put my hand on there and he turned it loose, and there I was flying the damn thing!

We flew on to Togiak. Now me and Wig neither were expecting this. We was looking out the windows, and we kept looking for the runway. Seen houses lined up on this side of a gravel road, houses lined up on that side of the road. We was coming down in between them! Well, I'd been used to landing on pavement, you know? I'd been on two or three trips before with Wig just landing in a normal airport. Wig was looking out one side and I was looking out the other. The closer we got, the more I kept looking at him, and he kept on looking out. Finally, his eyes met mine and we was both about that big around! We started hitting this gravel and stuff, and it was rough, you know,

In Togiak, Alaska, Ronnie Welch took this photo of a plane taking off from the main street of the town—the only landing strip.

Every morning, Ronnie and his new friends would go out together to the gill nets and collect the salmon they had caught.

and I was scared to death, and Wig was wondering, too. Hell, the pilot didn't warn us nor nothing. We landed right on the damn main street of Togiak! We were both flipping out. We got out, and the pilot turned around and took off, and there we were, standing on this gravel road which was the only street in town.

Had a real good time while I was there. I learned how to smoke salmon, which wasn't part of what we were actually there for, but. . . . I stayed up twenty-four hours a day. I ain't no kidding. Wig couldn't hardly get me to go to bed. It was daylight almost twenty-four hours a day.

This teacher we were staying with lived right at the back of the school. She and some of the other teachers, of course, done more than just teach there for a living. In the summer, when we were there, they got salmon. And I'd get up at four o'clock in the morning with them, and we'd go out in this little john boat and check the nets—get in all the salmon. Course they'd still be alive, and my job was to hit them in the head and knock them out. We'd get them back, and they sold them down in a little market. So from about four till six-fifteen, I guess, we'd be salmon fishing.

Come back and have to take a shower and get ready to go over to the classroom to work with the teachers and some of the kids. On

most trips, like at a conference, we'd give a speech for like an hour or
an hour and a half, and we never would really get into fine detail and
lay it out and show them step by step how it was done. [There were
too many people and not enough time.] But on this one, we went over
everything step by step with them, a lot closer than we did with other
people. And since we was working with the kids, too, they got just as
much information as the teacher did.

We'd stay in the classroom all day, and then we'd go eat, and Wig
and some of the teachers would stay there and talk, but I would just
go off and do my own thing. Hell, I wasn't all that big, but I knew my
way around—didn't take me very long. And me and the kids would
stay up during the night and ride bikes, and I'd go around and look
at all the things that was in the shacks and old buildings or whatnot.
This was things that I hadn't never seen before. It was real interesting, and I learned a lot about Alaska and Alaskan people. Like some
of the traditions that we have here, like making liquor, and rooster
fighting, making quilts, making soap, making shingles to go on top
of your house. Up there they have the same thing, except different. I
mean, they put shingles on their houses different. They fix fish
completely different than we do. It's just the same thing, except a
different perspective of it all.

It took some time to help the students understand about how to
go about getting a *Foxfire* started, but one day after we got off, three
of the kids that was there—and this wasn't planned or nothing—
three of the kids that was there was still really interested with what
went on during the day, and we went out and talked to their daddy
that evening. And he just naturally got off on stories because I wasn't
familiar with it up there. He was telling me his old way of salmon
fishing, and he showed me a different way to smoke salmon than the
other people did, you know, and just things like that. And it hit me
all of a sudden. We was sitting there and he was telling it, and it just
hit me. I said, "Right here is all it is!" They was looking at Foxfire
completely different than how it actually was. They was looking at it
as being in a classroom, and they still wasn't getting the point after
we'd been up there and been trying to teach them about it. But that
right there let them know what it was all about.

After I took those kids out that evening—I say those kids now; I
was one of those kids then—and that took ahold of them, why, they
went back and it was much easier from that point on because they
had kinda experienced what I had been doing back here in Rabun

County. The teachers even picked up on it more because it was all natural. It just all come into play. I guess that's when it really paid off. That's what we were after. We got accomplished what we went up there for. Everybody that we talked to while we was up there liked us. I feel like they got everything they were after, and I feel like we got accomplished what we were after. And now I have another check on my agenda—something I've done, something I'll always remember.

The first time I ever rode a locomotive was when I was with Foxfire. I rode from Toccoa, Georgia, to Washington, D.C., and from Washington, D.C., on up to New York on the *Southern Crescent*. That was interesting. I slept on the train on the way up there. That was sure enough a ride. *Foxfire 5*, in the introduction, Wig wrote about it— about how overwhelmed I was by it, and amazed. Said I put him in mind of himself back whenever he was a kid. That right there meant a whole lot to me. It makes you feel pretty good.

The train was about two and a half hours late. Me and Wig was standing out there on the concrete pad about to give up hope. We'd done let the other trains that went by run over so many pennies we was tired of that. He was on one side of the railroad track, and I was on the other side, walking the track to see who could walk the furtherest when it finally got there.

Well, I just had to see in that locomotive. Wig went on and got on the train, and I run on up to the front. Actually, Wig was worried about me. He always was whenever he took us off on a trip, but me, I was wide open, ready to see what was going on. I hopped up in the engine, and they were real nice, and I was scared 'cause I hadn't never been on one. But Wig had showed me which car he was going to be in, and I was interested to see what was going on, and I got right up there in the middle of them. Then I went back where Wig was.

We would pull into each station and slow down as we were going through there. If there was anybody, we'd stop and pick them up, but by the time we got there I guess a lot of people had done give up hope and gone. It was real neat, though, going down the track and seeing all the lights and wondering about this and that. I must of asked Wig a hundred thousand questions.

When we went to pulling into New York, there was just trains and train tracks going everywhere. I didn't know what to think about it. I thought it was a big mess, and that's what most cities are—everything crisscrossing.

In New York, we had to go over some of the paperwork and whatnot of making the *Foxfire 5* book with Bill Strachan at Doubleday. He showed me how they went about making the determination of whether the book would go, and what changes needed to be made. At the time, I really didn't understand a whole lot of that, but now I do. You see, it's a lot of those things that at the time I really didn't put into perspective until later.

You think about it, most kids don't get to do things like that at my age. One thing is getting the parents' consent to let you go. Once you get out there and make one safe trip, they feel pretty confident that you're in good hands. Many people, even the kids at school, were amazed at how come I got to go here or there, and they wanted to get involved with Foxfire. Then they found out, like I did, it was different, it was fun, it was interesting; you didn't have to do the same old thing every day.

I guess that's what made it so important and new for teachers and people all over the United States to want to get to learn about it. It's just a hell of an idea.

ᴡᴡ

KYLE CONWAY: Tom Nixon and I went to Los Angeles with Wig and did a talk before a group of California teachers. They were pretty impressed. Tom had never spoken before a large audience and BOOM, we stuck him up in front of seven hundred people. He did great. He talked about the music program, and I talked more about the classroom.

Joseph Fowler and I went to North Carolina and did another workshop and spoke to a group of teachers. A couple of those pictures from that got into Wig's book.

When I look back it's like, "Wow! I really did all this stuff in high school." It all gets kinda blurry. I guess when you're in the program, you're just going all the time. You lose track of what you've done and where you've been.

ᴡᴡ

SIDNEY DENNIS: My first trip was to speak to professors and students at Vanderbilt, which is a real prestigious university. We went to a country club to give the talk.

I remember I had been aggravating Wig, saying, "Take me on a trip."

Joseph Fowler and Kyle Conway answered questions like the professionals they were at a teachers' workshop in North Carolina.

He told me, "Well, if you go on a trip, you'll have to do an outline and give a speech."

I hadn't done anything like that, and there were two or three hundred people there! So I had to just start talking. It didn't really bother me. I'd thought I'd be scared to death, but I wasn't, and then they gave me a standing ovation at the end. They told me I'd be a success. They were really polite; I guess they liked some of my stories.

A funny thing happened on the way back. Wig and I were coming back on a country road, and he wanted to go see these people on the back side of Roane Mountain who believed there were witches. I saw this humongous hornet's nest on the side of the road, and I said, "Let's stop."

I chopped off the tree limb it was on in this man's pasture and got it and put it in the back seat of the car. It was the fall of the year and cold, and twenty miles later up the road, with the heat on in the car, we saw two hornets come out of the nest. One of them buzzed right over Wig's head!

Wig started ranting and raving. He was really upset! He said, "You better get that thing out of this car!" He almost ran off the road trying to get them off his head. I guess it got so warm in that car that the hornets were regaining consciousness. We were lucky: we didn't get stung.

It seems funny now, but when I look back on the incident, I realize that it wasn't funny or cute to him. It also wasn't really so funny to me at the time because I wanted to keep the hornet's nest, and he made me throw it out. The really funny thing is that as we were leaving, the car behind us stopped and the people behind us picked it up!

It was interesting to meet those people who believed in witches. They had symbols on their barns to keep the witches away, and I thought that was very intriguing. I hadn't known before that there were any people who still believed in witches.

Giving speeches for Foxfire was a real inspiration for me. When people give you a standing ovation, and when a professor, a real professional, comes up to you and tells you you'll become something in life, and he doesn't even know you're a tenth-grader, that really means something.

▓

AL EDWARDS: I did a bunch [of trips and speeches]. The first one, Wig and I went to Ramah, New Mexico, to work with a magazine there named *Tsa Àszí* that had gotten started back in the 1970s. Actually, Mike Cook had gone out there and spent the summer to give them a summer-long workshop on layout, interviews, photography, and the whole picture. So, he spent the summer getting the thing started. They continued along for a couple of years and then they ran into some financial difficulties. They shut down, and then that year they got some money and they began to grow, so Wig and I went out there and gave them a couple-day workshop, so we could get them fixed up again. They had a new teacher, so he wasn't familiar with what was going on. He needed to be introduced.

One summer I worked, Steve West and I went with Wig to Vermont to the Bread Loaf School of English. Wig taught a class with Dixie Goswami. Steve and I gave a talk in the Barn one night to the students and faculty, and then we went to New York after that. That was my first time in New York City. That was really neat because we got to be there for the reopening of the Statue of Liberty on July 4. We got to see the big fireworks and all that went on that weekend. The most intimidating audience [was when] I went to Hilton Head with Wig one summer to speak before the Georgia Association of Education Leaders. It was over seven hundred school principals and administrators, and our principal was there.

WW

OhSoon Shropshire: *Sometimes a Shining Moment* is a good book, and it has a lot of good points. I remember I went down to Sarasota, Florida, when the book came out with Paul Gillespie and Wig. We flew down there and did a conference for high-schoolers and a bunch of teachers who said, "I read your book and oh, it is just wonderful," and da da da.

Wig just became this monumental example that everyone wanted to be. It was pretty overwhelming to be with someone who got all that attention. I would have to answer to the teachers, because "You're his students and you should be perfect." I was like, "Wait a minute!"

I took a lot of trips. I took a trip to New York, and we had to do something with Doubleday. That was the first time I had ever been to New York City. Wig had to go to this interview with this bunch of men. It was in this men's club. He didn't know if we could get in. He had on a dress coat and we were just dressed in sweats and jeans. So, we just waited outside the door of this club for I don't know how long. Wig eventually snuck us in the back way. We felt really uncomfortable. Don't ever go to a men's club!

WW

Brooks Adams: I remember one time, this was with David Volk and Carol Chuplacheck, when we went to Atlanta to work on our circuit-riding preacher article. We were making a photocopy of a rare journal of a preacher who had worked in our part of the mountains in the 1800s. The Emory University Library owns it. We went down there and Wig had some speech to give, so of course, we went with him, and it was in this big hotel—a real nice, fancy, rich kind of place. We were touching the walls and everything. We realized what we were doing and that we were looking kind of silly, so we decided that from then on we had to look straight ahead. Don't touch the walls and don't look up. After that, every place we'd go, we'd just have to say that to ourselves. "You don't look up and you don't touch the walls." That was our culture shock, I guess.

Most of my trips were road trips. The time I got to fly, I flew to Washington, D.C., with Wig. Stanley Beasley and I went. While we were there we got to give a couple of talks. One of them was a really big crowd that we were talking to. Stanley and I worked together and wrote up a speech that we could give together. It was about fifteen to twenty minutes long with both of us. We made an outline of the things that each of us had done so that we could talk about the magazine class together. That worked really well. It was his first speech, so that helped him through his first speech. It was like to five hundred people, or something like that, so he got broke in right.

Then we went to St. Mary's College in Maryland. We had to make a two- or three-hour drive to the college and got to talk to some students, faculty, and the staff there. This time, Stanley and I decided to give our speeches separately. You see, I'd already given speeches, and I'd already gone through all that nervousness and everything, but Wig and I decided to let him do it himself this time. He got up there and he gave a darn good speech.

Another thing I remember about that trip is that they fed us like VIPs at this place. We had china and everything. It was one of those banquets you go to and they'll serve you and you can't really tell what it is, but it tastes good!

▟▙▟

STANLEY BEASLEY: I've got some real good memories [from my trips with Foxfire]. I got to go to Washington, D.C., twice with Wig. I got to go to New York to help them set up the Finger Lakes Teachers' Network. We met with the chairman of the Gannett Foundation to try to get some money for it. I really didn't know what Gannett meant at the time, but they own a bunch of television stations and newspapers. I didn't know how big of a thing it was. We were sitting in the conference room on about the top floor I guess it was. Rob Collier, the head of the foundation, asked us what we wanted [to drink]. I just said, "A Coke," and that guy had a Coke with me. It was just kind of fun to be there. I was all excited.

Later on in that trip we flew to Syracuse. That's the first time I got to ride on a small plane. [There were only] fifteen other people, and you could see the two pilots and everything they were doing. The plane would be going up and down and it was woozing your stomach.

I always wanted to be a pilot in an airplane [but that flight] made me think twice.

I think the first big speech I gave by myself was when me and Brooks Adams flew to Washington with Wig to speak at St. Mary's College. It is in Maryland, just outside Washington, D.C. [We made that speech for an audience of something] like five hundred people from the college. I was nervous and everything, but the people enjoyed it.

On all the trips, we gave speeches, and it felt real good being on the other end of the gun. Instead of teachers teaching you, you got to show them some things and [talk about] what it meant to you and things like that. I really enjoyed that. I think [the teachers] were most surprised to see that we could work on every little aspect like taking our own pictures and developing them, and just coming up with a whole article. They probably now appreciate that students can do more than teachers think they can.

vvv

MARY SUE RAAF: I went to Athens two or three times. Once I went with Julie Hayman and Tara Webster and we had the best time. That was my first speech, actually. [The audience] was all English teachers. I was very nervous, but that was a good [speech]. Werner Rogers, the state superintendent of schools was there, and he was impressed, and Wig was in a very good mood. We were really happy about that.

I remember, afterward, we were sitting outside and everybody wanted us to sign Wig's book, and we were like, "Why do you want our signature?" [They said,] "You're so wonderful—Foxfire students." We said, "Oh, okay."

David Volk, Kelli Marcus, and I went to a teachers' workshop [in Aspen sponsored by the Rural Education Association], and there were some other [presenters] too. We listened to them, and then we had our workshops. We got out all the interviews that we had. David got out his huge big article on land development, and Kelli and I got out our little ones, and we showed everybody what we had done along the way and explained the steps.

I always liked doing the workshops better than the speeches. I thought the workshops were more fun because there were less people and you could really get into what we did in the classroom. You could really explain it to them. I loved it.

That was the first time I ever realized how smart Wig was. I got an idea of how other people see him. Teachers would always call him Dr. Wigginton. They were always like, "Oh, he's so intelligent," and I just always saw him as Wig and never thought about it. He told a story to them about how a teacher had written a proposal to get funding to paint a map of her county on a cement slab on the school's playground, and had shown east, west, north, and south to get her fourth-grade kids to learn where they lived and about direction, and they were like, "Wow, what a good idea, you know." Wig showed them what she *could* have done, and suddenly it seemed like a terrible idea. She should have had the kids write up the proposal, gotten the kids to go out there and do the painting, and find which direction is which. She could have had the kids involved in it all the way from the start, and he was going on and on. His brain was working a mile a minute and that was the first idea I had of how smart he was.

It was neat because the teachers were in the same hotel that we were, so we got to talk to them a lot. We met this wonderful drama teacher, and Kelli and I were really excited about that because we were in drama. She was telling us about all these plays that her school had put on and she actually got our address and sent us a script so we could look at their play.

It always amazed me that I hadn't realized how far out into the country Foxfire had reached. I remember one year I went to Chicago for Christmas, and I went in a bookstore and there were the Foxfire books, and I was going, "Oh, my gosh!" I remember just being so impressed that everybody knew about it.

▀▀▀

BETH LOVELL: I went to Atlanta with George several times to play music and to give speeches. I gave a speech to the Atlanta Historical Society about doing radio course guides and making radio shows.

The first talk I gave, we were going down to the Trust Company Bank to give a concert, and later that afternoon we were going to the Georgia State class that Wig teaches. George didn't tell me I was going to have to talk to them. I just thought I was going to play music and that's it.

On the way to Georgia State, George looked in his rearview mirror and said, "Beth?" And I said, "What?" And he said, "You know you're going to have to give a speech down here. You're going to have to talk to these people about your Foxfire I class."

"No, man. Didn't know nothing about that."

"Yeah. Wig asked me if I would get you to talk to them"—because that was the time I was in Foxfire I and was going through the process. I said, "No way. You didn't tell me this. No, man. I'm not going to do this. You can't make me do it."

I was opposed. I wasn't a very outspoken person when I was in high school. I stayed in the background and barely ever said anything so that was going to about kill me.

I was determined to get them back for making me do a speech. I had made me some notes on the back of a McDonald's french fries carton, and I talked to the class about what all we were doing at that time in Foxfire I, and then I showed them the chart we had made in our class with Wig on the first day of school that was a list of the characteristics of a good teacher. We kept that posted on our classroom wall, but we had it with us to show it to the Georgia State teachers. I remember on that list—I think it was rule number three—was: "Teachers will not embarrass their students." I looked at George and Wig—straight in the eye—and I said, "Teachers will not embarrass their students." I thought Hilton was going to fall down on the floor laughing so hard. I got them back for making me give that speech!

# Transplanting Foxfire

WIG: Our involvement with IDEAS is important in this whole story because it's through them that we really began to connect with other teachers in a meaningful way. Before the first Foxfire book came out, I was trying to put together a group of respected authorities for our National Advisory Board. One of the people I saw was Sam Stanley, who worked with the Center for the Study of Man at the Smithsonian's Museum of Natural History. He agreed to be on the board, and after I left, he was visited by Brian Beun and Ann Vick from IDEAS—Institutional Development and Economic Affairs Service. They were looking for advice on ways to do something meaningful with other cultures in the way of education and/or community economic development. Sam said that it sounded like there was a close fit between our two organizations and that we might have some things to talk about. He urged them to call me.

At our first meeting, they saw right away that something like a *Foxfire* magazine might be a perfect marriage for both the educational skills, because of what it would teach students, and economic development, because a magazine and its related spinoff products can become a real business.

The end result was a grant to IDEAS from the Ford Foundation to start twelve magazines like *Foxfire* in twelve culturally unique and/or distinctive communities around the country to test the whole idea of whether or not a magazine like *Foxfire* could survive and prosper in places other than where it had started. The money from the Ford Foundation enabled them to send IDEAS staff members directly to potential communities that might want to do this, and paid for some of their staff costs, printing of the first issues that they put together, and student salaries for kids who worked on those first magazines during the summer. IDEAS found the first six magazine groups. The grant then paid to have students and faculty members from those sites come to Rabun County for training.

The Foxfire students were involved in running the training sessions to teach kids how to do interviews, make videotapes, transcribe and edit, do layout—basically they took the participants from the beginning to the end of the process. After that, each group represented there could extend an invitation to a Foxfire student to come back with them to spend the rest of the summer and work with a group of students to put a pilot issue together. Using that procedure, Jan Brown, Mike Cook, Gary Warfield, and folks like that were selected. Jan was in Montana, for example, working on an Indian reservation, Mike was out in the Southwest working with Navaho Indians, and Gary Warfield went to Philadelphia, Mississippi, to work with the Choctaw Indians. A number of those magazines continued for years.

As a result of that first workshop, each of the six groups put out an issue, so there was a second workshop here for six more groups who could also invite a student to spend a summer with them if they wanted to.

Thus, for the first time we had students, by themselves, away from Rabun for two months at a time, working as professionals, and proving we could trust students with that kind of responsibility. IDEAS even sent some of the kids to foreign countries like Haiti. Some of the most successful magazines are still going today. *Salt,* for example, is still being published today, eighteen years later. Most didn't survive more than six or eight years, but at least they proved that students could train other students successfully and that a *Foxfire*-type magazine could transfer successfully to other environments. And there weren't any parents whose children were invited to spend a summer away who wouldn't let them. It was really gratifying to see all the trust that had already been built up in the community at a time when we were still awfully young and green.

Then IDEAS began to put together training materials so that people who couldn't come here for a workshop could still get the information they needed to start something similar. They got me to write a small book for teachers called *Moments.* They also got Pam Wood from *Salt* to write a book called *You and Aunt Arie,* and they got

At an IDEAS-sponsored workshop in Rabun County, students from Haiti and the Virgin Islands watched Foxfire student Stan Echols conduct an interview with blacksmith John Conley.

some filmmakers to come down and make a movie called *Foxfire*, which is still being distributed by McGraw-Hill Educational Films. With all these materials, people who couldn't get to the workshops could learn some of the skills they needed to start something similar on their own.

IDEAS also began a newsletter called *Exchange*, and every time a new magazine was started, they would feature the magazine in the newsletter, along with special features like how to copyright, how to set up archives, and news from ongoing projects.

That connection with IDEAS continued until funding ran out and the point had been made. And it really *was* made. By that time, in the late seventies, there were even a half dozen projects in Alaska. We learned some crucial lessons through that grant, and we got stretched as an organization in some critical ways. And Ann Vick and I are still in touch with each other. She's still involved in education with diverse cultures, along with her husband, through their organization, the Education and Resources Group, based in Boston.

Those were fruitful, exciting, important years for all of us.

᠁᠁

JAN BROWN BONNER: During the summer of 1972, I went to the Flathead Indian Reservation in Ronan, Montana, and spent eight or nine weeks helping to start a magazine called *Dovetail*.

As best I remember, that spring Wig detailed to my parents and me his plan to send several representatives from Foxfire to places throughout the United States. The idea was very appealing. My parents agreed it would be a good learning experience, and so it was set.

I lived that summer with a high school teacher, Lorenza Normandeau, one of the advisers to the new magazine. I was given a small furnished attic room, and I was within walking distance of the school where we worked. Mrs. Normandeau had some unexpected surgery, so she was away part of the time, but I made friends with the high school students—especially the ones who had been at the Rabun County workshop—as well as others closer to my age. Although our cultural backgrounds were very different, the teenagers there were much like me.

My job that summer was as a student adviser; I explained what I knew about photography, how to construct an article, and once you're finished with the interview, how to piece information together. I think they listened because the students were more eager to learn with someone their own age showing them how. I didn't consider myself a teacher. I suppose I was, but to me it was like working on *Foxfire* here. I was sharing what I knew with new students. And I didn't go as an adviser with all of the answers because I didn't have them. I was mainly there as a resource. If they ran into a problem, I could tell them what we did at Foxfire. Then they could on their own decide what to do in their situation.

I was living on the Flathead Indian Reservation, so most of our interviews were with Indians. Everyone we interviewed spoke English. I remember one article we did on tanning hides to make moccasins. I can still recall the smell. When I left, the students I worked with gave me a surprise party, and the gift they gave me was a pair of moccasins the contact made. I still have them.

Days would go by without getting anything done. I can remember students playing stick ball in the classroom. When you're about the same age, you really don't feel like you have the authority to make them to sit down and get to work. That was hard, but we produced a magazine. I don't know how, but we did. I wouldn't trade that experience for anything in the world.

And I do remember my daddy when I came home. The only flight I could get into Atlanta was in the middle of the night. It was three o'clock in the morning when we landed. You know the ramp that you walk down from the plane to the airport? Daddy didn't even give me time to come down. He came up that ramp to be sure I was on that plane!

I still wonder what happened to those kids that worked with me that summer. I can still picture that area of the country very clearly. I never knew why they called Montana "Big Sky Country" until I went out there. That's the perfect name for it. The National Bison Range is out there, and there were a lot of buffalo and lakes and mountains. It is a beautiful section of the United States.

▼▲▼

MIKE COOK: The summer that I was nineteen, I was sent to New Mexico, Jan Brown was sent to Montana, Laurie Brunson was sent to Johns Island, South Carolina, and Claude Rickman was sent to Kennebunkport, Maine. Later on, people were sent to Mississippi, Hawaii, Haiti—all over everywhere. Students also helped Wig and Ann Vick start IDEAS projects in Alaska. I mean it was just a whole series of things—based on the idea of what we called "cultural journalism." We were not exploring an educational philosophy then so much, but rather the idea of having high school students do publications.

IDEAS paid me five hundred dollars for the summer to go to New Mexico. I wouldn't have missed it for anything. In three months, I helped get a magazine about ready to go, and it was really good. *Tsa Àszí* is still going, so far as I know.

*Tsa Àszí*, the Navaho word for the yucca plant, is a real guttural sound. I couldn't say it the way they said it. That magazine was done in the only Indian-controlled school in this country, or so they said.

All of the other Indian schools in the country were run by the Bureau of Indian Affairs, but that school was run by the Navaho tribe, which made it completely different from any of the others.

When I first got to New Mexico, the first thing that struck me was that everything is brown. Here, all you see is green. And there is so little water there. It was nothing for the temperature to reach a hundred and ten degrees.

I guess there were seven of us students living in a little adobe house. We went to things that white people wouldn't normally get to see. I remember going to a Kachina dance that was closed to whites. Tourists would come through to see the dance, but because they would mess up the religious aspect of the ceremony, the Indian tribes have gotten to the point where they close their important dances to whites.

The school was small. It was in an old building. The guy who had been there as the photography adviser before had stolen all of the equipment. I lived just right down the street, and all of the students I worked with were basically as old as I was. I didn't feel like I could tell them what to do because I was nineteen, just like they were. I didn't have any claim to fame over them. But we did several articles. One documented the creation of the Navaho cake. Men were not supposed to be allowed to watch the way it was done. It was all done by the women.

When we did that interview and the others, they were all done in Navaho. I couldn't understand a word. I couldn't help transcribe or anything. The people could speak English, but they didn't want to. That was a strange sort of thing to deal with.

I slept on top of a sleeping bag all summer—I couldn't stand to get in one 'cause it was so blessed hot. All kinds of strange things happened. I woke up one morning, and there was a guy standing over me with a knife in one hand and a chain in the other. I was lying on the floor and just opened my eyes and looked up and he was standing there. I closed my eyes and hoped he'd go away. He was an Indian that Tom Cummings knew. Tom was the teacher I stayed with. Some redneck cowboys had burned his parents' store about three days before, and he had gotten good and drunk and couldn't tell one white man from another, so he just came in where we were and was going to take revenge. Jack Hylen and I ended up getting up and talking to him, and he sort of listened, but he was too far gone even to hear us. Then he started smashing stuff with the chain. He broke all of the glass in the house. I finally realized that he was too drunk to know what he was doing, so when he was not paying attention to me, I just took him and held him up against the wall, and everybody got out and got in the car, and we just left him there in the house. I doubt that he remembered any of what he did. What would you do if somebody came in and burned you out? And you knew basically who did it, but the law couldn't do anything. He just felt helpless. He was in a rage, and he just got drunk and did it. But that was a strange experience. The summer was full of stuff like that.

The biggest thing for me, though, was for the first time having the responsibility to do something like the exchange, and getting a lot of good work done. The person in charge of the project was going through a divorce, so more times than not I was at the school with the students by myself. The hardest thing for me to get used to was that I was heading up the project by myself. That was difficult. I felt bad because at the end of the summer there wasn't an issue actually printed and gone, but seeing the progress that they made later on, I guess that the job got done.

All things considered, I made friends there that I still stay in touch with. I remember things out of that summer that are still important right now. I was suddenly thrown out there on my own and expected to do this thing. It's a wild experiment. Like I said, IDEAS paid for it, Wig had enough faith in us to send us, and we sort of didn't worry about it. We just went and did it.

ᐜ

CLAUDE RICKMAN: The first summer I worked in Maine, with a project called *Salt*. I was amazed at the kids up there. Most of them had had photography for probably two or three years. I mean some kids had their own darkrooms, and there I was trying to teach them how to do things like that, when some of them knew so much more than I did. But there was one good thing. I was smart enough to just let them do what they could do.

One of the articles we worked on was about lobstering. We'd go out on a boat and all you'd have for lunch was lobster and loaf bread. You started about four or four-thirty in the morning, or three depending on what the weather was like, and you got back about two. Of course, I'd work with some other kids in the afternoons. They were very good students, and it was easy. It just took off.

But you take a bunch of kids like the ones out in New Mexico. They liked interviewing, and they liked preserving their culture, but a lot of them had not had any background as far as tape recorder and cameras. If I gave them a tape recorder and a tape, they'd come in the next day, and it would just be recorded with music. I'd give them a camera, they'd just bring back the film and want me to develop it.

Mike had gone to New Mexico first. This was the second summer for the project. The Navaho were a real hard culture to work with. The kids were great, but they were maybe fourteen or fifteen years old, and they came from large families of sixteen to eighteen. They lived in houses that had no running water. The closest water might be five miles away. Some lived in little log houses chinked with mud, low ceilings. There were usually two rooms, twelve by twelve. No bathroom. No kitchen. A dirt floor with goat skins on it. That was it.

I had some problems, and I'm sure Mike encountered this same thing. You may have a kid in the classroom with you who has an article that is almost complete. Let's say he lacked two weeks' work and then he'd be through, and it would be in the magazine. That kid might go off on a Sunday afternoon and never come back. It could be a great kid that was real good to work with, and you'd never see him again. You'd ask the family about him, and they'd just say they didn't know, and they really didn't know. It was tough on me, and I'm sure it was on Mike.

Another thing that made it hard is the white people that were there were Mormons, and they didn't like you being there working with the Indians. If you walked anywhere with them, you had to walk either in front or behind them. They didn't want you walking together. It was about a mile from where we lived in this trailer to the school, and you had to walk, so that was tough.

I finished out there, and then I went from there to a group near Charleston, South Carolina, on Johns Island. It was a black culture that had descended from slaves. I worked with them part of the summer.

Then I worked in the Virgin Islands, and those kids down there were different from all the rest. If you had an interview [at four], and they got there by seven to seven-thirty, they would consider themselves early. They had a parade one time and the parade was scheduled to start at one, so I made them all be there at twelve-thirty, and they just thought I was stupid. Which I was 'cause I didn't understand their culture. The parade actually started at four. By the time the parade came by, we didn't have any film or any tapes left, so the students just got in the parade. It was just a long dance, about two miles, and we just danced down the road from one place to the other, and we lost the whole thing 'cause they'd used up the film before it started. You learn a lot from different cultures and different people. Every day at school that summer, you just got out at twelve to take a nap—just like a little kid! School was dismissed. You just went home, did what you wanted for an hour or so, and came back. It was a whole different thing, but it was a nice idea.

All of the places I worked with got out magazines. They say the one in Maine is still going on, but it's not part of the school system. It's a whole different thing now. But during those summers, there were probably twelve or fifteen different magazines going on at one time.

# The Circle Grows

WIG: By the late seventies and early eighties, literally hundreds of *Foxfire*-type magazines had been started, but it had become clear that many of the teachers had not been able to keep them going. In some cases, the students just didn't like the project, or the teacher who started it left and a new teacher came in who wasn't willing to pick up the work, or the money ran out. For whatever reason, lots of those efforts were failing.

Actually, one of the biggest reasons they were failing was because teachers had started these things without understanding the basic elements that had made the Foxfire project such a meaningful experience for so many students. Teachers, for example, had decided in advance that there was going to be a magazine, and they had simply walked into school on the first day and said, "This year we're going to have a magazine. Here's what the contents are going to be, and here are your assignments," assuming the kids would love the work, but violating all the while all the principles that had gotten the first group of Foxfire students so actively involved in, and committed to, that initial project. They had lost sight of the fact that if you use broader educational principles like collaborating with the students around kinds of projects that they might do together which would be completely appropriate to their own community situation, that all kinds of projects would be possible—and they might not look like a *Foxfire* magazine at all.

The whole thing made me sort of angry at first, but then I thought about it a little more and came to understand that the reason they had gotten off track wasn't their fault, but mine. When they had asked for guidance, all I had sent them were IDEAS manuals and newsletters that contained instructions for publishing magazines like ours.

Finally, in the early eighties, I decided that I really needed to put down on paper some of those broader lessons that we had learned about student choice, student design, a democratic classroom—those things that formed the bigger educational philosophy that we were trying to be an illustration of here that, if used by teachers in other locations, might result in projects not only different from *Foxfire*, but even more successful.

I worked on the book for a year or more, off and on, and I couldn't get anywhere because of the interruptions. It became clear that if I was ever going to get it finished, I was just going to have to go away and do it. I realized at the same time that, actually, it would probably be healthy for the organization itself if I did go away for an extended period of time because it would give all of us, myself and the staff and students, a chance to have a look at what might happen if something happened to me and they had to take over.

Around 1984, I went to Athens where I had been raised and rented an apartment. I turned my classes over to the staff members and locked myself in that apartment just to write. Leadership of the organization went to Paul Gillespie. Just as the year I was away at Hopkins, any of them could call up at any point and talk through problems that had come up. Periodically, Paul and I would get together. Actually, the organization ran very smoothly that whole year. As partial evidence, that was the period of time when Paul put together *Foxfire 7*, proving that with a new group of students, a former student could continue the same kind of work that had made us successful.

I think it also pointed up the real advantage of doing business in an organization in a democratic fashion because, with the weekly staff meetings, and with all staff members and students being involved in all the major decisions, there weren't any pieces of the organization that were hidden or secret. It was just business as usual, and it was rather like I was just away on an extended vacation. I found out about most of the problems that surfaced after the fact, and after they had been solved.

At about the time *Sometimes A Shining Moment: The Foxfire Experience* was published in 1985, one of two trustees from a family foundation called Mr. Bingham's Trust for Charity appeared in my office and said, essentially, "If you had some money to work with, what would you do with it?" Both had become increasingly concerned about the state of literacy education in this country, and they had set out to find some organizations that seemed to have part of the answer, and then give each a substantial five-year grant to refine their work and share it with teachers nationally. I described my frustration with the results of the work we had done previously with other teachers, and I laid out a different approach that I thought would correct my previous mistakes, and they liked what they heard. The end result was a grant for $1.5 million to work with teachers in a whole new way.

To make a very long story very short, the system I laid out was to offer a graduate-level course for practicing teachers at several carefully selected colleges of education. There, I would take the teachers enrolled through essentially the same planning and designing process I had taken my earlier students through, but refined and revised by the experience of the intervening years. At the same time, we would review the philosophical insights of such great teachers as John Dewey—material they had studied while they were learning how to teach but, in most cases, had forgotten immediately.

In each location, a full-time coordinator would be identified and hired. His or her job would be not only to participate in the course itself, but also then to continue to work with the participants after the course was over and they returned to their classrooms to try out and share the results of what they had learned. What I wanted, in other words, was hundreds of collaborators who would come together around some core ideas and then test them in diverse locations, kindergarten through twelfth grade, and with these students, help us refine those ideas for an even wider audience. To collaborate, in the best sense of that word.

The results have been amazing. We have ten networks of teachers, each with its own coordinator, each growing annually and each collaborating with us to refine a truly effective method of working with students. All kinds of materials for teachers are being generated: newsletters, books, a video documentary, descriptions of the course. In fact, the work is so intriguing that the DeWitt Wallace-Reader's Digest Fund has just awarded us a new $1.5 million grant to kick in when the Bingham grant expires in June of 1991 so that we can continue what we've begun. And I think this is going to make a difference.

All the evidence is there now that the kind of democratic, collaborative, problem-solving approach to the curriculum that led to the creation of *Foxfire* works—and works in just about any situation, rural to urban, and just about any course. And it works far better than the method so many of us are fond of which simply has the kids reading textbook chapters and answering the review questions at the end of each. But the eternal dilemma I and my staff members confront in every course is that teachers just don't know how to do it. In many cases, that's because they've never experienced such a process themselves as students. They can't imagine what it looks like, or what it feels like from the students' point of view to be immersed in it.

They're in just the same situation as the kids. The kids are intelligent, as are the teachers, but they don't have much experience in creating a manuscript for a publisher. So you provide the structure by which that experience can happen. Then the kids can build on that structure. Teachers often need the same kind of training situation. Once they've been through it themselves, they can transfer the skills acquired to a host of new situations—as can the kids.

But teachers aren't often trained that way. They study philosophy in text/lecture courses—the worst form of instruction—and they study it before they have actually taught, so they have no experience base to relate the information to. It's just like the kids, again, who are made to study enormous amounts of material without having any personal experience to relate it to, so it all goes right through their heads because they believe the information is useless stuff they'll never want or need. By the time they've reached the ninth grade, they're bored to death, and most stay in school only because their parents make them, or because they've been convinced that this bitter pill must be swallowed if they want to get a decent job—not because of any belief in the intrinsic worth of the material being studied. It's just dues you pay to avoid a blue-collar future.

The real irony is that the information about how and in what situations people learn best is all available. It's just not shared with preservice teachers in an effective way. Foxfire has not added a single new concept to what educational philosophers like John Dewey articulated at the turn of the century. The whole educational dilemma we now find ourselves in this country is crazy. We in education must either develop a collective memory, or consign ourselves to continuing to make the same mistakes over and over again and hurting kids in the process, turning them off and convincing most of them that they're stupid and inadequate. By the time they're in the ninth grade, they're so sick of school that they can hardly wait to leave. Is that the legacy we want to leave behind?

▀▀▀

HILTON SMITH: When I first got involved with Foxfire, I had taught at the high school level for twenty-five or twenty-six years. In fact, I had helped design and run an alternative public high school in Atlanta called the Downtown Learning Center, which successfully employed many of the same teaching strategies which Foxfire uses today.

I was finishing up my doctorate at Georgia State University and looking around for some other enterprise to get into that looked challenging and interesting, and not finding a lot of success at that point. Then I came across an ad in the *Atlanta Constitution* for an editor/educator in Rabun Gap. I started off at Foxfire Press working with students to help edit the series of Dutton books. Gradually I began spending more time at the high school. Initially, I was just filling in, but later I ended up with my own government and economics classes down there. I approached the classes in an open-ended way. We decided to use *Time* magazine as the primary catalyst for our class discussions. As a result of these discussions, the students began to develop a frame of reference to all the major institutional processes, laws, and personalities that are alive and current.

Then Foxfire received the Bingham grant. I was involved with Wig in writing part of the original proposal they requested, and when we received the grant, Wig asked me if I'd like to have a role in what has become our Teacher Outreach Program. Now I'm the coordinator of the program as a whole; I guess you could say I'm the coordinator of the coordinators.

In that capacity, I help teach the courses for teachers. After every course, then, there's a pretty extensive follow-up program because we have learned one lesson: you can't just conduct a two-week course and expect teachers to learn enough to be able to actually change the way they teach. That's where the networks come in.

As the teachers start to do new projects, they hit snags. They need somebody to answer questions for them, encourage them, and help them through rough spots. More importantly, we might say, "You know, there's another seventh-grade teacher with the same problem you have. Here's her name and phone number. She can help you if you'll give her a call." I also help manage the grants we award to student projects, and I help edit the issues of *Hand On* which feature the case studies that document what happened in these projects.

At this point there are ten networks: two in Georgia and Kentucky, one each in Washington state, Idaho, New York, Maine, West Virginia, and Tennessee. We're also conducting negotiations with interested parties in Louisiana, Florida, Illinois, and Australia. Each of the established networks has a coordinator, and so another of my main jobs is to organize and conduct their quarterly meetings, which are critical because each one of their networks is located in different areas with different laws and different state-wide educational situations and contexts.

In all cases, however, the goal is the same: to help teachers in all types of instructional situations employ and test the basic principles we all believe in. The main mistake people make is that they look for quick answers and ready-made steps: "First do this and then do that." It's not that simple. Every situation is different and constantly changing, with teachers and students constantly learning new things. But the basic principles of democracy, collaboration, problem solving, real world connections—all these remain intact.

BARBARA DUNCAN, COORDINATOR: I was raised on a farm in the country, and my grandparents lived on a farm, and you didn't separate the parts of your life the way people do now. Work wasn't separated from play, and work wasn't separated from family life. It was all a whole piece. When that happens in my life today, I like that. That rings a bell.

The connection with my life and with the way I grew up is the reason I became a folklorist. In college I kept feeling that most of what we studied about people had to do with stuff that was written by white upper-class men, and just from the way I grew up I knew there was more to people than that. So folklore was a way of validating my family and the way I grew up.

I first heard about Foxfire, I guess, when I was in college and the first book came out. My teachers in general thought that it was an excellent source of information on Appalachian traditions. I first made a direct connection with Foxfire when I was working for the Macon County schools from 1984–86. We had a grant to do a folk arts program there in Aunt Arie's home county. When the grant ended, and I had had a baby and was ready to go back to work, I called to ask if Foxfire was doing anything that I might be a part of.

I was hired as coordinator for the Blue Ridge Teachers' Network, which covers north Georgia. That job in itself is a lot of other jobs. I teach the graduate course for teachers at North Georgia College. I put out a newsletter for teachers. I keep the financial records, raise money for the network, and I administer minigrants to teachers. I act as a resource person/consultant. Sometimes I go out and visit classrooms, and sometimes I do workshops with students, like how to do an interview or how to use a camera. Sometimes I'll be the audience for student projects. I talk to principals and administrators. I would like to see school systems recognize that teachers are professionals who need release time to get together with each other and do professional sorts of things.

A lot of times I'm on the road, so I might get up really early and drive to do a workshop. Sometimes in the evenings I do a lot of phone calling to teachers, and get calls from teachers, because it's easier to reach them at home than at school. Often our meetings will be on weekends—there again, because it's easier for them to come to a weekend meeting than to get out of school.

But I like visiting teachers and students in their classrooms best.

It's all very interesting. It takes a long time for teachers to understand and integrate this into their practice, but among teachers I work with, there are a number who have been doing this long enough so that this approach is not limited to projects they do, but has filtered over into all of their teaching. The Foxfire approach also provides a way of teaching that you can mesh with almost any culture that you are working with, whether it's Native American or Asian or whatever, so to me that's exciting. No matter what the culture is, the values of the culture can come out in the students' input into what goes on in the room.

I'm also working with Susan Walker, the editor for a series of course guides for teachers, and we've been talking about folklore. I've put together a package of information that the other coordinators can try out in their summer courses if they want to. Susan and I have also been talking about quite a lot of interest in environmental projects among teachers and students. I would like to put together some kind of information on that. A lot of elementary school students have done gardens. A number of them have done recycling projects in their schools. Some of them have done research on rain forests. A class at the Asheville Alternative School, which is part of the city public school system, has put together a project where they sell products made from recycled paper.

It's really hard to say which project is the most impressive. They're all so exciting. I keep catching myself saying, "Gosh, you mean kindergartners do *that?* Did fifth-graders do *that?*" It just amazes me the potential kids have to do real stuff.

The most positive thing is that I feel really good about what we're doing as a whole, and being a part of that. When friends ask, "What are you doing?" I say, "Well, this is a job that I can do and my conscience feels really good about it." I feel like it's a positive thing for students, for the communities in which it happens, and for education.

ᙡ

ROSE BAUGHER: I'm a member of the Blue Ridge Teachers' Network. I teach special ed at Woody Gap School, in Suches. It's the smallest public school in Georgia—about ninety kids, K–12. Suches is small, too, and the school is basically a community center. Parents and families are very involved in their children's education. Most of the people who live here are farmers or mechanics or work in factories in Blairsville or Dahlonega.

It's really important for my students—any students—to feel good about something they've accomplished. I like for them to be able to say, "Hey—I did it. And I believe that I could do it again." Teaching special ed can be a frustrating job because if I hit it too high, it's frustrating; if I hit it too low, it's insulting. I can never settle down and say, "Okay, I got it. This is the way I'm going to teach it the rest of the year." It's constantly monitoring and constantly trying to feel out, "Okay, where am I going? Where are they going?" Hard things to work.

The biggest thing about special ed kids, especially mildly mentally handicapped kids, is that they can't think abstractly. So everything needs to be really concrete for them. And it has to relate immediately back to their own personal life. That's true of any kids, but to a greater degree with special ed. And the Foxfire approach does relate to their own personal lives and their own personal environments and so on. It's just a good teaching practice.

That hit us hard last year. One of the objectives that my high school students had was to start thinking about some career options for themselves and thinking about what they're interested in and what they want to be, and making plans for it now, rather than waiting till the last year or after. This is a small place, and they haven't seen many possibilities for themselves here.

To help us with this objective, we were using a textbook on careers. The kids read descriptions of different jobs, what the typical income might be for that kind of job, that kind of stuff. It was interesting for a while, but the book had jobs that we just don't have in our community. We don't have valet service in Suches. They realized it didn't relate to them at all. So after the initial excitement of the new subject was wearing thin, they were all but saying "Give me a break!"

So I was really honest and said, "Look, this is not working. I took this course over the summer, and this is what I found out." So then we started coming up with possible career projects—a movie, a book, a parent presentation, a slide show. And when they were ready to vote on it, they wanted to do a book.

So I drew a time-line on the board and said, "Okay, we're here. We want to get to the book. How are we going to get there?" And this is where they needed a lot of help, because they've never really planned things on their own. They're so used to having teachers say, "You have to do this, on such a day, and you have to do *this* on such a day." So they're really excited, and they say, "Well, we need to start interviewing people," and I said, "Yeah." So we started listing all the different possible jobs in Suches.

And they said, "But there's no jobs in Suches!"

But we started listing jobs they could think of, and we ended up listing twenty different possibilities. And we said, "Pretty good, huh?" They had thought they only had two or three possibilities, and this list kept growing. The biggest thing that surprised them was that a lot of people around here are very resourceful. They created jobs for themselves, which I think my students wouldn't likely have seen before.

In the interviews the kids were always surprisingly calm and collected. I occasionally embarrassed myself, though. We interviewed a trapper who brought in some traps, and he slammed one on his finger, and I screamed. It didn't hurt him a bit. He was illustrating how it really doesn't hurt the animal. We videotaped this thing, and the kids just loved it, and asked the guy to sacrifice another finger so I could scream again.

Four of them interviewed one person at a time, rather than doing individual interviews. The group went out to interview, came back, listened to the tape, took notes on their portion. So if a student's category was "risk," or "expenses," or "working conditions," they'd play the tape and take notes just on their category. And then they wrote their paragraphs just on their categories. Talk about an editing job. You take four writing styles and try to combine them into one. It's a nightmare!

After everyone wrote his or her individual paragraphs for each interview, we all read them together and gave suggestions about possible changes to make it flow better, that kind of thing. We put the paragraphs in logical order, and put a few transitional sentences here and there to connect the paragraphs together. One person wrote the introduction, and ta-dah! Doing it this way, it comes out surprisingly decent and coherent.

After that we went through the painstaking process of proofreading, which they aren't very good at. If you are dyslexic, do you want to try catching your own spelling errors? Everybody takes turns proofreading, so whatever strength they have they contribute. If one person is good at spelling, and one person is good at making sense, and one person is good at catching punctuation, and one person is good at capitalization, they all contribute their strengths—it's a collaborative effort.

After they proofread it, they retyped it. One person usually typed one story at a time. As soon as you proofread and finalized the paper, then we printed it out, and did the layouts.

The kids have been working on this project for two years, making a small book of careers in Suches. They're aiming this career booklet primarily at the sixth-, seventh-, and eighth-graders. It will be a resource for them, because during those years in middle school they take a course called Career Exploration. My students have completed sixteen interviews. They have four more layouts to do and they will be finished. We're at a point where we need to finish. The other day, the kids said, "Well, we could interview so-and-so," and I'm going, "Over my dead body!"

Probably the reason this project has taken as long as it has is their teacher has this horrible fault—perfectionism. I'll throw something back and say, "Back to the drawing board. Go and try again," rather than settling for something that's sloppy. Because when the book comes back, they're not going to feel good if it's sloppy and misspelled. It wouldn't be something they'd be proud of. And I hate for them to work so hard for two years and then come back with something that's just mediocre.

One related thing we did was a presentation at an international conference in Atlanta on career development for the Council for Exceptional Children. My students love the presentations. They act like they hate to do it when it's time, but they all do want to do it again.

Presentations are good for any student, not just my students. To be recognized and have people come up and say, "You did a fantastic job," makes their self-esteem skyrocket. They just feel wonderful. When I took the kids to Atlanta, three of them had never been.

Another benefit is that a presentation in the middle of a project gives them a chance to take a step back and look at what they've actually done, to reflect and assess. It gives them a chance to explain to other teachers what the Foxfire approach is, what steps we've taken to get to where we are. And they compare what it was like before and what it's like now in the classroom. The kids like feeling in control. They get to figure out what they need to do rather than me telling them what to do—what page, what section.

What was nice about learning about the Foxfire approach is I've heard all of these things before in college courses and I've read them in books, but it wasn't laid out logically. For me this approach provided an easy way to do it, a step one, step two, step three, step four way of approaching it. Letting the kids know what the objective is, then justifying that objective (and if we can't justify it, scratch it and go on to another), then coming up with ways to learn that objective, and then figuring out with the kids maybe a final product to go with it. And incorporating other objectives if you can. I could probably make a list of five hundred tiny objectives that they've been working on in this project. I'm not saying that they've accomplished all of them, but they have been initiated into them. After I took that course, I was ready to go back charged: "Okay, that's how I can implement this particular style." It wasn't any hit-or-miss kind of thing.

▜▛

MARIE BOND: I participate in the Seattle area Soundfire Teachers' Network. As a kindergarten teacher, in a small community near

Seattle, I had no idea whether the Foxfire process would work or not with children that young. It turned out that doing a Foxfire project really pushed them, but as long as it was practical, they could handle it really well.

We didn't actually start talking about a project until sometime in October, but the first day of school, at the end of the day, I called them all together and put a tape recorder down and we talked about what was it like to come to school. "Was it like what you thought? Were you kind of afraid this morning? What was it that you were worried about?" Then I just put it away and didn't do anything more with it until about October, when they knew what it was like to be in school.

Then I said, "You know, you talked about this the first day of school. Do you think that it would have helped you if there had been something so that you'd know what it was going to be like? Would you like to do something for next year's kindergartners so they won't be as 'scared' as you were?" And that's when we went into this discussion which led to the decision about our project. One early suggestion was to get on the telephone, and talk to the upcoming kids, but we had no telephone in the classroom. "So we'll make a book"—except of course that the kindergartners coming in wouldn't be able to read it, because obviously *they* can't read.

"We'll take pictures." Okay, we'll take pictures, good. "Now who's gonna explain what the pictures are about?" They finally decided that you could put it on a tape. "If you put a tape and pictures together, what's that called?" That's when they decided what they were going to do.

The finished video is in segments, and for each segment, the students wrote and illustrated a book which became the narrative basis for the video segment. For the first segment, the students chose the school bus. A student would give me a sentence like, "Stacy said she was afraid she'd get pushed off the bus," and I'd put that on the board. Then I'd transfer it to the bottom of a sheet of poster paper and the student would illustrate it. When we had a number of those, we bound the pages into our book about school bus fears.

When it came time to do the first filming, one of the high school teachers said he would come out and film it for us. He had looked at the students' book, and he wrote a plan for the shoot that said, "Based on what your kids have written here, this is what you are going to want to do." I took that and I threw it away.

I said to the children, "This is what you actually said. Now how are you going to show it?" At this point, I didn't know. Were they going to do it as a puppet show? Did they think they should do it in the classroom, and set up a pretend bus? And they said, "Well, of course, what we'll do is we'll use somebody's house, and we'll have the bus come, and we'll all show how you get on the bus and how you have to wait for the sign to come out, and so on." And they, in their infinite five-year-old wisdom, figured out exactly what the high school teacher had put down. But I hadn't even paid attention to what he'd said, because it was to be what the kids wanted, and they never found out he had sent a plan in advance.

On the day of the filming, we simply made arrangements for the school bus to come an hour early. We ended up borrowing the principal's camera, and the high school teacher rearranged his classes and filmed the students reading their script and reenacting the situations.

We used essentially the same process for each of the segments, and by the last one, when we were writing the book for it, they were able to revise it and edit it just as we went along. Somebody'd say, "We need to put in this," and somebody else would say, "Oh, before we do that we need to. . . ." It also shows in the video. The first segment was pretty hesitant, but they did it themselves. On the last one, they were so confident. Everybody participated in the audio part of it and they knew just what to say. It just was a huge growth in confidence.

We finished it up in April or May. There's always a district meeting of new parents and their kids, and that was the first showing of it. The parents thought it was wonderful. We have copies available now in all our elementary school libraries, and people will check them out and invite all their friends over with their little kids to see it.

I wouldn't teach any other way at this point.

✖✖✖

BECKY COLDREN LEWIS: I was a student in one of Wig's first English classes, and now I'm an English teacher and a member of the Skyline Teachers' Network in Atlanta.

After high school, I went to the University of Georgia for two years and began majoring in journalism. Foxfire didn't make me realize I wanted to major in journalism; it made me sure that that was what I wanted to do. I graduated in journalism, but my minor was in English

Education, and now I teach English at Fayette County High School, and I asked Wig to come to talk to my fifth period. Well, he came three hours early, and I hadn't expected him. He talked to all my classes and got them so excited that they wanted to do something using the Foxfire approach. I thought I could do it because I had been in his high school class, but it just didn't work well. I realized I needed more background on the philosophy, so I took a course at Georgia State from him, and then joined Skyline.

The Georgia State class that I took that fall made me very negative for a while. I was a very traditional teacher at that point, and every

At a recent public showcase of the Skyline Teachers' Network, former Foxfire student Becky Coldren Lewis explained her students' project to a visitor.

night I would go home and be so depressed. I would be teaching very traditionally during the day, and I would come to this course and find out that there was a better way of teaching, and I wasn't using it. Finally, my seniors and I started a magazine like *Foxfire* called *Fayette Portraits*. As I began to see the results of that, I began to move the same approach into my other classes, one at a time. I can almost graph myself getting more and more into the Foxfire teaching approach, but they're little steps; it's not been a huge jump. Today, I'm still teaching a *Fayette Portraits* class, but I am now bringing the Foxfire philosophy into all my classes.

The wonderful thing about Foxfire is that kids find out about so many more things than are listed on the state's ninety-three language arts objectives. They find out about politics, what works and doesn't work, and they have real-world experiences.

Last year my kids did an end of the year evaluation, and I found the big thing they appreciated was the trust they were given. They say, "Finally they're treating us like adults, and boy, isn't it time that they did." It's nothing startling to me, but it sure is to my students, and it is to other teachers. I think having been a Foxfire student has something to do with it. I remember having to go to the library and having piles of *Foxfire* magazines that we sent out, and these envelopes, and putting them in piles by zip codes. You had that kind of responsibility, and you wanted to get the job done right.

Two years ago, we got an invitation to go down to a National Historic Trust for Preservation meeting in Florida. So two of the kids and I went. When I was talking about Foxfire, I mentioned that I was an early Foxfire student. I said that my name was in the first *Foxfire* book, and that night, a man came up to me with a *Foxfire* book in his hand. He was real interested in the work that I had done in the book, and had me sign my autograph. Here I was having to autograph something I did in the ninth grade! I couldn't believe it.

Now, I'm helping my students have the same experience.

◤◣◥

LINDA BOYER: I'm a member of the Bitterroot Teachers' Network. In 1979, I was hired by the Lapwai, Idaho, school district as K–12 district art teacher, but many lessons are coordinated with math concepts, social studies, literature, heritage, science, health, and other subjects. Classroom teachers and I often work together on academic-arts projects.

The Lapwai School is located in a small town of a thousand residents on the Nez Percé Indian Reservation, and over 60 percent of the student body is Native American, As a child, I, too, attended the school.

[Last year my students did a calendar that illustrated Indian legends and local landmarks. This year they're working on a photographic book about the area.] The kids know all these people. We talked about the community and made lists in journals of family members that they knew who could be contacted for help. A man who worked with narrations of Indian legends came in and shared legends with the kids.

This campus is located right on an historical area, where Chief Joseph spent time. One of our kids is descended from Joseph, and he did the calendar page related to Joseph. He was just doing very little in our class before this project, and he had very little self-confidence. Well, he ended up being one of the boys on the street corner [selling calendars] the first evening the calendars came off the press. After our Foxfire project the boy had a very productive year. It was exciting seeing a project like this do something so special, so positive for a student.

One boy who wasn't motivated to do much and who has had a lot of trouble with the community has become very involved with the project this year. For the photograph book *Lapwai Area, Then and Now*, he wanted to concentrate on one particular idea. He hiked these hills, and it looks like he took pictures from an airplane. I could not believe all these photographs that he took with his little 110 camera. He has shots of North Lapwai and South Lapwai, and from the way they laid it out on their pages, it gives the whole panoramic view of the area. The kids said, "Where did these pictures come from?" They were surprised to learn that it was this boy who after school took these hikes with his camera and dog. And his parents, too, have given him a lot of positive support about his photography. With a unique shot of the wheat fields of this area, he just won a blue ribbon at the county fair. He's had many successes in photography since that first Foxfire project.

Five Foxfire-trained teachers are now using the approach in our school district. Because of Foxfire, a clearer understanding seems to be developing between the mixed heritages within our culture, and a closer bond between the youth and elders. And this approach also seems to work for nearly every learner.

◥◤◥

JUNIUS EDDY: Since the beginning of the Bingham grant, I've been working closely with Hilton, helping to guide the evaluation of the Teacher Outreach Program. Each time the basic Foxfire course was taught, we asked the teachers to complete surveys designed to tell us about their instructional approaches, their styles of teaching, and their attitudes about the educational process in general. Then we'd follow that up at the end of the course with a second survey to see how the course might have changed those attitudes. And now, we're trying to see what happens to them when they return to their classrooms: whether or not they've even tried to implement these new approaches, and if so, how and with what results.

Actually, I've been involved with the Foxfire program since Wig first walked into my Washington office in 1969. In the beginning, I wasn't sure if Foxfire was ever going to have a *national* impact on education. I was afraid that it might remain somewhat narrowly focused on Appalachian folk materials alone, rather than on the guts of the teaching-learning process itself. And I was also apprehensive that it might never go beyond the high school-language arts-and journalism level and wouldn't spread throughout the grades, K–12, or across the subject matter spectrum at the secondary level. Obviously these worries were unfounded. Through the Foxfire course *and* the networks, it has now spread throughout the entire educational curriculum.

It's a cliché, I think, to say that Wig has matured, but he has. When he walked into his first classroom and, early on, evolved the Foxfire approach, he was an iconoclastic young kid with a gorgeous idea that captivated everybody who heard about it. Now he's grown more thoughtful, more seasoned. I know he reads a lot more, and he's grown in his interest in a broad range of educational theory.

In fact, all the men and women on the Foxfire staff are pretty remarkable. They have commitment, but they also have a nice sense of humor about what they're doing. They're not so deadly serious they can't relax and enjoy themselves. They're also caring people— and they *do* get the work done. Wig's not always an easy man to work with, but these people have found ways to stay honest with him and still solve their mutual problems effectively.

The coordinators who work with the various Foxfire teacher networks across the country are equally remarkable. The other day, I was meeting with a group of these coordinators, and I was struck by their strong creative flair and genuine management skills. They learn well on the job, and they're flexible and patient.

I was especially impressed with these last two qualities—their patience and their flexibility. They struggle patiently with group decisions, trying to reach a consensus with which they can all be comfortable, and that's not an easy thing to do in as strong-minded a group of people as this. And their flexibility—some of these folks may be very vulnerable, but they're risk-takers, and somehow they don't seem badly upset or threatened by disagreement. They try an idea, and then if it doesn't work, they're willing to back up and say, "We've got to go in a different direction." They seem to have the kinds of personalities that are precisely what the teachers in their networks need when *they're* trying out this approach to teaching for the first time.

In some ways, it's a wonder that Wig has kept on teaching at all. He's stayed in Rabun County and remained essentially a teacher, on a public school salary, despite all the other demands on him. Many people in his position wouldn't have done that. They'd get pulled out of it after ten or fifteen years: they'd accept a job with a foundation, or run an educational think-tank of some kind, or head a graduate school of education.

Maybe, now, after *twenty-five years*, it's time for him to do something like that, but it's a good thing he did remain in teaching all these years. If he hadn't, he wouldn't have had quite the same credibility in working with the teachers in the networks, his own staff, and the hundreds of others he influences in American education every year. The very thing that qualifies him (and the rest of the Foxfire and network staff members) to teach courses about the Foxfire approach to education is that they are working, practicing professionals in classrooms. They're genuine master teachers, and they've had the practical classroom experience, and that's why they've made such a strong impact on the teaching profession.

In almost every instance, for example, our evaluations have shown that the Foxfire course seems to have motivated changes in the style of teaching that course participants ultimately undertake in their classrooms. The next step, in what we're calling Phase Two of our evaluation, has taken us into the classrooms of representative teachers who took the course and have been trying to implement these new approaches over the two or three years since they completed the course. Our purpose is to see to what extent, if any, their attitudes about teaching and learning may have changed. To see whether their classroom behavior has changed at all—whether they've grown and matured as teachers, or whether they've continued the instructional practices they were using before they took the course. (For some teachers, of course, the whole experience may simply have reinforced what they were already moving toward.)

So far in this, we've found that the vast majority of teachers *have* continued to use and refine the approach—and *that*, incidentally, has been one of the great benefits of these networks. These ideas and practices are being used every day in classrooms all around the country now—and anyone who wants to can go into one of these classrooms and see firsthand how well they're working.

And that's terribly important. People have to be able to observe such classrooms and see how different the teaching is from the old, bankrupt sit-down-shut-up-and-learn syndrome where kids are simply fed information without trying to stimulate their interest in any part of what they are being asked to learn.

There are enormous problems facing education today in this country—and they worry me. I alternate between optimism and pessimism about them. The big urban school systems may never be able to cope with the many educationally disruptive issues confronting them.

Often, parents simply abandon their kids to these systems—and one of the constructive things that seems to be happening in these Foxfire teacher networks is that parents and other community people become involved in, and contribute to, many of the projects their students are working on.

I do think, though, that if some of the various educational reform movements that are floating around today, such as Foxfire and the Coalition of Essential Schools, for example, could ally themselves with one another more closely, maybe we'd have some kind of major impact on changing the entire structure of schooling in this country.

Foxfire has shown, I think, that it's possible to change individual teachers. But trying to change an entire system or even one school building, where groups of teachers can begin to affect one another, so that slowly you get a more open structure in that school—that's the tough part. Educational change movements have indeed emerged in recent years that *are* trying to deal purposefully with the structure of schooling—while the work here at Foxfire (and in the networks) seems to be emphasizing changes in the individual teacher, and in the manner and substance of teaching and classroom instruction. Still other change agents are tackling the problem from yet a different standpoint, and maybe those various efforts can coalesce into a powerful movement that people in the hierarchies of education can't afford to ignore. Maybe none of these groups can ever really solve the problems effectively alone, but if they could find a way to get together, to combine their strengths and work in concert, we might really begin to provide some answers—and some hope—for teachers and students everywhere. Working with others toward that kind of joint enterprise may, indeed, be Foxfire's next critical step.

# "Then I Left High School"

JAN BROWN BONNER: The first two years after I graduated, I went to West Georgia College in Carrollton, Georgia, with the intention of majoring in physical education. Then I transferred to the University of Georgia and journalism. The summer after I graduated from Georgia, I married Olin (Sandy) Bonner, whom I had met while he was a boarding student during our high school years at Rabun Gap.

My first job was at Wofford College, in Spartanburg, South Carolina, where I was a counselor for an Upward Bound program that helped low-income, poorly motivated students through tutoring and enrichment activities. I worked there for two and a half years.

Then I began working at a weekly newspaper in Greer, South Carolina, where I wrote editorials, did wedding write-ups, proofread, and did layout. I also covered school board meetings and wrote sports articles. You name it. That was in 1976, and they were doing a centennial issue because Greer was one hundred years old. We did a huge centennial edition, with a lot of interviews on how things used to be. I wouldn't have known how to do the interviews if I hadn't worked with *Foxfire*.

My two children, Blake and Jill, were born during the time that I was going back to school, working on my master's in Librarianship from the University of South Carolina.

Now I work at Mitchell Road Elementary School in Greenville, South Carolina. People ask why I didn't stay in journalism, but it's amazing how journalism and library science interrelate. Being a media specialist, you're involved with books, computers, video, and all kinds of materials for children. In my first school, I coordinated

Jan Brown Bonner, who graduated in 1969, is now a media specialist at Mitchell Road Elementary School in Greenville, South Carolina.

and videotaped a morning show where every morning we'd have the children tell about the day and special events that were coming up. They would practice in their classrooms and then I would videotape it. It really corresponds with the kinds of things that I did at Foxfire.

The thing about teaching kids in a library is you don't have a set curriculum to go by. Teachers have massive textbooks and curriculum guides, but when you're in the library, you have nothing but your own ingenuity. You have to teach how to use the card catalogue, how to use an almanac, and how to find information in or outside of a library. I draw on my Foxfire experiences often in devising lesson plans. I find myself going back and thinking, "Well, we did something like this in Wig's class. Let me see if I can adjust it to what I'm doing here." It has been really successful. My job does consume a lot of my time, but part of that is my fault. I want to do a good job, which is another influence of Foxfire. I don't want to half-do something. I want it done right, and so I probably spend more time than is necessary.

Foxfire interested me in journalism and I found a love for writing I might never have known without it. I've made it through a lot of things I probably would not have made it through if I hadn't learned how to write. Success depends on the ability to communicate. I still don't have speeches mastered, but I feel comfortable with writing. Doing all those articles and learning how to organize my material really helped me with working for newspapers. Foxfire also taught me a lot about how to function in the professional world. It taught me about responsibility, deadlines, getting things done, being dependable, and following through on a task.

And I think Foxfire helped enrich my respect for the elderly, of course. I know everybody has to say that after working with Foxfire, but it's accurate.

Wig left a lot of decisions up to us. That's really true. Teachers are always asking, "Well, did he do the work or. . . ." Really, he left many of the decisions up to us, so I learned how to be a decision maker, too, in addition to everything else. You learn, when you're in the middle of something and don't know what's going on, that you can, through your own talents or through your own mistakes, find out what to do to work your way out of it. Foxfire made me feel like I was in control of my life in that it gave me self-confidence.

When *The Foxfire Book* was published, I was just totally in awe that something like that could come out of a little English class. Every time I go to a bookstore, I have to look and see what they've got in the way of Foxfire books. It's a real thrill to be able to see something that you have written in a bookstore or in a library. Every time one of those first few books came out I thought, "Oh, this is going to be awful." I still didn't have a lot of faith in myself. I knew I was going to find something that should have been done a different way. But I guess it turned out okay.

Everything about Foxfire amazes me, from the time that we initiated the idea to the time that we published the first issue, and then it sold out, and then we kept going with it. Within the school district of Greenville County, almost everybody knows about the program. A lot of times when I'm introduced, that's the way they introduce me. "She worked for Foxfire." Everybody is always so impressed. And I am, too. When I look back at that first class and think about sitting in that second-story English room with the windows open, and us discussing what we were going to do, it astounds me. When I read *Foxfire Reconsidered* and *Sometimes a Shining Moment*, I remain overwhelmed to think that it all started in that English class, and I was a part of it.

▀▄▀

GENELLE BROWN: You know, this goes even into a third generation. Our grandchildren this past year had teachers who talked about Foxfire and were very interested in Foxfire. So they got a copy of *Sometimes a Shining Moment* and had it autographed by Wig and took it to their creative writing teachers and their English teachers. It's gone on through the family. Everybody has had an interest in it through the years.

▚▚▚

JUDY MARINDA BROWN PLANT: After graduation from high school, I went to Reinhardt College in Waleska, Georgia, and then to the University of Georgia in Athens. I majored in public relations. After graduating from college, I married Gerald Plant. My first job was with the Georgia Chamber of Commerce in Atlanta, working on their tourism program, the STAR (Student Teacher Award Recognition) Program, and the Leadership Georgia Program.

My husband and I started our family in 1983, after a ten-year honeymoon and career pursuit. My son was born February 24, 1983, and two years and one day later our daughter was born. Life at home has not been dull with my two redheads! They are very interested in reading. One day I said to myself, "Oh, I just can't have them miss this!" I pulled out the very first issue of *Foxfire* and read one of my favorite stories, "Going, Going, Gone" by Brynda Clark. They enjoyed it and later they will be able to read about their own ancestors in magazines and books published by Foxfire.

Over the years, I have become very interested in crafts. As a result of Foxfire, I paid more attention to skills used by my grandparents and parents. At Christmas it was a special treat to get handcrafted gifts. Currently, I produce crafts for two stores in Stone Mountain, Georgia, one in Lawrenceville, and several craft shows.

I guess the main thing I learned from Foxfire was how to plan ahead. We had so many things we had to organize. And we got more encouragement, more positive reinforcement, in that work, than through any other activity. In some of the other things that I did in school, there were strongly set ways of doing things, and there was a lot of negative criticism. And some other encounters during high school were a struggle and full of brick walls you couldn't go around, up, under, sideways, or backward.

In Foxfire, we had opportunities to make decisions. We were faced with something brand new that had no set recipe or role model

Judy Marinda
Brown Plant,
1969, is a
craftswoman.

structure, so we realized we had an unpredictable end result. We had
to examine everything each step of the way to avoid mistakes and the
dreaded wrath of adults. It was a coup every time we did something
as simple as figure out when the subscription of a subscriber getting
a double issue would expire. We said, "We did it. We know it." "I can't
do it" had a limited use in our vocabulary! Getting young people at
any age to that level should be a primary goal in education.

The positive reinforcement continued long after I left Rabun
County. I had just one minor setback about the time of the movie
*Deliverance.* I remember being at a large dinner party in a downtown
Atlanta restaurant and feeling put down because of where I came
from. After the hick image of the movie dissipated, the glow of Foxfire
went on. As the news of Foxfire spread, so did the positive reinforcement I received when the subject of "where are you from" cropped up.

I really think it's a miracle that Foxfire has kept becoming bigger
and bigger. I think the fact that it's still here is wonderful and
amazing. In the early days, there would have been a hundred excuses
for it to casually close up. I'm so glad that didn't happen.

▀▀▀

GEORGE BURCH: After high school, I went to Young Harris College and got an associates degree in chemistry and physics. Then I got a degree in education at Georgia Southern. When I left there, I went to the Thomasville city schools and taught chemistry and physics for six years. Then I happened to get a job here at Woody Gap. I started teaching at Woody Gap during the 1979–80 school year. Now I'm the Woody Gap principal in a K–12 public school that has about a hundred students.

As I look back on Foxfire, it was a link in a chain. It wasn't the one thing that made my career choice. Mr. Philps's science class wasn't the one thing that made it either, but it was also a link in the chain. You have to look at what was available in Rabun Gap in terms of a vocation. You could work in the carpet mill, which meant you had a steady job unless orders fell off. I could work at construction, which was real good in the summertime, but I would starve in the wintertime. No way in the world I would have enough land to go into farming. But teachers seemed to be making a living and they had weekends off. Plus, I thought a great deal of Morris Brown. I wanted to be able to help people the way he helped me. Foxfire was just one of those links in that chain in building toward that decision.

I feel a lot of my job is making sure we have as good a school as possible. I spend part of my day completing paperwork to keep the school running. I spend part of the day consulting with teachers, and I try to spend at least a part of the day observing things. I'm constantly looking for ways to improve the school and keep it running on a smoother track. The nice thing is that instead of me looking at the education of students from grades nine through twelve, I look at their whole educational process, K–12.

I ran into Wig about ten years ago, and we had a good argument on educational philosophy. That discussion was about hands-on experience versus theory. I was a science teacher in upper-level courses, and I did not go with as much of the hands-on experimentation as Foxfire talks about, but in other classes I feel that it is very beneficial. I believe we have thirteen years in a public school that are going to change us for the rest of our life, and that, as educators, we have to give students as many opportunities to see as many different things as we can in that thirteen years.

Wig's basic premise is that everything has to be relevant at one point in time. Mine doesn't necessarily go along with that. I think that teaching basic knowledge does not have to be applied right at

George Burch, 1969, is now the principal of Woody Gap School. He was interviewed in the school's library with the editor's handbook he was given in high school on the table in front of him.

that time. It can and will be applied at the right time some time in the future. Projects have their place. They would not dominate the school that I would run, though. That's where Wig and I differ. One of the good things about education is that there can be differences without being right or wrong.

Wig had this way that I am a strong believer in now, and maybe it is part of what he taught me. It involves telling a kid what you expect him to do and expecting him to do it. He said, "This is what I expect you to do," and whenever he walked away, he fully expected you to do it. I think that's important. It was up to you, and you knew it was, so you did it.

That also taught me skills like organization, especially when Wig was gone and we had those deadlines. We figured out how we could meet them. My Foxfire experience also gave me the confidence I could produce something, and that I could work cooperatively with people. But I can also get stubborn sometimes. If you don't believe me, ask my teachers!

I remember what Wig wrote in this editor's handbook in 1968. He had a list of goals such as a scholarship fund to send students to college, a series of small books, and job opportunities for students who wanted to come home after college. The last paragraph right here says, "Admittedly, much of this is in the dream state at this point, but there's absolutely no reason why it couldn't work with dedication and determination on your part. You are part of what I hope will be a chain reaction that will light up this part of the world." It seems to have done it.

ᵂ

EMMA BUCHANAN CHASTAIN: After I graduated from high school, I studied cosmetology at North Georgia Tech. I started my own beauty shop in Dillard, which I've had now for twenty years. I got married, and that's all I've ever done except have babies and run a family and work on the farm; I'm a housewife, a mother, and a farm wife—and I run a business.

I wouldn't say Foxfire was an influence in choosing to study cosmetology. I was just looking for a career in which I could stay in Rabun County. Practically everyone I graduated with went away to find jobs, but I didn't want to do that. I plan to make it a lifetime career unless, of course, something really big happens to disrupt it.

Foxfire made me look around at what the Lord has given us— those gifts we have right here in the county. It made me notice the things that had been right around me, which I'd never known were there because I'd never paid any attention to them. I remember when I was in his English class, Wig did something new to us that no other teacher had ever done. Before, we'd never gone outside the walls of the school during class. But Wig would take us outside on the lawn, and he'd tell us, "Look around and write a poem about what you see." We might write about the wind rustling the trees, or a flower, or a bee, or we might look over toward Rabun Mills and see smoke going into the sky, and write about that. But the point of this activity was that it taught us to look around and appreciate what was there—to take time to smell the roses, so to speak.

It also opened up my eyes to the older generation. When I realized that my heritage was dying, and all of a sudden I saw it right in front of me written in a book, it made me appreciate it so much more.

Since I was the circulation manager, I learned how to keep rec-

Emma Buchanan Chastain, 1970, is a beautician in Rabun County.

ords. In my job now, I have to keep records of everything that I do, and I probably keep my records clearer as a result.

I also understand kids better, and I try to tell my kids to make the most of each day. They don't always do that; often they say, "Oh, I'm bored," but I try to prevent that as much as possible. I try my best to teach them to respect their elders and to be good citizens. That's what Foxfire did for me, and I try to do the same for them.

~~~

MIKE COOK: When I left Rabun Gap, I started at Georgia Tech. I was going to be an electrical engineer. I had been there for two quarters. But Atlanta drove me crazy. I was waked up in the morning by a pile driver across the street every day that I was there. So I transferred to Gainesville Junior College. I got into the journalism program there with intentions of going on to the journalism program at the University of Georgia. Having done Foxfire, I knew that I could write, and I loved to write. I also knew I loved meeting people, doing research and explaining things to folks—all the things you guys are doing right now putting this book together. So when I started casting around for an alternative to engineering, I knew I had one. The only other thing that I had experience in was teaching [which I also did with Foxfire during my summer jobs there] but I didn't want to teach at that time, so that made very little sense.

While I was at Gainesville Junior College, we started cable programming. We produced little half-inch videotapes which we gave to the Gainesville cable company, and they promised to show them. They never did. Nevertheless, at least we had learned the rudiments of editing and taking care of the equipment.

Then I transferred to the University of Georgia's journalism school. It was actually while I was there that Wig asked me to do this job because of my experience at Gainesville. Wig had begun to think about getting somebody to run the video program that had been started with our first NEH grant. The next thing I knew, Wig had said, "How about considering coming back up here and trying to start some kind of video thing? Maybe you can get cable access, and start doing programs like you have already done." So I went ahead and accepted the job, finished school, and joined Foxfire.

Mike Cook, 1971, now teaches radio, video, and magazine production in the Foxfire program at Rabun County High School. Here he is being interviewed by Leigh Ann Smith, Keri Gragg, and Jenny Lincoln.

From the beginning, Foxfire has seemed to be a neat, caring, human thing. If you helped build something, then you deserve to be involved in building it even further, and several of us former students have been hired to do just that. Paul eventually edited *Foxfire 7*. He also at one point served as Wig's right-hand man, vice president of the company. For me, it was like me being asked to be Br'er Rabbit in a brier patch, because I still had my interest in electronics. I also liked journalism. Asking me to come back and do something that was a combination of the two was like, "Are you kidding? Sure."

I really think the organization is tighter now than when I was a student in it. In a sense, more is being expected of the Foxfire students today than was expected of us then. [The students] are in charge. The book has to be out pronto, and they know it. Every day is a butt-buster. I don't remember having that kind of pressure. The Foxfire students today have videotapes, books, and magazines to get out, all of this simultaneously. I don't think it was as tough then as it is today.

The idea of Foxfire has gotten bigger than all of us. It's hard to keep up with it. I think the idea was one that, at the time, was right. As a result, it flew, and not only because the idea was good, but because people worked with it. It landed on fertile ground. But I still pinch myself about what's happening with this organization.

■■■

PAUL GILLESPIE: I took Foxfire very seriously. Of course I enjoyed it, and it was a diversion for me. But it was more than that. As it turned out, my work with Foxfire was part of what helped me to get into the University of Virginia, and that was a very difficult school to get into.

When I graduated from UVA, I came back to Foxfire and worked there for years. I had always wanted a law degree, though, so eventually I left Foxfire, and I went to law school at Mercer University in Macon, Georgia. I worked in Franklin, North Carolina, in a law office for a while. Then I got a job as assistant headmaster at a day school in Myrtle Beach, South Carolina. We had 230 kids at the Coastal Academy, and since I had a law degree, they let me teach a college prep course for seniors called Law and Justice. I also taught American Government, which was always one of my lifelong dreams. It's one of the easiest and most relevant courses that you can teach. I had resource people come in, like elected officials; and we also did role playing and mock trials. I took them to court. We had a great time.

Now I'm at Randolph Macon Academy in Virginia. We have always

Paul Gillespie, 1971, is the school development director at Randolph Macon Academy in Virginia.

tried experiential stuff and I think that is important, but I think the books are very important, too. When you prepare students for college, you've got to teach them to play out whatever game that is. I think you have to have a balance. You don't want to overdo anything. Here, we have math and chemistry and physics teachers who are all the time bringing in stuff. I know you can do it in social studies—if you don't bring in the real-world stuff there I think it is a crime—and the same thing can be said for all disciplines.

I happen to be in administration now, and I don't teach. I miss it, though, sometimes. It was a good experience, and I hope to be able to do it again. I'm Vice President in Charge of Development, and that involves a lot of different things. That involves fund-raising, but it also involves public relations. I don't land 747s in the fog and I don't take tumors from people's brains—I don't know how exciting my job is, but at this particular point, it is particularly fulfilling.

We attract people to our program because it is unique. We own a plane and we have seventeen-year-old kids flying airplanes by themselves. I think that's a good adult thing for them to do. I think there is a fine line, and I think Foxfire has always done a good job with letting kids be kids and doing adult things at the same time, because you do want to prepare them.

I don't know that I've resolved where the line should be drawn. I think sometimes young people are forced into being adults before they should be. Childhood moves so fast that I wouldn't want my children to be going through adult experiences just to make them be adults. Adultness comes as a product of age. People should be allowed to enjoy their youth and childhood, and have fun. At the same time, you can treat them as human beings, as people that have worth, and work on self-esteem. That's something that the Foxfire program always tried to do. But realize that students are students, and there's a balance. As long as the program remembers that these students are indeed adolescents, then it's okay. If it's positive.

I've always been open to different options, but at some point down the road, I will be in an educational organization either in a support role, or as head of a school. I also have an interest in educational law, and I hope someday that I can work in that. I've been involved with nonprofit organizations basically all of my life. I remember the term 501(c)(3)—I always heard that when I was in Foxfire, and when I was in law school I studied about that. I've got it down to law and education, and I think I'm getting to do a little bit of both. I always said one of these days I would figure out what I want to do when I grow up. And I'm almost there.

◆◆◆

CLAUDE RICKMAN: I went to Berry College in Rome. I had two quarters to graduate and left. I was planning on working a little bit and going back and finishing up, but haven't gone back yet. Had a good time. Learned a lot. It was a good growing-up time and it was a big social time. It was just a nice time to kinda get organized, 'cause life is a lot different after school. When you guys go home tonight, somebody's gonna tell y'all some things you can do and some things you can't. One day there's gonna be a time where you're gonna make all those decisions yourself. When you come home in the evenings, there's nobody to take the heat off of you except you. If you've done well, then you can relax. And if you haven't done well, then you'll pay for it.

After I [came back from] college, a lot of older people that I knew had died. I was gone almost four years, and when I came back they just weren't here. My dad got killed on his tractor right out there in the field while I was gone. That way of life had changed.

I went down to New Orleans. I didn't know anybody; just got in the

Claude Rickman, 1973, is a building contractor in Rabun County.

car and drove down and got a job on a boat. I was running pipe for oil rigs in and out on a barge.

I came home one weekend, and some water pipes had busted over at the Dillard House, and this guy wanted me to fix up them. I did that, and the guy wanted me to build a couple of houses. I was twenty-three then. I built those two houses and haven't quit yet. That's been twelve years ago.

I enjoy the building business. I've got a dozer and backhoe and trucks. It's just like any business. There are hard days and there are easy days, but overall it's a nice thing. It's a business that you can look back at the end of the day and hopefully see things that you've got done. I can go up on the Foxfire land today and look at those houses, and I can remember when we were up there on rainy days chinking those logs, and digging footings, and unloading sand. Millard Buchanan is dead, but you can still go back to those days. Working on the land and doing those houses helped out a lot with what I'm doing now. Anything that you can learn that's positive just gives you a better base for [what you need to do down the road].

For you fellows, whatever the job y'all decide, the biggest thing you'll need to do is find something that you care for. No matter how much you like anything, there are tough days in it. But if you enjoy doing it, when you get older and are at the end of your life, you'll look back and feel like you've got something done. But if you get into a job you hate and you go to work and you're not happy, then one day at the end of your life, you're going to be ill. You're not going to be able to see anything that you did. Life goes fast enough. You don't get but one chance, and you had better make it halfway good.

I was raised in two worlds, and I'm glad of it. Most people today are a lot less aware of those two worlds—how things used to be and how things are today—and they're almost helpless. I had some people who I built a house for call me one Saturday in a panic. They said, "Oh, Lord, our water's gone off." They didn't know what to do. What amazed me—and I don't blame them; they're used to a different world—is that they had a lake right in front of them and a creek right beside them. That'd be easy just to go carry you some water, but that's not the way we think of things. To me, it's not a big deal. When I was a kid, our water came out of the creek. We had a mule, and we'd go down there and haul the water up here. No problem.

I had some people in Sky Valley the other day, and the power went off, and they just. . . . I remember when we first got electricity. It was a box that was ordered from Sears—a kit with lights and wire and stuff, and you just put it up. Went out there one day and there was this box, tied with twine string, tied to the mailbox. That was in 1961. The power company cut a right-of-way through those pine trees up the old road—right there is the old road—and we ran the wires in the house and put staples in the walls through the old white porcelain insulators, and in about three days, we had power. We were amazed. Had about twelve lights in the house. That pole right there is the original one; it's never been changed, and I haven't changed out the old fuse box.

But when the power goes out here, I've still got the kerosene lamps, and I can light those and remember back to when it was like that. My mother and I still heat with wood in this house. We have two wood heaters, and that's it. My room is upstairs, and whatever temperature it is outside, that's what my room is. If I wake up and it's ten degrees outside, it's ten degrees in that room.

I also have a house over on Lake Burton, and it's got two heat pumps and running water and electric everything. But when something goes wrong, I can fix it, and if I can't fix it, I just light a lantern or two and don't worry about it. I can live either way. Doesn't matter. Whichever.

People think we couldn't live that old way again—we couldn't make it—but we could. It's a mental attitude. If you got married today and took your little kids to wherever and just started raising them up and everything around them was all hand tools and all, those little kids would adapt right to that. That's all they'd know. They'd never think a thing about it, until you spoiled them and took them to wherever and said, "Look, here's the easier life." Or we think it's easier. In a lot of ways, it is. I guess man always tries to make life better, easier, and sometimes I think he does, but sometimes I think he makes it harder on himself. It's like in this "easier" life you're exposed to so much stuff. I'll bet you 50 percent of Americans by tonight will know what the temperature was today in Iraq, and they'll know what went on today, and whether or not any hostages came across, and how much it cost today to help the military over there for another day, and what effect there was on the price of gas. My grandparents wouldn't have even known where Iraq was, and who cared, really?

We've got so much exposure to so much stuff. I guess it's good. We have a lot more choices. Of course, sometimes people make bad choices. If you had fewer choices, maybe your odds would be better.

▼▼▼

VIVIAN BURRELL McCAY: I was interested in journalism and photography when I got into Foxfire. I knew there were experiences I'd like to have, but I experienced much more than I expected I would. It was very worthwhile.

When I was in Foxfire, I first learned how to operate the 35-mm camera and do darkroom work. Then Foxfire helped me go to school and get my diploma in photography. Now I'm in advertising.

We had pride in our culture. Before, it was a stereotype of the Appalachian Mountains and the mountain people. The stereotype still exists, but Foxfire has done a lot to show respect for these people. You can proudly say, "Yes, I work with Foxfire, and, yes, I come from the mountains."

▼▼▼

Robbie Bailey interviewing Leona Carver, Kaye Carver Collins, and Phyllis Carver Ramey. Kaye Carver Collins, 1975, now heads the Community/Alumni Initiative for Foxfire. Kaye's sister, Phyllis, 1973, is also a former Foxfire student, and now works in the Rabun County Tax Commissioner's office.

KAYE CARVER COLLINS: I stayed in Rabun County and finished almost two years of college at night while working days at Sangamo-Weston, the Rabun County Library, and later at Gap Manufacturing. I got married and then went to work for Foxfire.

Basically, my job is Alumni Coordinator for Foxfire. That and programs researcher. The main reason I wanted the job is that I felt like the contacts were being ignored. I wanted to make sure they knew somebody did care. The local alumni group started a program called "Adopt-a-Contact." It's a project where the alumni group will stay in touch individually with the Foxfire contacts, and if they need anything, maybe we can connect them with the proper resources, or help ourselves. The only problem I foresee with this is that I don't want to help a contact, say fix his porch, and then have his son call and cuss us out because the son feels like he can take care of his own dad with no help from us. We also don't want to do anything to jeopardize assistance (like Social Security) that the older people qualify for.

The alumni group here in Rabun County is small. Anywhere from five to eight people show up for meetings. But it is a start! Part of my job in the future will be to figure out how to motivate more people. How to generate more enthusiasm for projects.

The alumni group is working on a former-student issue of the magazine. Hopefully, that will get a few more alumni involved. Where it will go from here, I'm not sure right now. But if we can build from this core group of volunteers, then anything is possible.

ᴡᴡ

Lʏɴɴ Bᴜᴛʟᴇʀ: A couple of things brought me into teaching. I was fortunate that I always had very good teachers. I think the idea first came to me when I still lived in New York. It was not until I was in the tenth grade, however, that I became convinced. Then I was able to go to the University of Georgia to study education.

I began as a substitute teacher, which is how you have to get started in New York City. I worked at Eli Whitney, which was such a scary place. Then I worked at Automotive High School. This was closer to where I lived, but it was also a scary place. The students were all guys, and they were not interested in academics at all.

Then I was hired at Bushwick High School to teach remedial English. They basically dumped the responsibility of the school literary magazine on me since they didn't know of anyone else who would do a good job at that. I used it as a motivation to get my remedial students to write. "If you all don't do something," I told them, "I'm not gonna have anything to put in this magazine." So we did a lot of writing. It turned out to be basically a poetry magazine, but there were also about two short stories and one article that was a write-up of an interview that we did in class with a Holocaust survivor.

I now teach at a special school where teenaged girls in the Brooklyn borough of New York City can elect to come if they are pregnant. It's one of five New York public schools for pregnant and parenting teens. My school is in a very depressed area of Brooklyn. It's not someplace you'd go to visit if you came to see New York City. We have eight full-time teachers, and about fifty to a hundred students each semester. My largest class has about twenty-three. I think one day I had twenty-two show up for it, but that was just one day. On the average, the students only attend about half of the time.

I first came here as a substitute. I liked it here, and after that I called the school every semester to see if they needed an English

Lynn Butler, 1977,
teaches today at
P.S. 67 in Brooklyn,
New York.

teacher. I didn't get hired there, however, until I sent them a copy of the literary magazine that I produced with my students at Bushwick High School. The magazine really wasn't a big deal, but for the people I wanted to hire me, it was. They got quite excited.

The girls, many of whom are junior high age, come into the school throughout the year. Many of them come in September, and a lot of them come in at semester break, but in general they come in whenever the guidance counselor at their old school finds out they are pregnant. About 90 percent of our students are black, and the rest are Hispanic. Certainly many of them have less than comfortable backgrounds; however, I can't say that they are what you'd call really poor, not for the most part. My students dress very well, most of them wear nice sneakers and humongous earrings.

These students need an unusual amount of counseling, so I'm glad we can provide that. Many potential teachers here turn away from an alternative school like this one because they're not really interested in doing counseling. It is something I feel strongly about, though, partly because I don't think I would have gotten through high school had there not been people I could talk to who were willing, and who I was able to trust. So I'm usually available after school or in the evening on the telephone. There are two guidance counselors and a social worker available for the really hard-core stuff, but the light-weight stuff such as, "My boyfriend is jerking me around, Ms. Butler. What do you think I should do?" I'm here for that.

After they have their babies, there is child care available downstairs at the school, and for students who do choose to keep going to school, the social worker makes a real effort to help them find child care near their homes or near the school. However, they still combine child care and schoolwork very poorly, for the most part. I don't lower my expectations for them, but I sure give them a lot more slack after they have their babies. If a student comes to me and says, "I'm sorry, I did not get this done because the baby was crying all night and had a temperature," I say, "That's okay, we'll manage that. I'll give you some more time." It's difficult; I'm a mother, and I also have to go to work full time, so I know it's hard for them. Maybe I identify with them.

The main thing that my students especially seem to need as distinguished from regular students are experiences which help them develop self-respect. That's what I try to provide in my classroom. The activities that we engage in and the things that we talk about are all more or less aimed in that direction. We're starting some new classes. I plan to co-teach a class in Language and Cultures with the social studies teacher. It will be like a seminar; we'll have longer periods. I'm also going to teach a film and communications class, which I have great hope for.

All in all, I use the methods of experiential education, democratic learning, and essential questions in my teaching. I know about them because of my experiences in Foxfire. Don't think I learned them at the University of Georgia, because I didn't. The only learning I had in experiential education was from Eliot Wigginton and Margie Bennett. The only training I ever had in essential questions was from observing lessons at Central Park East High School. Sometimes people are suspicious of these methods, but people's attitudes toward this kind of education are getting better, and more people are starting to hear about it. For example, my principal thinks John Dewey is right up there with God. If I didn't have that, I wouldn't be doing what I am now.

Two years ago was my first year at this school. We produced a newsletter together, which the students all respected. Most of the material for it came from the girls' writing in their journals. It was all basically creative writing until the very last issue. Then the students decided they wanted to write about baby and infant care. They did some research; they started talking to some of the nurses and other ladies who worked in the nursery downstairs. They even interviewed a pediatrician. So the newsletter evolved over the course of the year.

Right now the students in my class are working on a special book about different countries in Africa. When we began, each student had to select a country. Then each had to write a letter to either a mission or an embassy in New York City to ask for vital information about that country and invite a member of the mission to come speak to the students. Right now, the students are waiting for the responses. When these people come, they will interview them, and they will write the material up for the book.

Another project the girls have been working on this year is a soap opera called "Flatbush Avenue." They've developed the script them-selves—one of the scenes shows a confrontation between a guy and two girls who have just found out the same guy is the father of both their babies—and they've shot and edited the first segment. They plan to produce a show each term and share them with the other four schools. There's lots of good group work involved in that. When we're working on a video, for example, one group is acting and another group is taping, while one person is the director. One of the things the girls want to do soon is to go visit the other schools in the program and interview the girls there, and videotape those interviews. That's still in the planning stages. We will probably do that after we finish the project we're doing now about Africa.

Whenever a new unit is being planned, it's always a balancing act between the teachers and the students. My co-teacher and I look for literature, for example, that will motivate them to study their own cultures and relate those to their personal lives. But at the same time, if we use the Foxfire method of teaching, the real decisions have to come from the students, and that makes planning a course hard because we don't—and don't want to—know *exactly* what we are going to do. We want the students to shape it. At the same time, we and the students have to remember that at the end of what we do, every person has to show a certain level of mastery on certain skills. The State of New York has special objectives and mandates that the students are tested on by the system just like Georgia does. There's a fine line between being an educator and a boss; so it's like there's a balancing act between various agendas that sometimes seem to be in conflict.

And we do have disagreements from time to time. For example, we have had students who like to sit in the back and not do anything. To help with this problem, we've now arranged the desks so everything's in a circle now—there's no back and no front. And in general, the girls are very involved. I never showed the work I did with Foxfire to my students. I didn't want to seem as if I were saying, "Hey, here's what I did. Don't you want to do this?" I wanted them to come up with their own ideas. But if I hadn't been involved in Foxfire, I would never have become involved in something like this. I'd be your standard lost-with-a-lesson-plan teacher. As a result of that training with Foxfire, my refrain now is always, "Let the kids do it!"

At Foxfire, I also learned the camera inside and out. I learned how to use a darkroom, and I learned how to do layout and paste-up and stuff. I also learned how to write better than I'd ever done before. Prior to that time, I'd never disciplined myself enough. I'd been one of those people who said, "Well, writing is really not that important."

I was also more inspired to meet high standards and to do things right. Wig always told us, "You don't want your name on this if it looks like crap." And so I didn't want my name on an article with misspelled words and messed-up grammar. Wig pushed us; he pushed everybody.

Now, one of my two main hobbies is photography. I put together a darkroom at our school so I could share that interest with my students. I once placed in a photography competition in a magazine.

I'm also a writer. My husband is a screenwriter, and we do some writing together. We wrote an episode on speculation for "The Cosby Show," and it was one of fifty finalists in the Fox Comedy Competition selected out of five thousand entries. That's our big claim to fame so far! We also wrote one for "Thirtysomething," and we're working on one now for "Murphy Brown." I've also written one stage play, which I hope is going to turn into something. So that's what I do in my spare time. When I'm not running around with my daughter, I sit with a word processor and try to get a little work done.

I strongly believe in self-determination. I believe I made my life what it is now by a whole combination of factors. Perhaps the biggest factor of all is my background and upbringing. I was raised in a household that could best be described as "guilty liberal." I was endowed with a strong sense of social responsibility and a need to help other people in order to feel satisfied. My work with Foxfire was kind of an extension of that need, and my work now is a continuation of the same thing.

▓

JOHNNY SCRUGGS: Ever since about the second grade, I wanted to fly. I was growing up in about 1967 or 1968 during the Apollo missions. They were going to the moon, and all I could think about was flying— maybe even being an astronaut. But Clayton doesn't even have an airport, so there's not much opportunity for a guy that wants to fly to even be around airplanes.

Then, all I really thought about was playing football, girls, and having a good time. I didn't really respect the older people that much. But I gained a lot of respect for older people through Foxfire. And, of course, I finally got to fly. My first time was that flight to Monterey, California, with Foxfire. And that was it. I knew that was what I was going to do.

When I graduated in 1979, I went to Georgia Southern. Foxfire helped out with scholarship money. And I had started to learn to fly. I had saved some money one summer lifeguarding up at Sky Valley. I

Johnny Scruggs, 1978, is a pilot for United Airlines.

took flying lessons and got my private pilot's license. I didn't tell Mama and Daddy because they thought flying was very dangerous and they didn't want me doing it. So I just snuck off and got my license on my own.

The problem was that a poor old country boy like me couldn't afford to get all my ratings and the things that you are required to have to be a commercial pilot. There are too many hours involved, and it's just too expensive. I knew the military was the only way for me to go if I really wanted to fly. So after about two years at Southern, I started to talk to recruiters. They said, "We can take you now, and we'll let you finish your degree while you're on active duty." It all sounded too good to be true.

[The military is] very strict. Once you're in there, they make you learn. They spend a lot of money on you, and they don't want you to fail. The key is to get that college education, and become an officer. You've gotta be an officer to fly, and you've gotta have a college degree to be an officer.

So I went to flight school and flew helicopters and fixed wing, and I went to school three nights a week from five forty-five until ten-fifteen and finished my bachelor's degree at Monterey. It's hard, but I guess it was the best thing for me. I grew up a lot. I went in when I was twenty years old, and by the time I turned twenty-one, I'd gotten married. When you grow up fast like that, you have to make a lot of decisions, but if you really want to be a pilot, you can do it. I graduated number one in my class out of army flight training because [flying was] what I really wanted to do, and I set my mind to it. And if I can learn to fly, then anybody can. I really believe that actually you *can* be too smart to be a pilot, if you can understand that. You just have to have good judgment, good hand/eye coordination, good vision, and a lot of will power. You don't have to be a rocket scientist.

Now I fly for United Airlines. They say right now that the average guy getting hired by the airlines probably has four or five thousand hours in the air. If you get trained in the military, you have to stay in the military a minimum of six years once you graduate from flight school. They spend a million dollars teaching you how to fly, and they want to get their obligation out of you. Guys coming out of the military have about two thousand hours [flying time]. I've got, right now, nearly seven thousand hours—twenty-four hundred of that is in helicopters. That's why I'm an old man! [Laughs.] I'm thirty years old. That's a long time in the air. But a lot of the guys that I fly with have thirty thousand hours. If you figure it out, it probably comes out to be a couple of years of their lives in the sky.

I'm based out of Chicago, but I live outside Atlanta—in Acworth. When I go to work, I'll hop on a plane at Hartsfield and fly to Chicago [and] work for four or five days. I've got an apartment with four other guys there. These guys live in Texas, Alabama, Mississippi, and Florida. We all go in together and that's your home away from home, if you will. Then I catch a flight back from Chicago to Atlanta and I will be off for six days. A lot of pilots commute. You can live about anywhere you want to. We have guys who live in Australia and are based out of L.A. When they go to work, they fly from Sydney to L.A., and then they'll go to work for four or five days, and then they're off for six or eight days, and they'll go back to Sydney.

I like living close to Rabun County, so I'll probably always commute. There's talk of United putting a base in the Southeast somewhere, which would make my commuting a lot easier. If they put a crew base in Huntsville, Alabama, what I'd really like to do is get a home on Lake Burton [in Rabun County]. That would get me right back home. My parents are here, and my wife's parents have a place on Lake Burton now, so we come up to the lake and go water skiing and bring Brittany up to see her grandparents. It's only an hour and a half drive up here, so we come up a lot. If I didn't have to work, I would water ski, snow ski, and play golf the rest of my life. I'd be a happy man! But for me to drive to Huntsville four times a month, and be able to live here and raise my kids in this type of atmosphere would be worth it. It would be a little tough, but you've gotta sacrifice for your family. I'd sure do it.

One sort of ironic thing is that I fly over Clayton all the time. The sky is set up with imaginary airways, or highways, so to speak, and it's based on navigation equipment called VORs. As a matter of fact, there's one at Toccoa. If you weren't a pilot, you wouldn't even know about it. [One of the airways into Atlanta takes you right over the top of Rabun County High School.] Also, I still fly helicopters in the Georgia National Guard out of Atlanta so I'm up here all the time flying around. [Now all I have to do is figure out how to live here.]

I ran into Wig recently on the same United flight headed for Chicago. I was on my way to work, and he was trying to get to Seattle. It was sure funny seeing Wig. I looked and I said, "That's gotta be Wig. There can't be two guys in the whole world that alike." I hadn't seen him, I guess, in ten years. I asked him, "Do you remember the first time we flew together?" He did.

I don't know what I would have done if I hadn't been hooked up with Foxfire. I knew I wanted to be a pilot, but I had no idea I would be. I don't think I'd be standing here talking to you had I not been able to go to college. Foxfire afforded me the opportunity to at least go to college and try to see if I could make it in this old world. That opened up more doors. I met people and made lifelong friends. [I also] met the proper recruiter to get me in the service. Had I just stayed here in Clayton, I probably would have never met that recruiter who got me into flight school. I believe in destiny, and I believe that I was destined to do what I did.

By the time I was twenty-seven or twenty-eight, I had been around the world several times. China. Beijing. In the square where they had that big riot? I've been right there. Not when it was going on, but a year prior to that. I've seen the tomb of Mao Tse-tung and walked on the Great Wall of China. And it all started out on an L-1011 to Monterey, California, with Foxfire.

▼▼▼

LYNETTE WILLIAMS ZOELLNER: I went to college for one year, and I didn't like that, so I quit college and I went to trade school for a year and a half and I graduated from there. I got married and worked for a while, and then my mother and I went into business for ourselves.

We weave here. It consumes every waking moment, but I like being my own boss. I don't have to take orders from somebody. I have my own income and my own schedule most of the time. It's a whole lot different working for yourself than it is working for somebody else. There's no pressure. We never have any money is the only problem!

I used to be kind of shy and I didn't like to talk to people that I'd never met before. It was hard for me to come out and talk and meet people, and now that's what I do every day for a living. Foxfire gives you a lot more confidence about yourself.

Now I'm trying to teach my children the old things, too. My husband said I was born too late. I should have been born a hundred years ago. I like anything old and all the old ways. I'm trying to teach them that, too.

Lynette Williams Zoellner, 1978, is a weaver and craft shop owner.

Having worked with Foxfire, I knew that I could start my own business. I had the confidence that we could do it.

▼▼▼

BOB KUGEL: I was just down there as a boarding student from Detroit. I was sort of a delinquent. I was in a lot of trouble all of the time, until I got to know Wig. He helped me get out of so much trouble. I would have been a hell of a lot better off had I stayed in Rabun Gap. I learned more in one year at Rabun Gap than I would have in four years in Detroit. But I didn't stay. I didn't graduate. I quit school, but later I took my GED and moved to New York City.

You turn eighteen years old and you can come here and get a job driving a cab. It's like the guys that sell hot dogs on the street corner. You pay a few bucks and get a license. The first day when I got to New York I found this garage that hires you to drive a cab. They will fill out all of the forms for you, and they will send them down to the Taxi and Limousine Commission, and they will get you a license within three days.

When I first came here, I had about three hundred bucks in my pocket. I spent most of that getting the license. I stayed at the YMCA over on Twenty-third Street and Seventh Avenue. I think I was paying

Bob Kugel is a cab driver in New York City.

seventy-eight dollars a week. Then I moved to the Kenmore Hotel. I was working my butt off and saved enough money to get me a decent apartment. I just worked and worked and worked because that was the only thing I had to do.

Driving is sort of an art. I just found that I have a knack for it. It started out of necessity. I had to do it, and I had to get good at it because I had to make a living. In New York, that is very difficult because living expenses are so high. The better driver you become, the better you can weave in and out through all of the traffic. You get to know when people need a cab before they actually know they need one. And the better you get at it, the more money you make.

Before I went down to Rabun Gap, I was a wild punk on the street in Detroit. Foxfire sort of straightened me out and gave me a whole new outlook on things. It taught me about life—life beyond my own little world. There's people doing different things. Foxfire helped me to respect them. They're not necessarily people that you're used to associating with, but they are people. You learn about things like honor. Wig set his mind and got this whole thing started, and he's still going at it. To me, that's honor. He's gone through a lot of kids and has helped most of them some way or another. I was watching TV a while back and I saw someone interviewing Wig, and I thought, "Shit, that's Wig! And he's doing the same thing." Wig put things together on Foxfire, and for twenty-five years has made it a very successful thing. That's great, teaching kids, because the youth of America is the future of America.

It happened in Georgia—it can happen anywhere. You can teach these kids about their community and about the outside world. Foxfire interviewed local people. There's local people everywhere. There's local people in Rabun County, and local people in New York City. There are people that stay in their own little world. You get people, for example, in Manhattan that have never left the city. People in New York think, "This is it." Think there's nothing beyond the Hudson River. They think, "I'm a New Yorker. This is what's happening. This is where it's at. Ain't nothing out there." Which is a crock of bullshit! That's America out there. So what Foxfire has done is open my eyes up to see the whole world. It helped me respect my fellow man.

▼▼▼

SHAYNE BECK: I started to go to college, but I didn't want to. I'd had enough [of school] and really wanted to get out of school and I thought I'd just go to work, so my dad and I bought this store [Five Points Grocery].

My dad owned another store, and that's what I'd grown up doing [working for him in a store during high school], so I'd say my classmates expected me to be doing this.

I guess [the thing I like about my work is] when it's raining, I'm on the inside; when it's cold weather, I'm on the inside; and when it's hot, I'm in the cool. I'm my own boss and that's the main thing, 'cause I can make my own decisions.

I'm not very good in English, so Foxfire kinda helped me out. It helped me to learn. It made it a lot more interesting to learn about English, and not just sitting down with your head stuck in a book. Wig had a special way of teaching.

I think I'd be doing the same thing if I hadn't been in Foxfire. But I'm sure there are a lot of students that go through Foxfire that never

Shayne Beck,
1979, owns a grocery
store in Rabun County.

would have got their full potential out until Wig come along, 'cause he was able to get kids to give a hundred and ten percent.

♦♦♦

LORIE RAMEY THOMPSON: In Foxfire, I learned an appreciation for my home and family. I knew I didn't want to leave Rabun County. I wanted to stay here, make a good living, and do something constructive.

Where I grew up, there was a mountain behind my house. I loved to go up there. It had a gorgeous view. That's where I did my sorting out and thinking. Suddenly, the property became "For Sale." I was working as a secretary then. There was no hope for me ever buying it. If you want to make a living here, it's hard. The only solution I had was, "If you can't beat them, join them." Being a realtor was the way I was going to make a living in Rabun. Now I try to blend what I did in Foxfire with what I do now.

Lorie Ramey Thompson, 1979, is a realtor in Rabun County and a member of the Foxfire Community Advisory Board.

I was heavily involved with environmental studies in the outdoor ed. program. I was concerned about the clear-cuts that were being done in the county. And in Wig's class, we did one thing that was great. We did a slide show about trash up and down Highway 441. I am all for sign zoning now. If everyone had the same sized sign on their businesses, they could get rid of sign pollution on this road. We're starting to look like a tourist-trap city. I think that's a shame. The people who visit don't see the beautiful part of this county until they almost get out of it.

[I think about all that, and I try to do something about it. At the same time, I also stay involved with Foxfire by being on the Community Advisory Board. It keeps you thinking.] By making a comment, Wig puts you to thinking of aspects you would have never thought of. That's what makes a teacher—not so much what they can teach you, but what you can learn by yourself. With the Community Advisory Board meetings, there'll be lots of discussions on a subject and lots of different opinions. When Wig speaks up, he never says, "This is what I think." He'll say, "Well, have you thought about this side?" That's someone who can communicate and make you think even farther. That's a teacher.

I feel so strongly about the Foxfire program. I want it to be around when my child is born. Through the Community Advisory Board, I can actually take a part in it. If you're going to take, you need to give back. That's what I'm trying to do [now]. I want to give back to the program what I can.

**w**

TOMBO RAMEY: I worked for Foxfire one summer restructuring the cabins, resealing wood, and putting flooring in. I got interested in cabins and wanted one for myself. Working with them that summer gave me some ideas of the process of tearing it down and rebuilding it.

Foxfire had known about the building before I did, and they even have some of the old furniture from it up at the village. The owner said he wanted to sell it, and I ended up buying it from him. It took me six months, by myself, every day, taking down the siding, and numbering it. I hired some help to take down the logs, and I have it stored in some box trailers. I hope to get some land and make a nice little home out of it someday. I even got the history of the cabin itself.

Tombo Ramey, 1979, is a builder today in Clayton.

Right now, I am living here in Clayton, building homes with my family. We build homes for sale, and we have a lot of rental property. I'm doing a lot of construction work, and basically that's what I have been doing for the last couple of years. I did work for Georgia Power for three and a half years after I got out of college, but I was working in Atlanta, and I just got tired of the city, and came back to these mountains. I imagine in the future I will be some type of builder, developer, or be in real estate.

▚▚▚

JOHN SINGLETON: For two years, I received a Foxfire scholarship to go to Young Harris College. I was hating college. I was just studying and playing tennis at the time, and I kept thinking, "You know, maybe I should just scrap this." I didn't know what else I was going to do. I wrote Wig a couple of letters early on. I remember every time I'd write him, immediately I would get a letter back. He never said, "John, stay in college." He just talked to me about, "Well, here's what your options are, and here's the benefits of each." And he would tell me about when he was in college. He would write home and tell his father, "I'm having trouble, Dad. I'm studying hard and I'm making C's."

His father would tell him, "Well, son, if this is really the case, maybe college isn't the direction you should be going."

I can remember that story, because when Wig went on to study education, he graduated first in his class. I think the lesson there is at some point, you have to grow up and make some decisions.

I stayed in and got an undergraduate degree in journalism with a minor in political science from the University of Georgia. I was going to save the world. I thought I was going to make journalism my lifelong career. I remember sitting on Christmas Eve at a television station in Greenville, South Carolina, where I was doing my internship. I was sitting there with about twelve or thirteen reporters between the ages of twenty-five and thirty-five, and they were all running their hands through their hair and smoking. I thought to myself, "I don't want to be like this. I'd rather be a bum than sit and do this all day." Nothing about it seemed appealing to me. I said, "Well, now what am I going to do?"

I decided to go back to school. I went back to Georgia and got my master's in Education, and Foxfire had everything to do with it. I don't know if it was a good idea or not because I haven't taught yet, but, you know, it was strictly thinking back to the one thing that I could take from my youth [and build on] that made me want to try it.

[Foxfire] also absolutely [helped me] with editing skills, and grammar, and the whole environment of learning, [and] how to study and apply something, and *finish* something. You know, no term paper in high school or in college was as difficult as putting together the Ben Ward article. Nothing ever compared to that one.

Now, I plan to teach political science, geography, and history in high school. I have family in Alaska. I would prefer teaching up there. I guess at some point I'm still going to save the world, but don't worry, it's not going to be anytime soon, so y'all are still safe!

▙▟▛

VAUGHN ROGERS: I always showed a responsibility about myself, and so Foxfire didn't change me as much as some students who gained confidence in themselves and really turned around academically. My academics were already there.

Vaughn Rogers, 1981, works in his family's hardware and building supply business.

But the main thing Foxfire taught me was that if you want something, then there are all different ways to get it. Instead of sitting back and saying, "I can't do this," well, "Call so and so and maybe he can help you. If he can't he's going to tell you where you can go." The main thing is not to be scared to ask people for what you need. It wasn't just the classroom learning. It was learning *all* the resources that were available outside of our realm. When John Singleton and I were having trouble on the articles about his grandparents, that happened. We had a general store ledger that was hard to read. Some of the symbols and stuff we didn't understand, and instead of just dropping it and saying, "Okay we can't figure it out," Wig says, "Let's go to the State Archives in Atlanta, and they can probably help us figure what the symbols are." So instead of just giving up, Foxfire taught you there were resources out there to give you answers.

When I graduated from college, I went into the real estate business with my father here, and things were pretty tight. It was hard to get started in the real estate business at that time because everybody had gotten in it by the time I graduated from college, and it was real cutthroat because there were so many of us.

So I got out of that and I went to work with the family business, which is hardware and building supply. I went into outside sales, dealing with the contractors, figuring their house plans, and telling them how much it would cost them in material to build the house, going to the jobs, and taking orders for supplies.

Right now, I do plan to make this a lifelong career. It's a family business, and our grandfather has pretty much counted on the younger generations to carry on what he began in 1928 when he started it. I'm content with it, and proud of what he's done, and proud to be able to carry on the business. It fit in with what I had studied in college. It's a good steady opportunity, and it's there as long as I want it to be. I'm not saying that if something came along I would refuse it, but most likely I want to stay in Rabun County. It's a good place to raise your kids. It's the place that I'm content.

▚▚▚

WESLEY TAYLOR: I had Foxfire scholarship money when I was in college. It helped me pay for a lot of my education at the University of Georgia. I did a lot for Foxfire, and I thought it was great to get something back.

I graduated from there in 1984, and I took a job down here in Wilkes County teaching agriculture and that's what I'm still doing. I finished my master's degree in 1987. I graduated with my specialist's degree in 1989 in agricultural education from the university. I got married in 1989. My wife teaches kindergarten, and we're both employed by the school system.

Everybody on my father's side was in agriculture. My great-grand-father was an agriculturist; my grandfather was an agriculture teacher in the twenties and thirties; my father is a farmer. On my mother's side, just about everyone is a teacher, including my mother. So I just put the two together.

A teaching philosophy is very important because you've got to have some benchmark to work from. My objective as a teacher is to provide as many varied experiences as I can for the students—let

Wesley Taylor, 1981, teaches public high school and is mayor of Tignall, Georgia.

A group of Wesley's students are building a barn on the school's campus.

them learn something to help them reach their potential and learn things that will be useful to them in life, no matter what they do—whether they're a clerk at City Hall, a lawyer, or out plowing the field. I use the same hands-on experiential education methods that have been used by Foxfire to make it what it is today. In my agriculture class we go out here and build a barn, and we work with livestock. We've got hogs coming in next week. Many things we do are outside class because you learn better by doing, and that's a Foxfire tradition. I just hope something I relate to them will help them forever.

There are many things that you can get in school besides math and English skills—things about life, about having to deal with society, being on time, having responsibilities. You set the values for these kids, and if you don't teach values, you don't teach. Employers will teach you the technical things you need to know, but they want somebody with integrity and responsibility. If they are supposed to be at work at nine [they should] be, and they should work for a day's pay. Foxfire instills that in students. If you two guys interviewing me right now were sorry, you would be off swimming somewhere. But instead you've got responsibilities that have to be met, and y'all are meeting them. We used to have to go to town and take money and write checks. It was our responsibility to see that get done and give it 100 percent. When you start something, you hang with it and finish it. Questions in a book aren't going to help you learn any of these things.

Most students *will* do something productive. I've never had a student that won't do anything. They might not like what you're doing at a certain time, but something will come up that they will like. The kids who are borderline and probably aren't going to make [it] are the ones I like to help. If I can help someone that really needs it, that really satisfies me. That's what I like about teaching. And all of the things they learn in the process are like gears in a transmission: they all work together. Each piece in the total education system is important.

I've also been the mayor of Tignall, Georgia, since last October. Some people wanted me to run for mayor, and I decided I would. At first I didn't think I had a very good chance. Some people don't like outsiders [and they were] kind of mad because I wasn't from Tignall. I stayed away from the polls, and when they counted [the votes] up it was a dead tie. So they had a run-off [election], and I won by six votes.

I'm glad I did run, because it's been an interesting job. [I'm the youngest mayor Tignall has ever had,] and that has its advantages and disadvantages. I've had good luck with it so far [but] it's a lot of work. Before I was mayor, I used to be able to [complain], "Well, them dern police. They didn't do this or that." [Now people call me and say the same thing.] Someone will call me and say, "My phone's out of order." I'll [answer,] "Yes, ma'am," and call the phone company for them. I'm not the phone man, but I do what I can. I've gotten out in the middle of the road and directed traffic for a funeral before because the police officer was out at that time. [I just do whatever I can to help people.]

Everybody ought to be in a public service, but dealing with people—that's something that you learn to do on the job. We were involved with a lot of people in Foxfire, and that helped me with being mayor. Right now we are working on a sewage system—getting one installed. We just got it approved the other day. To start a project and to keep working on it uses the same principles in about anything you do.

**~~~**

KIM HAMILTON MCKAY, DANA HOLCOMB ADAMS, AND ROSANNE CHASTAIN WEBB:

KIM: After high school, I went to Young Harris one quarter. My grandmother was real bad sick and was in the hospital, and she ended up dying before I got through with that one quarter. I transferred from there to Truett-McConnell College because it was closer, and someone at that time needed to stay with my grandfather because he had been so dependent on her. I went there two quarters and ended up working at Reeves Hardware in the daytime and going to night school about two years, taking accounting and computer courses. I got married shortly afterward and worked for John Dillard for a while doing bookkeeping. I got the job because I had a bookkeeping/accounting diploma with computer background.

Then I had a baby, stayed with her for nine months, and by that time I was ready to go back to work. I took a temporary job to help down at the luggage plant. Helped them out a little over six months while two of the office employees were sick. From there I went to the bank and I've been there ever since in the bookkeeping department.

DANA: After I graduated from high school, I got a full scholarship to college from Foxfire. I can remember Mom and Daddy fussing

(Left to right) Dana Holcomb Adams, 1982, is a legal secretary; Kim Hamilton McKay, 1982, is a bookkeeper; and Rosanne Chastain Webb, 1981, specializes in public relations. They are looking through back issues of *Foxfire* they worked on. Beth Lovell, Julie Dickens, and Jenny Lincoln interviewed them.

because I'd stay after school so much, but I had been told that if I worked real hard, then when it came time to go to college, they would help me. Now my folks realize that if I hadn't had that scholarship, I wouldn't have gotten through school—unless I had gotten a job while I was going.

I think it was Margie and Bob Bennett who made the biggest impression in my life. They kind of showed me the direction to go, helped me and were there when I needed to talk to somebody. Margie's the one you could ask anything, no matter what it was. When you're fourteen, fifteen, and sixteen years old, you've got to have somebody like that. That's the good thing about her; she didn't lie to you. If she didn't think it was something you should be doing, she would tell you.

KIM: It was like you had decided it for yourself, and she was just helping you make the decision. I think that that is the problem with a lot of parents today. Instead of helping their kids make their own decisions, they tell them no, they can't do it, and that makes the kids want to do it anyway. I think that was one of the talents that Margie had. She made everyone feel like an adult or on the same level as her.

DANA: Now I work as a legal secretary in Clayton, typing up all of these legal documents. I've learned a lot about real estate and finance. Partly because of Foxfire, I'm more comfortable working with older people than I am people in their thirties and forties. I felt like when I was with [older people] in high school, they really enjoyed it, and their eyes kind of gleamed. So I like for somebody that's older to come into the office. It makes me feel like I can help them. When I was younger, I felt like they helped me a lot by giving me time. [Now I can give it back.]

KIM: And I think our typing skills in Foxfire really helped us in our jobs now. Working with Ann Moore, doing bookkeeping, and running a business, I think, was what helped me the most. Now I'm a book-keeper here [and both of us have been able to stay in Rabun County]. I think I'll retire here in the county. All my friends are here, and my family. And I want my girls to get involved with Foxfire.

ROSANNE: I've decided that I want to stay here, too. If I don't find a job in public relations, I'll free-lance and do magazine articles. Before I got involved in Foxfire, I didn't think I could write at all. Then I went on to the University of Georgia, where my major was journalism until my husband got a job and we had to move, and I had to transfer to Brenau College where they didn't offer a journalism major. They did have public relations, though, which is like a mixture of marketing, journalism, and advertising, and so my major became PR. I did my internship at Foxfire. Then my senior thesis was how PR works in a nonprofit organization. I based it on Foxfire and four other nonprofits that have the same size staff, like the Highlander Center and the Atlanta Historical Society and the Georgia Conservancy. Then I did a lot of research on larger nonprofit organizations like the Red Cross, and what they do for PR, and then I put all my findings together to show where PR could fit into Foxfire.

At graduation in May, I won the Senior Thesis Award for the best thesis. We didn't know who had won it until the last minute, and when they got up to present it, they said I had learned to write before I got there because of Foxfire. I had an advantage over everybody else.

◤◥◤

DONNA BRADSHAW SPEED: After high school, I got married. Then I opened my own craft shop. I had no idea I'd be going into crafts, though. When I was in high school, I didn't realize how important it is to learn and record what the people around me knew how to do,

Donna Bradshaw Speed, 1983, is a craft shop owner.

like making their own quilts and crafts. I didn't care. I was too busy having fun and chasing boys. I don't know what my classmates thought of me. I was voted "wittiest" in my class, so they all thought I was nuts anyway.

Now I love crafts. To me, each is something special. There's a piece of somebody in everything in this shop. There's a lot of work in it, but there's also a lot of love in what they do, so it's not like people are popping out stuff like in a factory just to make lots of money. They really care about their finished products. But for many of them, it *is* how they make their living.

In this job, you learn a respect for people who make things. I've never met a crafts person who didn't have a good heart. And they aren't snobby people or hateful, bossy people. People who make crafts are caring, sharing, and giving people—they really are. Everybody I work with is fun. I enjoy running my mouth, and I get to do that a lot with people who come in here! I guess Foxfire helped a little there. I learned to run my mouth in front of people without being hacked out and nervous.

I also learned how hard it was for people to live back then before microwaves and electric sewing machines. It was so tough; I would have hated it. I would have liked it a lot better that things didn't cost as much, but I would have hated getting up and building a fire to cook breakfast and keeping that fire going all day long in order to have dinner and supper cooked. All of those quilts and pillows are pretty, but back then making them was simply something people had to do. It was survival.

But *everything* you do in life changes what you are—everything. Everything influences you, and it's hard to pin anything down as being the result of only one thing. Foxfire didn't influence me to start the craft shop, but what it did was to make me appreciate what people do.

Foxfire also helped me realize that I should take pride in being in Rabun County. There are not many places like Rabun County anymore. The people here are so friendly. I love where I come from. I wouldn't trade being from Rabun County for anything. And if I have children, and if Foxfire is still there, as I hope it will be, I hope very much that they get involved in it.

ŴŴ

RONNIE WELCH: From high school, I went on to the Army. Could of went to college, and I would have, but I've always been real independent and hardheaded, so I took on off on my own and went into the service. Traveled around. I tell you, part of what made me go into the service, though, was the fact that whenever I was with Foxfire, I got to travel around, you know, to different cities, and I didn't feel like I wanted to stay right there in Rabun County all my life without getting out and seeing the rest of the world.

I worked on heavy equipment while I was in the service, and I was a truck driver and a little bit of everything. Now, I work for a company that's called Heavy Machines, and we have a contract with the Lands Railroad yard in Atlanta. You know the trailers that tractors pull? Well, we lift them on and off flatcars with cranes. I maintain those cranes that's down there on that yard.

I was down there one night, by myself, working on them, and I was doing an air pressure check. Usually, there's a train engineer in the locomotive, but there wasn't that night. I hopped up in that thing, and just like an instant, I was back in Toccoa on the *Southern Crescent*. It was the same thing.

Ronnie Welch,
1983, works as a
large-equipment
contract service
technician.

I got in there and monkeyed around and figured out how to rev it up and get my air pressure built up to do my brake test. I used to tell Wig that I'd like to be a train engineer, or work around trains, and I am now. I have discovered that ain't what I want to do forever. As a matter of fact, here I am twenty-five years old, and I still don't know what I want to do forever. I've been around quite a bit. I've been a lot of places, seen a lot of different things. Still don't know if I'm through or not. Probably not.

Whenever I started down there, I was working for another subcontractor for the railroad. At the very first, they were in charge of six trucks and three cranes, and no trailers and nothing else. They got bigger, and as they got bigger, I got bigger. Eventually I was shop manager. I had four guys working for me, twenty-two years old. Made good money, too—$640 a week. They had a real hard time finding anybody that could put up with everything that goes on down there, but I really didn't have any problem doing it. By that time, though, we had fourteen trucks to take care of, 332 trailers we had to do federal highway inspections on. It's a twenty-four-hour-a-day operation. They don't stop for nothing. I held the job for two years.

Then they decided that they would give up the crane maintenance, and whenever they did, Heavy Machines took it over, and I went to work for them. Now we've got five cranes and that's all I do. This is not your everyday heavy equipment. They're on huge rubber tires. My head probably sticks two or three inches over the top of the metal wheel [hub] in the tire. The boom will go twenty-eight feet high down to about eight foot. I figured up its weight one time. In my maintenance manual, it don't give you a total weight. It will give you the spreader weight, the mask weight, the frame weight, the wheels and tires weight, and all the major components. I think I figured it weighs three hundred and twenty thousand pounds. It's got three cabs.

And one of those cranes will lift a maximum of ninety thousand pounds. That's not actually their maximum. It's recommended maximum. They don't want you to go any higher than ninety thousand pounds, but I know for a fact that it will lift a hundred and thirty-four thousand 'cause they overload a lot of those trailers down there, and the cranes still pick them up. I put a set of scales on one one time just to see, 'cause I was getting a lot of unusual damage to my cranes. So I put a set of scales on there and showed them. I had to prove to them what my problem was. They didn't believe me.

And they work those cranes hard. They lift on and off down there an average of about twenty thousand trailers a month. That's grown since I first started there from forty-one hundred lifts a month. That's just in the past five years. It seems like I jumped in there whenever it first started, and now it's booming.

On a crane, I do everything from changing the oil and greasing it to completely tearing down the crane. Whatever it takes. I'm in complete control. It's a different job for me, because I have to deal with people—have to deal with truck drivers coming in and out of there to get trailers, have to deal with the politics of the railroad, and I also have to deal with my job as far as what's got to be accomplished. I guess it's pretty much an everyday routine job except you're on call twenty-four hours a day. Just when you think you know it all, there's something else that will knock you in the head, and that's pretty good. I guess that's why I've been there five years.

Looking back, I guess Foxfire taught me to be a professional, but it also taught me a lot of different ways to do things other than just the ordinary way. The first real job I had was up there on the Foxfire land. There again, I didn't see the whole outlook and aspect of it all then. I was just real involved in what I was doing at the time. Now I see that it helped me out a lot. I had a little bit of extra money coming in, and there again, that was the whole start, I feel like, of my life from that point until now. It gave me something to look forward to, and I guess that's what made me so independent now. I felt like I was on my own making money to buy my school clothes. I would give my family money. I stayed interested and involved in something all the time. That's probably why I've turned out like I am today. I'm not bad to drink, never did any drugs. If I hadn't got involved with Foxfire, and me being straight across from the beer joint with all the commotion and whatnot going on over there, I could have got involved in some, I feel like, not very good things. Maybe turn out to be much less than what I am today. But I feel like I am somebody today, and I've come a long way and learned a lot, and I have a lot to give now from what I've learned. I guess Foxfire changed my whole life—just put me on a perspective of life—and I've followed through the best that I know how, keeping that knowledge with me along the way. I'm sure it has made a good-sized portion of how I look at and treat people. I know it has. The way I was treated, it makes you feel like you are somebody and not a snot-nosed kid. It gives you a certain amount of responsibility. I felt like I had an obligation. I just had something to do all the time, and it was important to me for them to let me do something and feel like a grown-up.

I guess just to wind it up in a nutshell and say it all, without Foxfire, and without the way that they did go about treating me whenever I was in the class and whenever I was out of the class, I have no idea of how I would have turned out—what I would be like today. That's how big of an impression Foxfire had on me. It gave me the initiative that I've got as far as seeking out, finding new things, and teaching people what I know. I use it in everyday life with my wife, and people I know, with my job, and with my outlook on life. I feel like a lot of the ways that Foxfire taught me is the way that I would like to carry on and teach other people. Foxfire worked real hard to put that in our heads, and there again, I didn't realize it at the time what y'all did. Y'all got me involved in doing it, and I didn't even realize it. I was going off with Wig and everybody, and teaching people then how to teach what y'all were teaching me. So it definitely sunk in, and yeah, I do use it in everyday life. It works.

Foxfire helped me a lot not only in knowledge but in caring. There was plenty of love and caring up there on the mountain. There always has been. And if I need something today, I can go up there and see any one of them and they will help me any way they can or steer me in the right direction. They're more like a family than anything in every aspect. That's exactly what happened between you'uns all. Y'all took me under your shoulder; whether y'all knew it or not, and whether I knew it or not, that's what happened. Turned out pretty good.

▀▀▀

ALLISON ADAMS: The college I went to was Agnes Scott, a small, selective women's college in Atlanta with a strong emphasis on academics. I wanted a small college, and I thought a women's college would be a good place to go to, too. I didn't want male competitiveness in the classroom because I think that's a silly attitude. I loved the idea that I could go to class with a sweatshirt, sweatpants, bushy hair, and no make-up. There's a great deal to be said about that kind of atmosphere.

There was also something I had learned to appreciate by becoming involved in Foxfire: the close contact and friendly relationship with the staff members. When I came to Agnes Scott, I found I could establish the same kind of relationship with my professors because it has a small ratio between teachers and students.

Agnes Scott is quite a selective college. When I was a senior in high school, I submitted my application, and they accepted me. The

Allison Adams, 1985, is
director of publications
at Converse College in
Spartanburg, South
Carolina. Here she's being
interviewed by student
editors of this book, Jenny
Lincoln and Leigh Ann
Smith.

acceptance letter said, "Along with your acceptance to Agnes Scott, you're a semifinalist for the scholarship competition." So I went down for an interview, and they asked me, "Allison, what have you done?"

I replied, "Well, I've got two books with my name on them published with Doubleday and Dutton. I'm a real published author!" Then I told them all about Foxfire. I won the scholarship, and if it hadn't been for that, I wouldn't have been able to go because my family wouldn't have been able to afford this expansive private education.

I knew from the time I was a sophomore in high school that I was going to major in English because the only thing I could really do very well was read. I've always told people, "I'm not a writer; I'm much more of a reader." In Foxfire, I learned a great deal about reading material critically, and this really helped me in college. To write a research paper for college English class involves exactly the same skill you use in preparing an article for the *Foxfire* magazine. You take information, organize it, and present it in a form that is coherent to the reader.

I love doing research papers. All the way through college, as I worked on them, I would say, "Well, this is great fun. It's just like a scavenger hunt!"

People would look at me and say, "You're insane! This is boring; it's hard work!"

And I would reply, "Not if you make it fun." It *is* like a scavenger hunt. You have clues and you have to figure out where the clues lead you to and find the gold mine of material. When you bring the wealth back to your desk, it's all confused and messed up, so your job is to take all that scratch stuff that you've thrown down on little three-by-five cards and make a point of it, get it to make sense. Being able to put research papers together was what got me through college. One of the biggest papers I ever did was on the problems and solutions in education in the southern Appalachian mountains.

One of the most special and exciting parts of my Agnes Scott experience was when I was chosen to do the oral history project when the college was about to celebrate its centennial. One of the professors had heard about me being in Foxfire, and she recommended that I be in charge of that project. This turned into a summer job between my junior and senior years in college. I just took what I learned from Foxfire and adapted it to a new situation.

I interviewed many older women who had graduated from Agnes Scott. I also interviewed former staff members. I interviewed a former dean, and I interviewed a really cute man named R. Mell Jones who was the head of the security staff and had been on campus for twenty-five or thirty years. He had some of the funniest stories to tell, especially about running off stray boys.

The day before I graduated, Agnes Scott signed a contract with a small company, Susan Hunter Publishing, to publish the commemorative book. This was a publishing company that I had had an internship with before my junior year, so I was delighted that the contract was signed. Some of the material in this book is the work I did for the oral history.

You may recall that earlier I told you that I'm not really a writer; I'm much more of a reader. That's why I went into editing. My first job after graduation was at a small publishing company in Atlanta called Longstreet Press, which publishes a variety of nonfiction books. If it hadn't been for Foxfire, I might not have gotten this job. This is how it happened. When I was a senior in high school, I spoke about Carolyn Stradley, who I told you about earlier, at my STAR student banquet. The speaker at the banquet, George Berry, Georgia's Commissioner of Industry and Trade, was so impressed by my words about Carolyn that he gave me his card after the banquet. He told me, "Call me in four years and I'll help you." After I got out of college, I called him, and that was how I ended up getting this job.

That job included a variety of different tasks. Since I was just out of college, for a while I was the "low chick on the totem pole." As an editorial assistant, 20 percent of my job was answering phone calls. The rest of my work was public relations, and assisting the editors. In April 1990, I was promoted to be the assistant editor.

Then I left Longstreet. I moved to Greer, South Carolina, to start a new job. As of June 25, 1990, I am the director of publications at Converse College in Spartanburg, South Carolina. Converse is another woman's college, of whom the president is an Agnes Scott alumna. The four years I was at Agnes Scott, she was the academic dean, and I know her pretty well. I am responsible for publication of the alumni magazine, a newsletter for parents, and multiple brochures. [Even though I consider myself more a reader than a writer,] I'm doing plenty of writing in my new job!

ᴡ

FELRESE BRADSHAW CARROLL: One of the biggest projects I did in Foxfire was the research project about who owns the land in our county. We went to that tax digest in the courthouse and worked for weeks and wrote down everybody [and how much land they owned and whether they were local or from out of town]. Now, in the job I do today, I have to do property searches on everybody, and I have to go through the tax digest. That's one of the basic parts of my job.

Foxfire helped in just all kinds of ways you can't think of. It seems like through Foxfire, I came to be very interested in the community. You start to realize how important your community really is, and that's one reason I am still here doing the kind of work I'm doing now—helping people in the community.

ᴡ

TOM NIXON: When I went to Kennesaw as a freshman, a Foxfire scholarship paid for most everything. I was going through some family problems, and the next year I stayed out for a year. Later, when

Felrese Bradshaw Carroll, 1985, is a social worker with the Family and Children's Service in Rabun County.

I went back, Foxfire reinstated the scholarship. I've been full time for the past year at Piedmont.

I've got a major in middle grades education, with a specialization in math and a minor in music. I hope to do my practice teaching and graduate within a year. Of course I decided music because I enjoyed it, and I got into math because I liked math, and I've done pretty well at college with it. I got math on my degree so I could get a job. If I'm a music teacher, well that's great, but they need math teachers more.

Piedmont really puts us through a music program. I gained a lot more respect for other types of music, though I liked them all anyway. But going in depth in music theory, and understanding how it all works, and analyzing different pieces, and going through all the music history from medieval to Romantic to twentieth-century music just gives more of an understanding, and you start to appreciate it more. You hear people say, "Well, I don't like country music," and it's usually, "Because my friends don't like country music," or, "I just

Tom Nixon, 1985, is
majoring in education at
Piedmont College.

don't like the way it whines around." But if you understand more
about music and how it works, you appreciate it.

I wish I could play music all the time—enough to make a living at
it. The Foxfire Boys have been together going on ten years soon, and I
think that's an achievement in itself. And the chemistry when we
play: I've played with a lot of people on stage, and it's just not the
same as our certain kind of sound. We thought about trying to go big
time, but we would have had to change our style of playing to become
more commercial and cater to a wider circle. We'd have to go to
Nashville, and there's so much competition.

So I would like to teach and incorporate what Foxfire showed me
about education. Of course, when teaching math, you have your
textbook, but you can apply math to the real world. As far as music, I
couldn't think of any other way to teach. What I went through with
George was good [as a teaching model]. Of course, I would have state
guidelines to go by, but I would like to incorporate that informal
methodology: kids teaching kids, kids realizing that they need to

learn a certain skill or information, and also asking, "Why am I learning this?" You know they want to know why. They're always saying, "Well, I'll never use this." Well, sure. But have you all ever said, "Why do I have to know English?" You know why *now*. You're putting out this book. [I have to help kids make the same connections with math.]

Rabun Gap Community School is where I would like to do my practice teaching. They have been working with the community—with Trout Unlimited, the Forest Service—and they've been doing food plots out there, and they've cleaned off creek banks, put up stream structures in the creek, and all that type of thing. Now Rabun Gap Community School is interested in becoming a model Foxfire school, and that's why I want to practice teach there. It will be interesting if it takes off.

Because of Foxfire, I'm definitely more confident, as far as believing in myself and having confidence in other people. I also made out real well in English in college. Wig's College English class was a big help to me as far as the ability to write and rewrite papers and see what you did wrong. I just took an English proficiency test down at school, which is like the Georgia Board of Regents exam, and people take it sometimes six times before they pass. I passed it the first time. I just went in there and reeled it right out. Being able to write and organize your thoughts on paper is important.

Probably the biggest lesson, though, is learning to *do* what you have to do, and do it well. The band has learned some things about being professional. With the Foxfire Boys, it is just constant grinding. You've got to crank it out and do it right. That's what it's like in the real world. You've got to get it. If you don't get it, that's it. It's not like taking a report card home and saying, "Well, I didn't pass." You don't say, "I passed going to work today," or "I passed this fiscal year at Burlington Mills." It's not like that. You've got to meet your deadlines. You've got to do it and do it right. When we're really tight when we play at a show, it just feels good, and all that practice pays off. I guess being professional is that sense of doing it right, being more than adequate, being the best. That's what Foxfire taught me.

**W**

KYLE CONWAY: I always knew I wanted to get out of Rabun County. I'm not a native of here. I don't have the old family farm. I don't have an extended family that lives here. I appreciate it. I'm glad I grew up in Rabun County. But it wasn't ever a question of whether or not I was going to stay or leave because there was really nothing here for me to do. What Foxfire did do for me was make me more comfortable in taking charge of my future. I was always going to do that, I was determined to do that.

The Air Force Academy was the only place I had ever wanted to go, for some strange reason. I can't really explain it. I was probably the only sixth-grader that knew that he wanted to go to college, and what college he wanted to attend.

I got into the academy, which everybody thought was a big deal, and once I got there I did fairly well, which everybody thought was a big deal, also. I guess it was, but being there and doing it, I had a different perspective on it. It's just me, it's just Kyle. I'm just doing my thing. I graduated from there with a political science major and a minor in Russian. I've taken classes in just about everything under the sun because you have to: all sorts of engineering, as well as

Kyle Conway, 1986, is a graduate student in the John F. Kennedy School, Harvard University.

political science, behavioral sciences, math, chemistry, physics. I've jumped out of airplanes and I've flown gliders. Been all over the world. Went to England one summer; last summer I spent six weeks in Belgium working at the military headquarters of NATO; this summer I'm going to Vienna. Next fall I'm going to graduate school for two years at the Kennedy School at Harvard, which was a big dream come true for me. That's kinda nice.

The academy was a unique learning environment. I didn't have the freedoms that some of my contemporaries had when they were going to school. That takes some getting used to. I'm used to the lifestyle now. You don't cut classes. You don't get too much sleep. We wore uniforms. Going to a civilian graduate school is going to be a change of pace. It's like finding out what all I missed in college.

Four years at the academy was pretty much four years full time. I really had to work hard. I never considered myself a brainchild, or some genius. I met people who could just do everything in their heads and did not have to do the homework, and were just incredibly smart. I'm not that kind of guy. I'm a workhorse. I have to sit down and do the homework.

But I appreciate the opportunities that I've had, and the successes that I've had knowing that I pushed myself and made it. I keep doing things I never thought I would be able to do. It's exciting, too.

My parents thought Foxfire was really worthwhile. Of course, the opportunities that I got were just invaluable. Foxfire definitely pushed me in the right direction and gave me the skills I needed to get there. I think Wig has had a big influence on me. That has always been something that I've been thankful for.

Writing was the number-one thing. That's what got me through college and has gotten me where I am today. You'd be surprised at the number of people that I know who graduated at the top of their class and still can't write worth beans. The things they can do in their minds will melt your socks, and yet they can't put it down on paper.

I remember one experience I had just this past year. It was an upper level political science class. It was a paper a week. It's like, "Here's a sixty-page article; read it and write a two-page summary."

One time, after my teacher graded our papers, he walks into the class and sits everybody down, and says, "Okay, we need to have a come-to-Jesus talk about these papers." Everybody's looking at him. He wrote out the grades he had given out. He had given one A plus, a couple of B's and the rest C's and D's, and he failed a couple of people. That was kind of scary. He says, "We've got a lot of work to do this semester. You guys can't write." He passed back all the papers. I flipped mine over, and I had gotten the A plus. He said, "No comments, I can't find anything to take off for, keep it up."

It all comes back to being able to write. That's what made the breaks for me. I'm convinced that's what got me into graduate school. There are only four people going to Harvard from the academy, and I'm one of them. The essays I wrote for the application are, I know, the kickers that got me in. It pays off in the long run.

▄▄▄

SIDNEY DENNIS: After I graduated from high school, I went to trade school and got a degree in electricity. I got a job, and I made good money. But I felt that it just wasn't me. I was working at a mill driving a loader, but I knew I wasn't happy. I just wanted to get out of the area. I left Rabun County with a negative feeling. I was really down on it. I said, "I'm leaving. I'm going to places where nobody knows me." So I went to Southern Union College, in Wadley, Alabama, for a year.

But I missed so much down there. I didn't have my parents, and I didn't have my brother. That experience made me grow up some, and it made me want to come back home. Now I really appreciate and love these mountains more than I ever did. I think everyone needs to leave home awhile. It really is an experience that makes you grow. Right now I'm a sophomore at a junior college. I'm going to be a junior at the University of Georgia this fall. It's been a dream. I really look forward to entering.

In college, my major's going to be public relations. Every time I did a speech for Foxfire, I really liked it. I was relaxed; I didn't get nervous. Wig told me, "Sid, you get along great with people, and you ought to consider going into a job which involves that." So that's why I chose public relations. It's a field where you have to deal with people. That's one thing I can do. I can convince people. I can make people laugh, and I can make people understand an issue. I talk so much, finally I said, "Well, I'm gonna get paid for talking one of these days."

My original intention was to join the armed forces, but I had to have a back operation that limited me. As a result of it, I can never join the armed forces. From my perspective now, however, it's probably the best thing that ever happened to me. I'm thinking about going to Scottish Rite Hospital. That's where I'd go if I had the choice. I'd go there and be in the P.R. department and tell the kids before they have the operations that they're not so bad. I'd like to encourage them—to tell them they can become something in life if they can stick their minds to it and not let anything get them down. This is because that's what I needed when I was there—encouragement. They need somebody like me who's gone through the same experience to say, "Look, you can become something. This is not a setback. This will help you, and you'll be a better person."

That was the great thing about Foxfire. It set it in my mind that I was going to be something. It made me feel successful, and it made me feel good about myself. Just because I'm from the north Georgia mountains doesn't mean I'm going to be a failure. I can conquer anything.

Mike Cook was good at encouraging people. In fact, he was the reason I went to college. He showed me he believed in me. He told me I was smart enough to go to the University of Georgia. I'd been out of school a year, and I said, "Mike, I think I want to go back to college."

He said, "Sidney, you're smart enough. You'll make it. You'll be something. You really should go back to college." He'd told me the same thing my last day of high school. Nobody else at the high school ever told me that. They cared, but not like that. That's one reason people took the Foxfire classes—you could tell that the Foxfire people really cared about your life.

In most classes, kids are divided into categories. There are the intellectual, college-bound people, and there is the social group, and there is the artistic group, and there are the jocks, and there are the farming and construction-type people. I think it's wrong to have it all set like that. In Foxfire, they had a variety of people. It didn't matter if you were smart or dumb or what you owned. They just took you as a person, an individual.

I learned a great deal of responsibility. While I was in Mike's class, I was operating a one-thousand-dollar video camera. You just don't drop something like that! I also learned to be inventive. In George's class, I learned how to make instruments. That made me use my mind and become more creative.

I respect older people more as a result of being in Foxfire. Wig would kick you out of his classes if he caught you laughing at them, so you learned to respect old people. You learned to give them patience and kindness. You didn't talk when they talked. You learned to be sincere, and, above all, you learned to be responsible.

My parents were really glad I was in Foxfire, and they will cherish the interview with my grandparents for the rest of their lives. But the neatest thing of all will be for my kids. I can say to them, "This was your great-grandparents, and you have the opportunity to listen to my interview with them." I can take them to the archives, where they keep all the records, and get that interview with my grandparents. And I can show them the book, where their words are captured and printed forever. I would have loved to listen to and read the words of my great-great-great grandfather!

One day, I'll be able to repay Foxfire. I'll be able to help somebody. I'll get someone to go to college. I'd like to show them that you can still make something of yourself, even if you're from the rural north Georgia mountains. As long as God gives you ability, use it. If you can play an instrument, play it. If you can sing, you should sing. Since I can talk, I'm going to talk.

ᗯ

LAURA LEE: I'm currently a junior at the University of Georgia, majoring in biology. College is more exciting than high school. It's an opportunity to learn just for yourself and not because your teacher's

Laura Lee, 1987, is majoring in biology at the University of Georgia.

going to take you to the office and kill you if you don't learn it. You have to make yourself go to class. Most of the teachers don't take attendance, and there's a big temptation not to go—to just lay out.

I have a busy life. I have class for three hours a day, and then I get home and I have my little girl, Jennifer. It's hard to take care of her and study at the same time and also get all my housework done.

When people ask me where I'm from and I say "Rabun County," the usual response is, "Where's that?" If they don't recognize landmarks like Clayton or Tallulah Gorge, I tell them Rabun County is where the Foxfire books come from. Almost everyone knows what I'm talking about.

One day my philosophy professor was absent from class so that he could attend a lecture Wig was giving at UGA. The next day he asked the class, "Do any of you know who Eliot Wigginton is?" I said, "Yes, he was one of my English teachers in high school," not thinking that Dr. Granrose meant, did any of us know he was the founder of Foxfire. Dr. Granrose was impressed with Foxfire's use of video in the classroom. He said he was going to try to incorporate video into future classes of his own.

When I went on an archaeological dig with my anthropology professor, we got to talking and I discovered Dr. Kowalewski also was interested in Foxfire, his work of preserving the past being similar. He seemed very impressed, and gave me a compliment by asking, "Is that where you learned to write so well?" And yes, it was.

In high school, I never realized Foxfire was so well known. Now people are always interested when I say I was involved. I consider it a credential, something to be proud of.

▼▼▼

OhSoon Shropshire: I originally came to the University of Georgia because of my experience with Foxfire, and I got a Foxfire scholarship the first three years that I was here. Right now, I am going into my senior year in college. My major right now is psychology. I probably will get a degree in child psychology with a minor specifically in child hospital therapy.

I am working two jobs now. I do the medical records at the health center. When students come in, I create documents for them, edit the computer printouts, and admit people.

The day-care job I have is really because I need more contact with children. This is a day camp, but the parents have gotten rid of them for the day so they can go to work. They want to be listened to, 'cause often they're not. By giving them an ear, or just a little bit of attention, you get a lot more out of them than if you just ignored them, just like with our Foxfire contacts. They love being listened to, and by having someone being interested, it gives them an outlook on things they've done in their lives.

I like the little kids the most. They're so precious. You're just amazed at the things they say and do. If you smile you liven up their world, because attention to them is more precious than gold. The world is so big and they're so small. It's hard to realize that. I think the thing I hate the most is that you have so few materials. I have classes of sixty children in one class. It's really hard. You can't get enough construction paper for these kids. You don't have glue, enough macaroni to make necklaces, and things like that.

[All this is] really gonna help me in my job because I am really interested in children. Diseases like child leukemia and emergency amputation are real, real traumatic experiences that children aren't prepared for. Sometimes they're never gonna get well. But that's what I want to do.

I would like to work with something like Foxfire as a nonprofit organization. I like that idea—like working for a hospital that doesn't require a profit. I don't like giving out help and feeling guilty about it. I'd like working somewhere that has a little moral fiber to it. I think that would be part of my goal.

My classmates always thought I would be an artist, which, when I actually got to the University of Georgia, I was taking. But you have to be a little conceited, in my opinion, to be an artist, in order to think your work is better than anybody else's. The only way to get ahead is to believe that you're good enough to beat someone else out of a graphic arts job, and I'm just not into that. I want to leave this world feeling what I've done has helped and has been right.

ALLYN STOCKTON: I went to Abraham Baldwin Agricultural College after high school and I just transferred to the Southern College of Technology. I'm wanting to become a surveyor. After college, I'll have to work under somebody for four years before I'll be able to get a license. I hope to be with the DOT somewhere near and come back to Rabun.

I had two different classes where I had to give speeches—one was a speech class and the other was a business communications class. I'm not a great speaker by any means, but I was way ahead of the rest. After my first speech, my professor said, "Have you ever had experience giving speeches before?" I told him I had Foxfire in high school. He said that he has had students who were under Wig before.

My last speech, I brought a box in there with Foxfire books in it, and talked about what I did in high school. I started handing all these books out, and their mouths dropped. They couldn't believe that we'd done that in high school.

▓▓▓

BROOKS ADAMS: When I graduated, I started school at Georgia Tech, and I have a co-op job with Michelin Tire Corporation. I go over every other quarter and work with their engineers and electricians. My major is electrical engineering.

Brooks Adams, 1988, is an engineering student at Georgia Tech.

My parents pushed me to start Foxfire. I don't know if it is the reason Allison got involved in it, but after they saw what Foxfire did for her, they wanted me to get into it.

My dad is a mechanical engineer, and I've been influenced by that all my life. I think that I chose electrical engineering, though, because I got to work with all the equipment at Foxfire, and I'd worked with it on my own. Then when I discovered electrical engineering, it turned out that it was supposed to be a real good field to go into. I thought, "Well, that's convenient, so we'll go with this."

And today companies are looking for engineers who can write because that has been a big problem in the past. Engineers have got great ideas, but they can't communicate what they need to in writing. When I applied for my co-op job with Michelin, I told them about Foxfire and what I had done with all the interviews, and being able to put articles together. I told them about the radio shows and told them about the research paper I had done in my senior year. I guess they believed me when I told them I could write. I got the job.

There are steps in designing something. First of all, you have to be able to understand what somebody is wanting you to design, so you have to be able to interpret what they want. That can be either through writing or verbally or pictures. After that, you have to look at what you have to work with and what you need as an output to go back into the machine. You usually work it out with a mathematical equation to come up with a solution to the problem. Before you can actually build the solution, you have to write a report including what the problem was, how you went about coming up with the solution, telling why your solution is good, and how you plan on implementing it, and you have to be able to write that up like a sales pitch.

When they give us design projects at school, you have to have them done in a certain amount of time or you start getting points counted off. Foxfire helped me put together an itinerary of things that I had to have completed at a specific time in order to have what I needed done, done. It showed me how to do that. Since I have gone through that process with the radio shows, I know how to do that. That's what engineering is. It's designing something and going through a process to get to a final product.

Foxfire has also succeeded in a democratic process of treatment, freedom, and responsibility. It gave us responsibilities, and if we didn't fufill them, we fell on our faces. If that happened, though, we had to get back up and try it again.

Foxfire helped with my self-confidence. It showed that I could put together an article, get up in front of a couple thousand people, talk to them, and do anything I wanted to do. We're the ones that made the decisions: what we were going to do with the articles, how they were going to be done, made contact with the people that we wanted an interview with, and wrote everything up.

When I graduate I'm not sure what I want to do. I either want to try to get a job or go to graduate school and continue with electrical engineering in their graduate program or get a master's in business administration.

My parents gave me control of my life, and Foxfire taught me to take control. It let me be in charge of what I was doing.

**ᵂᴬᵂ**

STANLEY BEASLEY: I enjoyed coming to Foxfire class every day. In all the classes before you'd do grammar year after year after year. You didn't get the time to know what you were strong in. When I got in Foxfire and started using all the things I was good in, I could see what

Stanley Beasley, 1988, is majoring in horticulture at the University of Georgia.

I needed help in. Wig and Margie would help you in your weak areas. They probably helped me the most to prepare for college. I don't always use proper English when I talk, but I started being conscientious about those articles and college English papers. Because of Foxfire, I made A's in my first English class at Piedmont.

Now, with a Foxfire scholarship, I'm in my junior year at the University of Georgia and majoring in horticulture. A lot of people really don't even know what horticulture is. I get mad sometimes when they say, "Oh, you're going to be farmer." Horticulture is not even close to being a farmer. I was always interested in horticulture, which is why I always did real well in horticulture classes in high school. It's a hands on thing. You get to grow plants and it's something you can put your hands on. You can see the fruits of your labor; kind of like doing an article for *Foxfire*.

Horticulture is a big field. There are four different areas in it. You have your flowers and shrubs, and then landscaping. Then, fruits and vegetables. Also, you can teach at the graduate level. I can go in any different direction.

While I was in Foxfire, I think my parents were proud that I was helping to preserve the old things and ways of their time and day. I wasn't just interested in moving on and getting caught up in everything modern. I was also the only person in my family to go on to college. I tried to do everything the best I could in high school. I made my parents real proud with Foxfire and going on to college.

In Foxfire, I got to see that I really could do things on my own, and I wasn't too young to actually do things that were beneficial. I can take a lot of what I learned in Foxfire and use it even in horticulture. You can apply the lessons to so many different things.

▼▼▼

TONIA KELLY: I'm majoring in aerospace engineering at Georgia Tech, and also going to trade school in the summers taking metal trades.

College is really hard. All through high school I had straight A's. I came out with like a ninety-six point something average for four years. In college, I'm making mostly C's. If I had to do it again, I would probably go to a smaller school for the first year and get used to it before transferring to a larger school. At my very first class at Georgia Tech, I walked in and saw two hundred people there. I was like, "Oh, my gosh!"

Tonia Kelly, 1989, is an aerospace engineering student at Georgia Tech.

[In addition to helping me with my English skills,] Foxfire has given me confidence in myself. I did that long Conway Watkins article, and before, I would never have thought I could do something like that. It just gives you confidence that you can take on something that seems overwhelming and get it done. I don't think I would have chosen somewhere so big, and a major that is as challenging, if I hadn't been challenged by Foxfire.

[Foxfire also] taught me that teachers were humans and that you could talk to them, and they would work with you instead of against you. I remember I used to think that teachers were somebody that you didn't approach—that they were just there and you listened to them and then you left. But that's not true. You can know your teachers outside of a classroom. You can meet them and talk to them and get help. At the same time, however, I also learned to rely on myself to get something done. Wig didn't stand over us and say, "Do it!" like some teachers do in high school. It's like that in college. They're not going to stand over you and tell you to do it. If you turn it in, that's good, and if you don't, oh well. It's nothing to them. Wig [did care] but he wasn't going to stand there [and force] you to do the work. It was your choice to do it [and if you chose not to, then it didn't get done]. When you did do it, however, you felt good. [So, in general,] Foxfire helps to teach responsibility, get your assignments in on time, and maybe to take on more than what you normally would—to go more in depth with something. If you're told to write a paper, you don't just skim over the top. You get into it more.

▞▞▞

MARY SUE RAAF: I'm going to the University of Georgia now. I have a Foxfire scholarship. I'm majoring in psychology, and I have a job at Charter Winds in Athens, which is a drug and alcohol rehabilitation center. I work on the adult substance abuse unit.

I had a good year for the first year in college. I was scared to death. Then I started. Everything seemed to work pretty well. It was the weirdest thing to walk into a classroom and not know one person in there. When you walk around campus and see somebody from Rabun, you get all excited. People you never really knew in high school will come up and talk to you for a half hour.

I've decided I want to be a psychologist because I want to work with alcohol and drug-related problems. Some of that interest has to do with my Foxfire research paper on bulimia. I got really interested in addiction. I loved that Foxfire College Research class. That sounds weird because everyone else hates that class, but I really liked it, and I was really glad that I had had *Foxfire* magazine first, because the students who hadn't were all really nervous about their interviews and things, and I wasn't the least bit worried about the interviews. All that really helped me with my first two Englishes in college. I had to write a big paper for one class, and I got a ninety-five.

When I first came to Rabun County in the ninth grade, I was really unhappy because it was just such a culture shock. I was from Chicago, and it was just so small here. I didn't fit in because I didn't have a Southern accent. We lived with my uncle Jack out in Persimmon. He was dating Brad Haynes's mother, and she kept telling me, "You just have to get in Foxfire, Mary Sue," and I was like, "Okay." She died that summer. I'm really glad she got me into Foxfire or I wouldn't be in college right now.

So in tenth grade I got into Foxfire. I started making a lot of friends. I started feeling like I fit in more after I got involved in Foxfire.

At first, I felt like Wig didn't like me because I was from Chicago, and I didn't think he thought I was going to take it seriously. Then we had this big final with questions about Rabun County. I went all out and worked really hard on it and I got an A plus. I was really happy, and after that I had a different perspective on things, and I learned so much about Rabun County that I never would have known. I ended up loving it. I thought it was so neat that people knew who their great-grandparents were, and knew who their third cousins twice removed were.

In eleventh grade, I took Foxfire II. We really felt responsible for the magazine. We felt like it was our magazine instead of Wig's magazine. The democracy involved in Foxfire makes you feel like you're in charge. Foxfire helps you to develop responsibility in other classes, too. In a regular classroom, you can get by and not do anything. If you have a test, lots of times they'll be multiple choice and kids cheat. Foxfire is something you can't cheat on. You can't cheat on an article.

Now I respect older people more than I used to, and I just feel like they have so much knowledge. When I worked as a nurse's aide, there were a lot of older people there, and they would always get to talking about how things were when they were little. Old people have so much to share with people, if we'll listen. There's a lady at the hospital now who hardly ever talks or anything. Nobody can get her to talk. They don't like her very much. I was sitting there one day, and I was trying to talk to her, and I asked her what she liked to do. She told me she liked to fish, and that she used to do all this stuff. She started talking to me, and she'd never talked to me before. It makes you realize that just because they're old doesn't mean that they don't think, care, or feel anymore. They still do. Foxfire makes you realize that. It helped me learn how to deal with all kinds of people.

I figure that majoring in psychology, I will still have chances to write, and I'll still have chances to give speeches, but I'll be able to work with people, too. I think that field is a perfect match for me.

◆◆◆

BETH LOVELL: The reason I joined Foxfire was so I could learn to play music, and then once I got into George's class, he advised me that I should take Wig's Foxfire I class. I wasn't particularly thrilled with school. I always hated it, and he seemed to think that if I got into Wig's English class, that that would help me out a lot, which it did. I

Beth Lovell, 1989, is majoring in political science at
Truett-McConnell College.

enjoyed all of it. Michelle Speed and I did an article about the Kelly
family for *Foxfire*. In the music class, I got good enough on the guitar
that I did a lot of teaching my senior year. I gave some of the students
lessons after school for a long time.

My senior year I also took Hilton's social studies class, so he and I
became good friends. Hilton did one of the nicest and sweetest things
anyone has ever done for me. I had a problem with reading when I
was in school. George had helped me out with my reading when I
worked with him. Then Hilton [picked up from there]. We used *Time*
magazine in class, and he would go home at night and read the
articles for me into a microcassette tape recorder. He would bring the
tape to school the next day and let me take it home, and I could listen
to the tape and follow along with the article at the same time. I
thought that was one of the sweetest things anybody had ever done
for me; now I can read on my own, and this fall I'll be going to college.

While I was in Foxfire, in school, the staff members had their
weekly meetings in the classroom after school every Tuesday afternoon. A group of students met with them. We were called the A Team.

I was a part of it for two years. We made some pretty big decisions about who got to go on trips and things like that. After I got into the A Team, I used to think it would be nice to be on the Foxfire staff. I liked all these people, and I thought I'd like to work with them.

I never dreamed that I would be working this closely with Wig or any of the Foxfire staff, but I am now, and when I start college, I'll probably still work part time in the evenings.

Right after I graduated from high school, I worked one week at the Clarkesville Mill and decided I wouldn't work in no mill all of my life. That was the pits. In August, I came up to Wig's office one day and asked him if I could come to work in the fall part time and go to Piedmont College part time. He said he'd take it to the staff.

So, I came down to the staff meeting that next Tuesday, and they talked about it and hired me back for part-time work. Things didn't turn out good for me at Piedmont, so I ended up working at Foxfire full time in December. Now I'm doing all kinds of good stuff—things I probably wouldn't have even dreamed about doing when I was a senior. I'm putting together a new sales brochure now. We're going to do a major marketing flyer for the Twenty-fifth Anniversary products, the Christmas book, and the anniversary book.

Now that the former student alumni group has been formed and Kaye Collins is out on maternity leave, I'm doing most of what she was doing. I'm calling the meetings, holding them, writing up the minutes, and following through on what comes up at the meetings. Right now, we're working on an issue of the magazine put together by former students. I'm making sure that we're going to have enough articles coming in. That way, the students can concentrate on this book.

Foxfire has taught me a lot of responsibility, dealing with pressure as far as time goes, meeting deadlines, and working with people. Working together—and especially with as much as there is to do at Foxfire—you have to be a member of the team. You can't take it alone. You're not the only one in the boat if something goes wrong and you're not the Lone Ranger.

But I have to get back to school. I have a scholarship this year, and I'm going to Truett-McConnell College in the fall. According to Ann Moore, I got the largest sum of money that Foxfire has given at one time to a student. It was the Community Advisory Board that did that, and I know all of them. I feel honored that they recognized me enough to give me that.

I think I would have turned out differently if it hadn't been for Foxfire. I probably wouldn't be going to school in the fall. I would be working at Bi-Lo checking people out. Foxfire showed me that you don't have to settle for working at a fast-food place or working in a mill.

Being around Wig, Hilton, Susan, George, and Mike—all of these people have degrees and they know how to use their degrees. That's something you can look at, especially if you're around them all day. You learn to appreciate that, and say, "Hey, I want what they've got."

And people like Robert over here, he's the "million-dollar Murray." He's a good one to work around. He tends to not see things just in his own way, but he sees all sides. He's very objective when he looks, and I'm learning to do that; to look not to see just straight ahead but to get the whole circle and the whole picture.

I'm learning to be more in control of my life right now. I'm learning to make a decision like go to college or what I'm going to get out of college. Instead of going through and getting a C or B, I'm determined that I'm going to make A's.

# Creating *Foxfire: 25 Years*

An interview by Beth Lovell with the editors of *Foxfire: 25 Years:*
Robbie Bailey, Scott Cannon, Lee Carpenter, Julie Dickens, Shannon
Edwards, Keri Gragg, Chris Nix, and Leigh Ann Smith.

**Q: When you all first started out in Foxfire, how big did you
think it was? What did you think it was?**

SCOTT: When I first started two years ago, I didn't know about the
Foxfire land. I didn't know that they had land and property in Mountain City. I just thought it was this one little old six-hundred-foot-
square room in the high school.
  That's when I was in Foxfire I. The only thing that we were doing
was small interviews that were going into the magazine. Now we are
doing this book.

**Q: What does Wig do to you all to get you ready to tackle
something as big as putting a book together?**

KERI: Well, the first thing is that Foxfire is so different from a
regular class. Even the classroom's different. You walk in here and
you see quilts and stuff hanging all over the walls. The atmosphere is

so much more relaxed. If you sit on the floor, Wig's not going to shout at you. Furthermore, we don't call him "Mr. Wigginton." We call him Wig. We call all the people on the Foxfire staff by their first names.

SCOTT: Wig lets us know from the time we first come into the class what the state requirements are, and we have charts and posters detailing those requirements. The semester when I was in Foxfire I we did projects. For each project we did, we had to write a project report. At the end of these project reports, we had to tell whether the project met the state's requirements. So we had to go back and look at the charts.

"Well, yes, yes, yes, it met these."

Sometimes it was, "No, it didn't meet this," but, you know, that's going to happen to everybody a little bit because every project won't meet every requirement. Even if a project's great, it's not going to be perfect every time.

LEIGH ANN: In Foxfire I, when we split up into groups, one of the projects was to read a book of Appalachian literature and then write papers and keep reading journals about what the book was about and what I was interested in. The other day, I was just looking at the books on the shelf in our room, and I found one that I liked. I took it home, and I'm reading it right now. It's nice to get interested in these books, even though you might not be interested in all of them all of the time.

SCOTT: In your regular English classes, you learn just what's in the textbook, and that's it. In Foxfire, we go beyond that. We learn all the writing and grammar, and we also learn how to use a camera, how to use a tape recorder, and how to develop our own pictures. Then we go from projects that use those skills into actually putting together an issue of *Foxfire*, and that's all in that one year Foxfire I class.

KERI: We don't even use a textbook. It's all hands-on learning. Wig never says, "Open your book to page such-and-such and do this many questions." Instead, he says, "This is how it works. Do you understand?" The only time we use an English book is like a dictionary. It's just a reference book, it's something we get information from.

LEIGH ANN: Lots of things we're learning in Foxfire just can't be

The primary editors of *Foxfire: 25 Years:* (standing left to right) Robbie Bailey, Scott Cannon, Chris Nix, Lee Carpenter; (seated left to right) Julie Dickens, Leigh Ann Smith, and Jenny Lincoln. Missing from photo: Shannon Edwards.

shown on a regular test. We don't fill in the blanks or blacken ovals on a multiple-choice test. Basically, the magazine is our test. It's not a test per se, but it's evidence of our work.

ROBBIE: I look at that whole year as a test. The magazine represents a whole year of learning. The test is whether you can take those skills you've learned and write an article in the magazine that people will want to read.

LEIGH ANN: Of course, I feel bad if I look at the mag and I find I have the caption on a picture wrong or something. But then there's the whole article. And, of course, we're all imperfect. One of the things in the Bible that I always remember is that I'm never going to be perfect.

ROBBIE: working on the *Foxfire* magazine and on the books leads you into other books, especially when they are about experiences you have shared in your own life. It's really important to see what other people say about the same experiences you have. Being a writer yourself with Foxfire enables you to feel a sort of communication with other writers and other people, even if they're from other times in history.

KERI: Last week I went to see a play called *The Reach of Song*. It's about this man named Herbert Reece. In the play, he wrote three or four books, and then he was a teacher at Young Harris College. He committed suicide. Mama drove me off to see this play, and I thought, "I really don't want to see this."

But when I got there and started watching it, I found that it was so much related to Foxfire that it was unbelievable to me. I just really got into the play. After I started thinking about it, I really came to enjoy it. It was a great play. If I hadn't taken Foxfire, I wouldn't have thought anything about it. But because I did take Foxfire, it made me think about a lot of things the people were saying.

ROBBIE: What I'm trying to say is that during these last two years in Foxfire, I've learned more English than I learned throughout grade school and all the years before. I could probably take a test right now based on the last two years of what I've learned, and I think I'd probably do pretty well on it. I would probably be in the top 10 percent.

✴

**Q: How did it work doing *A Foxfire Christmas* and this book back to back? Was it confusing?**

SCOTT: It wasn't confusing. It was more of thinking about what you were going to be doing next. We laid the Twenty-fifth [book] down at the beginning of the [1989–90 school] year because the Christmas book had to be [delivered to Doubleday] in November. We didn't have nearly enough Christmas material [to fill a book], so we just laid the Twenty-fifth down to get that one completed, and when that one was sent off to Doubleday, we picked back up on the Twenty-fifth.

✴

### Q: Didn't some of y'all go up to Doubleday and deliver the Christmas book?

JULIE: Four of us went to Doubleday: Chris, Lee, and I, and Jenny Lincoln, who isn't here today. I remember us going in there and somebody would look at the manuscript, somebody would number the pages, somebody would cut and paste, and somebody would add pictures. [We assembled the final manuscript and added the photos in one of their conference rooms.]

**⋓**

### Q: Has there been any pressure on you to get this new book finished?

SCOTT: Deadlines. Meeting all of the deadlines. We're trying to get this book out before school starts this year.

CHRIS: This summer, we were hired mainly as editors. We tried to devote most of our time toward editing. At the beginning, we were transcribing and editing. As the weeks progressed, we began to get bogged down with transcribing because of the large number of people that we were interviewing. Wig said he didn't want us doing that, so he hired some transcribers to help us along.

**⋓**

### Q: What was the most interesting interview that you went on?

LEIGH ANN: The most interesting interview that I went on was the one with Allison Adams. It took us forever to find it. If her dad hadn't come down the driveway, we would never have found that house. One lady told us it was a brick house, and we had heard it was a white house. It ended up being green, and barely even had a brick on it!

SCOTT: I guess one of my favorite interviews that I went on was with Johnny Scruggs because he was just a plain and simple fellow; but it was funny, because he told us to go to the forks of the road and turn left, and we ended up way up on Screamer Mountain. I mean we went to the top of the mountain. Then we ended up being behind Carver's Chapel Church. He told us to look for a red Toyota, so we stopped at this house with a red Toyota pickup. Chris and I went up and knocked on the door for a while, and as we were about to leave, we heard somebody yell out the window. I asked him if this was Johnny Scruggs's residence. He said, "No." We never even saw him. He just stood somewhere in the house and yelled out of the window. I just stood there asking him where to go, but I was yelling to the door because I couldn't see him. I'm glad somebody didn't drive up, because they would have seen me yelling at a door!

When we finally found Johnny, we asked him where he wanted to do the interview, and he said, "Let's just do it on the back of the pickup." We just stood out there for one and a half to two hours and just talked to him about the old times. It was fun.

CHRIS: After the interview we stayed and talked for another one and a half hours.

JULIE: Don't ever do an interview in a gas station.

SCOTT: Don't ever transcribe it because you always hear this bell going ding, ding! Wig said from day one, "I'll set an interview up with Claude Rickman. Don't worry about it, guys." Well, we've got about four more days to go, and we still haven't interviewed Claude. I can understand it, though, because of his schedule. I honestly don't see how Wig does it. He is gone all the time and still has time to keep us in line and make sure we don't go crazy on him. There has been so much going on that I've thought about committing suicide!

CHRIS: Wig did get it set up a couple of times, but Claude canceled on us the first time, and then the second time we got there right on time. He wasn't there.

SCOTT: So, we went chasing dogs and scaring cows after that.

JULIE: On that interview we did with Al Edwards, the Georgia Public Television crew was there. We got set up on the porch. They had to take those microphones and stick them down our clothes and bring them through at the other end. They hooked them all up and everything, and we were ready to start the interview. Al stands up and says, "I have to go to the bathroom."

LEIGH ANN: Then there was the time we had the interview with Wesley Taylor. There was about ten of us.

SCOTT: I remember the first time that we went to interview Wesley. Mrs. Taylor drove Robbie and me down there. Wesley is a teacher and mayor of the town. We interviewed him where he was building a barn, at the school, and at the county office where his mayor duties were. After the interview was over, he took us back to his house, and that was where Mrs. Taylor was. She asked him to go over by the head of a deer that he had killed so we could take a picture. We also got a picture of him and a table that he had built because Mrs. Taylor thought that it would be a good idea.

I had a lot of fun on that interview. One reason was because of Mrs. Taylor. She was just so full of energy. It was a barrel of laughs. It was fun just to watch her. That was my favorite interview without a doubt. She's a fun person to be around.

JULIE: I asked Tonia Kelly on an interview about the wrong thing. Before the interview, I gathered information from the articles she had done. When we got there I said, "Tell us about the article you did on how to raise chickens."

She looked at me and said, "I don't remember doing an article about chickens. I did an article on how to raise *children*." Scott looked at me like, "You dummy!"

**w**

## Q: What did you learn from former students through this project?

SCOTT: The former students offered a lot of encouragement. I learned from those former kids that in the beginning, they must have had a lot of dedication.

CHRIS: Helping put this book together, I've seen that a lot of the same things that happened to the former students have happened to us. They learned a lot about the people and their heritage from the people they interviewed. I've learned a lot about the people that I've interviewed as well. One lady said that if she hadn't had Foxfire, she wouldn't have learned about the people in Rabun County. I agree with that, too. It's interesting for me to see how the things that happened twenty and twenty-five years ago are still happening now with Foxfire. Putting this book together has been one big learning process for us all.

SCOTT: When you interview these people, it's like you see the same things happening to yourself. They talk about all these little stories that happened when they went on trips, and when you think back on the trips that we've been on, it seems like we have the same little stories to tell when we get back. History is just repeating itself. You know just what they're talking about. The trips have probably been one of the funnest things. On trips, you get to learn how to do a lot of different things besides giving speeches. I remember when Robbie and I went to Boston. We had to do a workshop at Harvard, and everybody there would come up to us and tell us that we had to go and see the city. So we said, "Okay, just tell us how." They told us to go to the subway station, get on the red line, go three stops, get on the blue line, go two more stops until you get to the orange line. Beetle and I were so confused. We were supposed to meet Wig back at the hotel at six-thirty to go and have dinner with some friends, and at ten minutes after six we were ten miles out of Boston. We did make it back, though; don't ask me how, but we did.

CHRIS: When we were at Sydney, we visited a place called the Powerhouse Museum. Lee and I looked around for a while and decided that we wanted to go to the Hard Rock Café. Wig wanted to stay there for a while, so we told him that we would meet back at the hotel. Lee and I got lost. It took us twice as long to get to the Hard Rock as it normally would. We barely made it back to the hotel in time. We went up to this guy, and said, "How can we get to the Hard Rock Café?" He said, "You're from the States, right?"

JULIE: When I went to New York, Jenny and I got lost in Central Park. It was funny because Chris and Lee went to Radio Shack. We didn't want to go. So we start walking, and I thought, "Sure, I can find my way back." I didn't realize that it was so big.

So I asked a policeman where the Omni Hotel was, and he said, "There's only three here." I had to go and call the operator and all kinds of things.

SCOTT: When Chris and I went to New York, we had to give a workshop in Harlem for pregnant and parenting teens. The night before, I was sort of worried because the news said that there were nine murders in nine hours up there the night before. That had me a little worried. I was thinking, "Let's get in here and get out and get back to the hotel!" It wasn't as bad as I thought it was going to be when we got there, though.

On that same trip we also had a meeting with Doubleday. They showed us the finished cover for *A Foxfire Christmas*, and then they wanted to know how we were coming on this book. I think they were pretty worried about it. We told them, and then they and Wig started talking about some other stuff.

I remember it was nice and cozy in that room. Chris and I didn't get much sleep the night before. Then we got up early that morning. We were so tired and sleepy. I didn't act sleepy, but I was about to fall out of my chair. I knew Chris was about the same. You all know how it is when Wig and some other people are talking. They are way above your head and it's hard to stay in the conversation. There was a break in the meeting, and they asked us if we wanted some tea. So we went back there and got some tea, took a sip of it, and it was so hot that I had a red streak on my tongue. I couldn't taste anything for the rest of the day!

▀▀▀

## Q: What other kinds of things did you learn from the former students?

LEE: They kept saying that if they hadn't had Foxfire, they wouldn't have been in college, or they wouldn't have a job. All of them didn't say that, but when you hear people who are saying it, it really makes you feel appreciative.

JULIE: All of them talked about when Wig was gone. Wig's been gone a lot this summer, and I can see how things have stayed the same. It affected us the same way it affected them.

SHANNON: They told us that they learned a lot from Wig and how to keep the magazine going. We've had to work without Wig this summer, and we've learned a lot.

CHRIS: I've learned how to edit a whole lot better, and put the pieces together to make it fit better. Working on the book has been a big step up for me. It's not like working on the magazine. I've taken on a lot more responsibility while working on the book. There were times when Wig wasn't around, and it was up to us to get this stuff edited on our own.

▚▚▚

**Q: Do you think you could take on another book without Wig?**

LEIGH ANN: I don't think we could take on another book as challenging as the Twenty-fifth without Wig. It's never really been without him. He's always there, but not all the time. But I'm glad we got some time to ourselves. Wig makes you sit still.

▚▚▚

**Q: How do you all feel about Wig?**

SCOTT: He's all right. He's married to Foxfire. I don't think one teacher could be more dedicated to a project than he has been with Foxfire. There's no way. It's impossible.

LEIGH ANN: I think he's a tortured man!

JULIE: I was transcribing Lori Ramey, and she said that she thinks that Wig's first love in life is teaching students in Foxfire, and I think that's true.

CHRIS: I don't think I could ever fill his shoes. I couldn't handle the pressure.

ROBBIE: I know Wig's a teacher, but he's also a friend. Any time I have any problems, it's usually him I go to first. If I had a problem in school, I'd never dream of going to a regular teacher and talking, but you can go to Wig and sit down and have an adult conversation. Wig says, "If another teacher paddles you, you come straight to me."

LEIGH ANN: Wig is very demanding, and you get intimidated by him because you know he's so smart. But in a way that doesn't matter because he's so nice. You can communicate with him; you can tell him what you think, since he treats you like a person with a right to your own opinions.

SCOTT: If I could choose the four people who've changed my life the most, one of them would be Wig.

I think that it's funny how he makes big deals out of little things, because he wants our input to be important. He will never tell you what to do; he'll just lead you on until you make the right decision. He could just go ahead and make all of the decisions, but he don't. I think that is one of the most important things as a teacher, letting students have input in the class. I think that's what makes him such a good teacher.

And he stays a step ahead. It's just unbelievable. What I don't understand is his ability to stay at these workshops for a whole day without stopping. I go in early in the morning and talk till about lunchtime and then go and see the city, but he stays there all day. Plus he may have two and three workshops a week like that. Now that's dedication.

CHRIS: Lee and I got a little taste of what it's like when we went to Australia. We were there for two weeks.

LEE: They ask you the same questions at all the different workshops and it gets old, and he's done it for twenty-five years. After two weeks we were ready to forget workshops.

▼▼▼

**Q: What have you all learned? To work together? How to fight?**

SHANNON: We work together, fight a little bit in the process.

SCOTT: If I was doing something and I wasn't having fun, I wouldn't want to be doing it. I like having fun in everything that I do, and this summer has been a lot of fun for me.

LEIGH ANN: We got into this big fight one day. All of a sudden, Scott starts shooting these dadblasted rubber bands. I said, "Scott, would you please stop?" And then he hits me with one, and I said, "All right, I can't stand this anymore." So, Shannon and I packed up the computers and took them to the other room. I couldn't stand it no longer. We got settled in Mrs. Ramey's room, and opened the windows to get a breeze going. I hear this knock on the door, so I went to open it, and it was Scott and Chris carrying one of the large wooden statues from the Foxfire classroom. Scott said, "I'm moving the Foxfire room." I was so mad I slammed the door in his face. Then George comes in and wants to know what's going on. I told him we moved for the betterment of the class!

CHRIS: I remember Scott would run out into the hall outside Leigh Ann's room and clap his hands and whistle real loud, and then take off running just to aggravate Leigh Ann. Scott had a lot of pleasure bugging Leigh Ann.

JULIE: George said, "I thought it would be wild this summer with seven sixteen-year-olds working together, but I never dreamed that they would be shooting rubber bands at each other!"

LEIGH ANN: There was the time that Chris and Lee were going to take us down to the Clayton Café, and they said, "We're going to get a Coke." Shannon and I looked at each other and said, "Uh, oh!" We ran out the door and they were already down the stairs on their way out. They left us at the school. I was so mad. We decided that we were going to roll Chris's truck [with toilet paper] to get them back. We were mad at the time we did it.

CHRIS: I didn't know that they did it at first. I didn't think that those girls would do something like that. It really surprised me to find out that Julie and Jenny were in on it. I could see Leigh Ann and Shannon out there fooling around with my truck, but I couldn't imagine Julie and Jenny out there. Mrs. McNeil, the assistant principal, told them to use cheese and shaving cream! I'm glad they didn't take her advice.

Then there was the day we all ordered pizzas from the Pizza Hut. We all brought our lunch from home, too, but the pizza filled up everybody but Scott. He was still hungry. So he had his pizza, plus two sandwiches, some Little Debbie cakes, an apple, and some potato chips. He got severely sick. He had to go home. He was saying, "Oohh,

Chris Nix's truck after Julie Dickens, Jenny Lincoln, Shannon Edwards, and Leigh Ann Smith rolled it.

I'm sick." We tried to tell him that he would get sick if he ate all that food. I was teasing him while he was sick and he'd say, "Leave me alone, Nix, I'm sick." The funny part about it was the fact that he was making this terrible moaning sound. I laughed my head off.

▚▚▚

**Q: Looking back, through these former students, would you change anything about Foxfire?**

SCOTT: I would keep it the same. There is no way it could be any better than what it has been. I was transcribing Wig's interview about *The Foxfire Book*, and he talked of the many coincidences that have happened. He said that at the time the book came out, America was wanting to know all about folklore and crafts. It was a fad. The book couldn't have come out at a better time. He said that thousands and thousands of books were leaving Doubleday, and people just couldn't get enough of them. That's amazing. It's hard to believe it happened in a little place like Rabun County. I don't think they could have done any better than what they did.

LEIGH ANN: Actually, a lot of the processes *have* changed. Instead of doing everything by hand, we use computers now. It makes it a lot easier. But the events that have happened are just too good to change.

ᴡᴡᴡ

**Q: I guess the publication of this book, and the birthday, is going to be kind of an event. How does that make you all feel?**

CHRIS: It makes me feel glad I'm in it. It's been similar to working on *A Foxfire Christmas*, but more of a challenge. The part that makes me feel the best about it is the fact that I'll be able to use my work experience with the book on my college application. It's going to help me get into school, so I'm really going to do my part and work hard on it. And of course it's going to be something that I'll look back on in the future and be proud of. I feel very fortunate to be a part of Foxfire and the crew putting the book together.

ROBBIE: I feel like I'm part of a milestone because we're the stepping-stone to twenty-five more years. I feel really good about working on this book. It's going to help us get into college. It's hard to get accepted there these days, but when we send the admissions officers copies of the book, they're going to say, "Wow, that's pretty good."

Wig told us one time that sometimes when he goes to bed at night he dreams of a student being in a college admissions office, being grilled by an admissions person. He or she gets asked the question, "Well, what have you done for the past four years?"

The student answers, "I've written a book that was published by Doubleday. What have you been doing?"

JULIE: I remember before Wig, Chris, and Lee left for Australia, Wig said that this is one of the biggest projects that he's ever left with a group of students before. That really makes you feel important, that you've been a part of it.

CHRIS: I wouldn't leave a book to seven kids. Shoot, no!

ROBBIE: Foxfire makes you more mature. I do feel like I still act like a kid, but doing this stuff is making me into more of a young adult. When you go to college, you have to be sort of professional, and doing a book for Doubleday definitely makes you more professional. I've learned more in the past two years I've been in Foxfire than in the whole ten years of school before that.

SCOTT: I guess that makes you feel responsible, because if he can depend on us to accomplish this, I think we can accomplish anything.

And, as Beetle said, It's a *milestone.*

LEIGH ANN: I hope somebody reads these books, and the teachers who read these books will learn that classes like Foxfire have really been useful to a lot of people. They can do this too, if they just take the time to understand it.

ROBBIE: When I graduate from high school, I want to look back on my high school years as joyful and happy. If I hadn't had Foxfire, I just don't think that would be possible. Foxfire certainly has helped me a lot. I've got to go on now with my life, using what Wig's taught me, and see if I've done my job.

ᵛᵃᵛ

## Q: Where are you going from here?

CHRIS: I hope to go to Georgia Southern for two years and then transfer somewhere else and get an engineering degree.

ROBBIE: I'm thinking of engineering, journalism, and teaching. I think I'd like to teach back here in Rabun County. I'll either go to Tech or Georgia Southern, or Georgia.

SCOTT: I'm thinking of Georgia Southern, Clemson, and Georgia.

LEE: I'm hoping to go somewhere like Embry-Riddle.

LEIGH ANN: I'm thinking about becoming a teacher.

JULIE: I want to go to the University of Georgia.

SHANNON: I don't know what I'm going to do.

# Afterword

Morris Brown, principal: I haven't been formally associated with Foxfire for about fifteen years now, since it moved to Rabun County High School, but I am still an onlooker. I keep up with things as best I can. And it seems to me that its objectives when it was first started and now are the same. It's just expanded some. For example, when I was involved with Foxfire, there was not a music program, but the basic philosophy has stayed the same: make education interesting, and learn by doing things rather than just reading about them.

Wig and the students did everything concerned with Foxfire. All the credit goes to them. The only thing the administration did was to help provide the environment which could give birth to such a project. And I doubt very much that it could have happened in a typical public school at that time. It would have been very, very difficult to get something like Foxfire started there; it was too new. At Rabun Gap School, on the other hand, we had a little more leeway. The county authorities, the superintendent, and the school president were all very supportive of Foxfire. Also influential was the fact that it was the sixties. People were interested in returning to nature, and learning about old cultures. People really wanted to read Foxfire. There have been occasions when people have written letters to *Foxfire* saying, "Once I started reading the magazine, I couldn't put it down till I finished it!" It's so unique; it's not just a regular high school literary magazine with short stories and haiku poetry. When people read it, it brings back memories of their childhood. So I think Foxfire should go on doing basically the same things and publishing the same sort of information—the county, the experiences of our forebears, sharing our culture with other cultures. The original objective

356

is still just as new today as it was then. Every time you pick up a magazine, there's always a new story and a new person. It's not like reading yesterday's newspaper.

Another thing that was a key element in Foxfire's success was the personal relationship that developed between the teachers, the students, and the community. The people of Rabun County had confidence in the school, Wig, and the administration. It's difficult for any enterprise in a school to get off the ground unless it's supported by the community.

There's no question that hundreds of students benefited enormously from being in Foxfire. Foxfire seems to bring out the best in people. I remember that many students were shy and insecure, especially living in such a rural area as Rabun County, and by giving them the chance to go out and interview people, it made them more self-assured. As a result, they developed much more rapidly. They were able to zero in on what their skills were and what they wanted to do.

I've seen many students who were just so-so, lackadaisical about their work; they didn't seem to care whether they passed or not. Then they became involved in Wig's classes and they just seemed to wake up. They learned new skills, and found whole new desires and goals. Even the students who were not directly involved got some benefits by seeing it in operation, and knowing that students just like themselves really were involved in running a serious operation.

We had one student who enrolled in college and was taking a sociology class, and the textbook was *The Foxfire Book*. The instructor said, "This introduction says it's done by high school students, but there's no way they could have done it. They're just saying that to sell it."

The student immediately stood up and assured the teacher that it was a high school project.

But it wasn't just the students that benefited from Foxfire. It was something that the whole school and the whole county—parents, teachers, administrators, and the community itself—could be proud to be a part of. There has been a great deal of favorable publicity not only to the school, but to the whole Rabun County area.

In our family, the effect even goes into the third generation. Our grandchildren this past year had teachers who talked about Foxfire.

All in all, I think the school and Wig came together at the right time.

# Former Students
# Interviewed

| *Student, Date of Graduation:* | *Profession:* |
|---|---|
| Jan Brown Bonner, 1969 | Public school media specialist |
| Judy Marinda Brown Plant, 1969 | Craftswoman |
| George Burch, 1969 | Public school principal |
| Emma Buchanan Chastain, 1970 | Beautician |
| Becky Coldren Lewis, 1970 | Public high school teacher |
| Mike Cook, 1971 | Public high school teacher |
| Paul Gillespie, 1971 | Private school development director |
| Claude Rickman, 1973 | Building contractor |
| Gary Warfield, 1973 | Veterinarian |
| Vivian Burrell McCay, 1974 | Sales director, advertising |
| Kaye Carver Collins, 1975 | Staff member, Foxfire |
| Bit Carver Kimball, 1975 | Office manager, plumbing company |
| Lynn Butler, 1977 | Public high school teacher |
| Johnny Scruggs, 1978 | Airline pilot |
| Lynette Williams Zoellner, 1978 | Craft shop owner |
| Bob Kugel | Cab driver |
| Shayne Beck, 1979 | Convenience store owner |
| Lorie Ramey Thompson, 1979 | Realtor |
| Tombo Ramey, 1979 | Builder |
| John Singleton, 1980 | Graduate student, education |
| Rosanne Chastain Webb, 1981 | Public relations |
| Vaughn Rogers, 1981 | Sales, building supplies |
| Wesley Taylor, 1981 | Public high school teacher, mayor |
| Kim Hamilton McKay, 1982 | Bookkeeper |
| Dana Holcomb Adams, 1982 | Legal secretary |
| Donna Bradshaw Speed, 1983 | Craft shop owner |
| Dean English, 1983 | Blueprint dry mounter |
| Ronnie Welch, 1983 | Large-equipment contract service technician |
| Frank Dyer, 1984 | Sheriff's deputy |
| Danny Flory, 1984 | City policeman |
| Allison Adams, 1985 | College director of publications |

Felrese Bradshaw Carroll, 1985 — Social worker, Family and Children's Service

Tom Nixon, 1985 — Student, Piedmont College, education
Kyle Conway, 1986 — Graduate student, Harvard University
Sidney Dennis, 1986 — Student, University of Georgia, public relations

Al Edwards, 1986 — Free-lance photographer
Laura Lee, 1987 — Student, UGA, biology
OhSoon Shropshire, 1987 — Student, UGA, child psychology
Allyn Stockton, 1987 — Student, UGA
Brooks Adams, 1988 — Student, Georgia Tech, engineering
Stanley Beasley, 1988 — Student, UGA, horticulture
Tonia Kelly, 1989 — Student, Georgia Tech, aerospace engineering

Beth Lovell, 1989 — Student, Truett-McConnell, political science

Mary Sue Raaf, 1989 — Student, UGA, psychology

PRIMARY EDITORS:

Robbie Bailey
Scott Cannon
Lee Carpenter
Julie Dickens
Shannon Edwards
Jenny Lincoln
Chris Nix
Leigh Ann Smith

OTHER STUDENTS INVOLVED:

Rabun Baldwin
Bruce Beck
Chuck Clay
Scott Crane
Tammi English
Keri Gragg
Holli Hickox
Amy Nichols
Anthony Queen
Rob Stockton

The interviews that comprise *FOXFIRE: 25 YEARS* were conducted, transcribed, and edited by high school students in Georgia. The students' work was supervised by their teacher, Eliot Wigginton, who started *Foxfire* magazine with his ninth- and tenth-grade English classes in 1966 and still teaches in the mountains of north Georgia. Mr. Wigginton was voted "Teacher of the Year" in Georgia in recognition of his important contributions to education. In 1989, he was awarded a MacArthur Fellowship.